ADVANCES IN HOSPITALITY AND LEISURE

EDITED BY

JOSEPH S. CHEN

Indiana University, Bloomington, IN, USA

Emerald

United Kingdom – North America – Japan
India – Malaysia – China

Emerald Group Publishing Limited
Howard House, Wagon Lane, Bingley BD16 1WA, UK

First edition 2017

Reprints and permissions service
Contact: permissions@emeraldinsight.com

British Library Cataloguing in Publication Data
A catalogue record for this book is available from the British Library

ISBN: 978-1-78635-616-1
ISSN: 1745-3542 (Series)

Printed and bound by CPI Group (UK) Ltd, Croydon, CR0 4YY

ISOQAR certified
Management System,
awarded to Emerald
for adherence to
Environmental
standard
ISO 14001:2004.

Certificate Number 1985
ISO 14001

INVESTOR IN PEOPLE

ADVANCES IN HOSPITALITY AND LEISURE

ADVANCES IN HOSPITALITY AND LEISURE

Series Editor: Joseph S. Chen

Recent Volumes:

CONTENTS

RESEARCH NOTES

LIST OF CONTRIBUTORS

Robert J. Blomme	Nyenrode Business Universiteit, Breukelen and Open Universiteit, Heerlen, The Netherlands
Joseph S. Chen	Department of Recreation, Park and Tourism Studies, Indiana University, Bloomington, IN, USA
Jeen Filz	Hotelschool The Hague, Amsterdam, The Netherlands
Yvette N. J. Green	Lester E. Kabacoff School of Hotel, Restaurant and Tourism Administration, University of New Orleans, New Orleans, LA, USA
Zulhazman Hamzah	Faculty of Earth Science, Universiti Malaysia Kelantan, Kelantan, Malaysia
Jue Huang	College of Humanities and Social Sciences, United Arab Emirates University, Al-Ain, UAE
Mei-Ling Huang	School of Tourism Development, Maejo University Sansai, Chiang Mai Province, Thailand
Henry G. Iroegbu	School of Business and Public Administration, University of the District of Columbia, Washington, DC, USA
Min-Seong Kim	Department of Tourism, Recreation & Sport Management, University of Florida, Gainesville, FL, USA
Soon-Ho Kim	J. Mack Robinson College of Business, Georgia State University, Atlanta, GA, USA

Sonja Kinski   School of Business and Management,
                             International University of Applied
                             Sciences, Bad Honnef, Germany

Christoffer   School of Business and Economics,
  Wanga Krag   The Arctic University of Norway,
                             Tromsø, Norway

Dong Hun Lee   College of Health and Human
                             Performance, University of Houston,
                             Houston, TX, USA

Winitra Leelapattana   School of Tourism Development,
                             Maejo University Sansai, Chiang Mai
                             Province, Thailand

Willy Legrand   School of Business and Management,
                             International University of Applied
                             Sciences, Bad Honnef, Germany

Maryati Mohamed   Department of Technology and Heritage,
                             Faculty of Science, Technology and
                             Human Development, Universiti Tun
                             Hussein Onn Malaysia, Johor, Malaysia

Uysal Muzaffer   Department of Hospitality and Tourism
                             Management, University of Massachusetts,
                             Amherst, MA, USA

Nina K. Prebensen   UiT, The Arctic University of Norway,
                             Tromsø, Norway

Bruce Prideaux   School of Business and Law, Central
                             Queensland University, Cairns, Australia

Fiffy Hanisdah Saikim   Institute for Tropical Biology and
                             Conservation, Universiti Malaysia Sabah,
                             Sabah, Malaysia

Philip Sloan   School of Business and Management,
                             International University of Applied
                             Sciences, Bad Honnef, Germany

Weerapon Thongma	School of Tourism Development, Maejo University Sansai, Chiang Mai Province, Thailand
Arjan van Rheede	Hotelschool The Hague, The Hague, The Netherlands
John A. Williams	College of Business Administration, University of New Orleans, New Orleans, LA, USA
Ming-Hsuan Wu	Department of International Business Studies, National Chi Nan University, Nantou County, Taiwan
Chunyu Yang	School of Business Administration, Guizhou University of Finance and Economics, Guiyang, China

AIMS AND SUBMISSION GUIDELINES

Advances in Hospitality and Leisure (AHL), published annually since 2004, attempts to promote seminal and innovative research outputs pertaining to hospitality, leisure, tourism, and lifestyle. Specifically, this journal will encourage researchers to investigate new research issues and problems that are critical but have been largely ignored while providing a forum that will disseminate singular thoughts advancing empirical undertakings both theoretically and methodologically.

This 12th volume includes eight full papers and two research notes. As for data collection, all papers deploy either a quantitative or qualitative approach. The contributors to the present issue come from night nations/regions entailing Australia, China, Germany, the Netherlands, Norway, South Korea, Taiwan, Thailand and the United States.

For submission to future issues, please review the following guidelines.

Originality of Manuscript: The manuscript should represent an original work that has never been published elsewhere nor is being considering for publication elsewhere.

Style and Length of Manuscript: 12 pt Times Roman font; double spacing; APA; 7,000 words (Full Paper) or 4,000 words (Research Note).

Layout of Manuscript: First page: title of paper and author contact information; second page: title of paper, an abstract of 120–140 words, and keywords; third page and beyond: main text, appendix, references, figures, and tables.

Text of Manuscript: For literature review articles, please include introduction, critical literature review, problems in past research, and suggestions for future research. For empirical research papers, please include introduction, methods, findings and discussions, and conclusion.

AHL requires electronic submission. Please send an email attachment with a Word format to the editor Dr. Joseph Chen (joechen@indiana.edu) or send a CD to Tourism, Hospitality and Event Management, Department of Recreation Park and Tourism Studies, School of Public Health Building #133, Indiana University, Bloomington, IN 47405-7109, USA.

FULL PAPERS

THE EFFECTS OF PERSONALITY TRAITS AND CONGRUITY ON CUSTOMER SATISFACTION AND BRAND LOYALTY: EVIDENCE FROM COFFEE SHOP CUSTOMERS

Soon-Ho Kim, Min-Seong Kim and Dong Hun Lee

ABSTRACT

Coffee shops are becoming more aware that brand loyalty can be an effective strategy for securing a competitive edge in business. To supplement current understanding of the importance of coffee shop branding, this study investigates the role of personality traits and congruity in the formation of brand loyalty. This study finds that personality traits have direct effects on congruity and customer satisfaction, the two defining factors of brand loyalty. Overall, our results suggest that the interaction of personality traits, congruity, and satisfaction is essential to the process of influencing coffee shop customers' brand loyalty.

Keywords: Brand loyalty; congruity; coffee shop; personality traits; satisfaction

Advances in Hospitality and Leisure, Volume 12, 3–33
Copyright © 2017 by Emerald Group Publishing Limited
All rights of reproduction in any form reserved
ISSN: 1745-3542/doi:10.1108/S1745-354220160000012001

INTRODUCTION

Self-congruity is a key concept in the consumer behavior literature that reflects consumers' perception of a product/service or brand in terms of its functional and psychological attributes (Kressmann et al., 2006). Consumers' motivation to express themselves is often what drives them to purchase the goods and services of a particular brand (Sirgy, 1986). Thus, Kressmann et al. (2006) emphasize the importance of self-congruity in consumer decision making and define it as "the match between consumers' self-concept (actual self, ideal self, etc.) and the user-image (or personality) of a given product, brand, store, etc." (p. 955). Nam, Ekinci, and Whyatt (2011) developed and tested an integrated model with a focus on self-congruity as an antecedent of consumer satisfaction and brand loyalty. Coffee shops have been rapidly expanding their market share by attracting new customers and luring others from competitors. In the United States, for example, coffee and snack shops have grown in popularity, with over 50,000 coffee shops in existence and a combined $31.12 billion in annual revenue in 2015. Global coffee consumption has increased, and over 2.25 billion cups of coffee are consumed daily in coffee shops around the world (Coffer, 2014).

Previous research has paid special attention to the importance of developing self-congruity, which encourages brand loyalty (Jamal & Al-Marri, 2007). Brand loyalty is essential to an establishment's long-term success and is one of the most common topics in the marketing field (Brakus, Schmitt, & Zarantonello, 2009). Consumers with high brand loyalty are less sensitive to price and are less likely to be influenced by a competitor's advances. A coffee shop brand manager often spends millions of dollars annually in order to create and support the brand image. The impact of brand symbolism depends upon the interrelationship between a brand's perceived image and the consumer's self-image (Jamal & Goode, 2001). According to Graeff's (1996) study, "the more similar a consumer's self-image is to the brand's image, the more favorable their evaluations of that brand should be" (p. 5). Therefore, consumers are more loyal to brands that have images compatible with their own self-perception. Although the self-congruity theory has been tested across some products, such as soft drinks, beer, and alcoholic soft drinks (Allen, Gupta, & Monner, 2008; Branaghan & Hildebrand, 2011; Hogg, Cox, & Keeling, 2000), few studies have investigated the impact of self-congruity on brand loyalty in the coffee shop industry. Previous studies in the service area have mostly focused on the antecedents of brand loyalty, namely service value and customer satisfaction, as they are regarded as core determinants of long-term success for businesses (Hu, Kandampully, & Juwaheer, 2009; Lai, Griffin, & Babin, 2009; Lin, 2010).

Thus, this study specifically investigates the effect of self-congruity on customers' brand loyalty to better understand how self-congruity influences customers' responses (i.e., satisfaction with the coffee shop and brand loyalty) in a coffee shop context. This study also aims to examine the antecedents of self-congruity using the personality trait theory as the fundamental theoretical background. Some hospitality and tourism literature has examined how self-congruity predicts hotel brand loyalty (Han & Back, 2008), customer retention for restaurants (Kwun & Oh, 2006), and destination choices (Sirgy & Su, 2000). However, the research on the relationship between personality and self-congruity is quite limited in the hospitality context. Personality traits are relatively enduring patterns of thoughts, feelings, and behavior that apply to most consumers (Roberts, Walton, & Viechtbauer, 2006). Since brands have their own particular personalities, consumers tend to treat brands like human beings and are likely to use the brand in line with their own personality traits (Lin, 2010). Based on this theoretical background, this study applies a conceptual model of consumer-based brand loyalty, which expands the symbolic consumption of brand evaluation by incorporating personality traits into Nam et al.'s (2011) models of brand loyalty and congruity. Overall, consumers associate with the use and consumption of the brand by expressing both functional and symbolic attributes that lie within congruity (Batra, Lenk, & Wedel, 2010; Romaniuk, 2008).

The personality trait theory has been emphasized in many brands and products, including durable goods, consumable goods, entertainment and luxury goods, and so on (Govers & Schoormans, 2005; Kumar, Luthra, & Datta, 2006; Mengxia, 2007). However, few coffee shop brands have used personality traits as the marketing research target. Therefore, the effect of personality traits on brand loyalty should be examined based upon consumers who have had direct experiences with a coffee shop brand. Given the recent incorporation of personality traits in the field of marketing, and the lack of agreement on the exact link between personality traits and consumer behaviors (Kim, Suh, & Eves, 2010; Vazquez-Carrasco & Foxall, 2006), this study considers it essential to shed more light on this phenomenon. Specifically, this study examines the partially mediating roles of congruity and customer satisfaction based on the relationship between personality traits and brand loyalty.

To the best of the authors' knowledge, there has yet to be conclusive studies that have examined the mediating roles of congruity and customer satisfaction within the coffee shop industry. This study also contributes to a better understanding of how congruity influences customers' satisfaction and brand loyalty. It is crucial for coffee shop owners to find ways to set their products and services apart from others due to the highly competitive market environment, where a coffee shop's products and services have reached a similar status (Lee & Yeu, 2010). In reality, branded coffee shops achieved a higher net operating income during the global economic recession (Kang, Tang, Lee, & Bosselman, 2012). Several scholars have also suggested the use of self-congruity as a source of differentiation, revealing branding as one of the most competitive advantages in the coffee shop industry (Jang, Kim, & Lee, 2015; Kang et al., 2012). In particular, customers view the act of visiting brand coffee shops as a form of self-expression and a way of communicating their self-identity (Kang et al., 2012). From a practical perspective, this study will help a coffee shop management establish a congruity between customers' self-image and the coffee shop brand in order to generate positive customer responses. This study uses the personality trait dimension as the independent variable, congruity and customer satisfaction as the partial mediating variables, and brand loyalty as the dependent variable. This theoretical framework using personality traits and self-congruity provides a new approach for brand managers to segment customer markets and "brand" the coffee shop.

THEORETICAL BACKGROUND AND HYPOTHESIS DEVELOPMENT

Our conceptual model is graphically shown in Fig. 1. The model illustrates that the personality trait dimension contributes to brand loyalty and that the relationship is partially mediated by two variables: congruity and customer satisfaction. Our research model is based on two theories: the trait theory and the self-congruity theory. In this model, customers of a particular brand who can identify with the brand's personality are likely to feel more loyal toward the brand because they are emotionally connected and satisfied with the brand. The dimension of personality traits is closely related to emotions. Personality traits can be understood as a dimension of arousal, which is a core facet of human emotion and affect (Viktoria Rampl & Kenning, 2014).

Gordon Allport, an American psychologist and the founder of personality psychology, described the personality as "a real person." Additionally,

Allport states that the personality is a dynamic organization of psycho-physiological systems that create a person's characteristic pattern of behavior, thoughts, and feeling (Allport, 1961). A personal disposition is defined as "a generalized neuropsychic structure (peculiar to the individual), with the capacity to render many stimuli functionally equivalent, and to initiate and guide consistent (equivalent) forms of adoptive and stylistic behavior" (Allport, 1937, p. 373). Some personality trait researchers believe that personality traits are inborn and are stable, but other researchers argue that personality traits continue to evolve and even change, even if the inborn temperament does not change (Sternberg, 2000).

Trait theory is a major area of study in personality psychology. The trait theory can be divided into two schools (Lin, 2010). The first school believes that all individuals have the same set of traits, but they are different because the level of each trait is shown differently. The other school believes that individual variance comes from the trait combination, which varies from one person to another, so that everyone has his or her own set of specific traits (Sternberg, 2000). The personality trait dimension is a useful variable in examining coffee shop consumer's choices of brands because successful brands are usually in compliance with a consumer's personality (Lin, 2010). Consumers are attracted to a particular brand because successful brands usually demonstrate and express the consumers' own personality (Govers & Schoormans, 2005). Therefore, personality traits can differentiate one coffee shop brand from another. The leading coffee shop brands, such as Starbucks and Dunkin' Donuts, have maintained their advantage over other competitors in a saturated coffee shop market by developing the brand power to keep their patrons coming back. Due to the strength of their brands, these coffee shops continue to dominate markets all over the world.

According to the self-congruity theory, individuals act in ways that maintain and enhance their self-concept (Sirgy, 1986). One way individuals do this is through the products they purchase and use. A consumer's self-image can be defined, maintained, and enhanced through these products (Aaker, 1997). Consumers achieve "self-consistency" by holding positive attitudes toward, and purchasing brands that are perceived to be similar to, their self-concept (Graeff, 1996). Essentially, consumers are more inclined to hold a set of beliefs about themselves and subconsciously act in ways (i.e., purchase and use goods or services) that reinforce those beliefs. Behaviors and events that result in self-perceptions inconsistent with one's self-concept cause dissonance — a state of mental stress that motivates individuals to restore consonance. This motivational tendency has been coined as the need for self-consistency (Epstein, 1980). Consumers' need for self-consistency motivates purchase behavior and brand loyalty. Self-congruity is the match between a consumer's actual self-image and the user-image associated with a particular good, service, or store. Consumer behavior research has demonstrated that actual self-congruity (the match between a consumer's actual self-image and the user-image associated with a particular good, service, or store) is positively related to consumer behavior constructs including brand attitude, brand preference, brand choice, purchase motivation, purchase intention, brand purchase, brand satisfaction, and brand loyalty (Beerli, Meneses, & Gil, 2007; Kressmann et al., 2006; Sirgy, Grewal, & Mangleburg, 2000; Sirgy & Su, 2000).

The self-congruity theory can be applied to the context of the coffee shop industry because self-congruity is a process of matching the symbolic image of a coffee shop and a customer's self-image (He & Mukherjee, 2007). In addition, self-congruity has been proven to be antecedent of customer attitude toward a brand and a predictor of their actual behavior (Kang et al., 2012). Thus, customers intend to create meaningful and personal bonds with the coffee shop brand by matching the images of the brand with themselves. The congruence between coffee shop brand and customer self-image is defined as self-congruity. When coffee shop customers identify the coffee shop brand image as congruent with their self-image, they accept that the coffee shop brand can represent their identity, thus causing them to form a favorable attitude toward the coffee shop (Lee & Hyman, 2008).

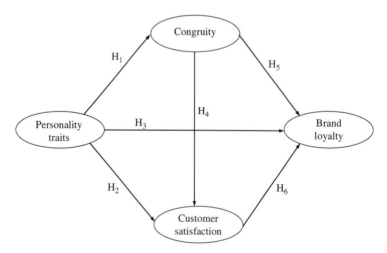

Fig. 1.   A Proposed Model.

Personality Traits

Personality psychology could be described as possessing two types of traits: (1) main traits that convey important values, and (2) complementary traits that are only present in some situations (Seimiene, 2012). Aaker (1996) uses a main and complementary trait model for analyzing a brand's image. According to Aaker (1996), if a brand operates in several markets, it has the same main features; however, complementary traits work differently. Therefore, consumers are able to use personality traits not only to describe themselves, but also to differentiate between brands in order to relate certain brands to themselves (Aaker, 1997). Personality traits influence consumer preference and patronage, leading to stronger emotional ties to a brand (Aaker, Fournier, & Brasel, 2004) as well as greater brand loyalty (Chen & Phou, 2013).

Personality traits have been defined as "an individual's characteristic pattern of thought, emotion and behavior, together with the psychological mechanisms – hidden or not – behind those patterns" (Funder, 1997, pp. 1–2). Thus, personality trait is a prominent factor in the explanation of human behavior. Personality predicts job performance (Tett, Jackson, & Rothstein, 1991), marriage stability (Karney & Bradbury, 1995), and even mortality (Roberts, Kuncel, Shiner, Caspi, & Goldberg, 2007). Research incorporating personality traits in the consumer context can help us to develop integrated conceptual frameworks for understanding consumers (Westjohn, Singh, & Magnusson, 2012) as well as better targeted communications (Baumgartner, 2002).

The marketing literature offers evidence on the effects of self-image congruence on brand choice, preference, and loyalty (Wang, Yang, & Liu, 2009). Some studies have connected the congruence between store image and self-image on product perception and purchase intention (Bloemer & Oderkerken-Schroder, 2002; D'Astous & Gargouri, 2001). Although substantive evidence is lacking regarding self-image congruence with personality traits, a considerable number of prior studies have suggested that personality traits result in higher congruity. High congruity occurs when the personality traits of a customer match the personality traits of a company or product brand (Hsieh, Pan, & Setiono, 2004). For example, Branaghan and Hildebrand (2011) proposed that self-image could be thought of as a person's network representation personality traits. Thus, in a scenario of high congruity, company or product brand personality traits have a high degree of relevance to each other (Ahluwalia & Gurhan-Canli, 2000).

Following Cervone and Pervin (2010), this study views personality traits as the study of what is generally true of consumers by examining consistencies in individual difference variables. This study focuses on personality traits as the variable of interest for studying coffee shop customers because of the common meaning of individual traits over time and across many different situations (Lounsbury et al., 2012). More specifically, Solomon and Jackson (2014) suggest that the personality trait dimension is an antecedent of relationship satisfaction and that both constructs should be positively associated with each other. In addition, Liu (2014) found support for this proposition in the context of leisure participants. Rosowsky and Sega (2012) argue that the personality trait dimension reflects the functional aspects of marital satisfaction. Furthermore, their research demonstrated that consumer satisfaction mediates the relationship between personality traits and long-term marriage. They found that individual behavior, which relates to personality traits, had the strongest impact on marital satisfaction.

Due to theoretical and empirical evidence that personality traits and affect are strongly related (correlations between 0.63 and 0.83 from Clark & Watson, 1999; Zimmerman, 2008), a number of studies have established relationships between personality traits and affective behavior (Matzler, Bidmon, & Grabner-Krauter, 2006; Mooradian & Olver, 1997; Pirog & Roberts, 2007). Consumers are likely to use brands that mirror their own personality traits (Govers & Schoormans, 2005) in order to express themselves (Herstein et al., 2012). In addition, a brand may become part of an individual's self-concept by evoking strong cognitive and psychological attachments. Several researchers have demonstrated that a brand can evoke strong symbolic values that usually depict customers' personality traits (Ekinci, Sirakaya-Turk, & Preciado, 2013; Hultman, Skarmeas, Oghazi, & Beheshti, 2015). Thus, coffee shop brands with strong personality traits are likely to evoke congruity by effectively reflecting customers' desired self-image. As a result, marketing activities are aimed at helping consumers to believe and recognize brand personality traits, which reinforces the communication between the brand and the consumer in order to enhance brand loyalty (Lin, 2010; Matzler et al., 2006). Based on this information, we propose the following hypotheses:

H1. The personality trait dimension has a positive effect on congruity.

H2. The personality trait dimension has a positive effect on customer satisfaction.

H3. The personality trait dimension has a positive effect on brand loyalty.

Congruity

Self-congruity as a symbolic benefit of products has been well-documented in the marketing literature (Das, 2014; Helgeson & Supphellen, 2004). Self-congruity is defined as "how much a consumer's self-concept matches the personality of a typical user of a brand" (Helgeson & Supphellen, 2004, p. 206). Self-congruity theory proposes that consumer behavior is partially determined by an individual's comparison of the image of him or herself and the image of brands, as reflected in a stereotype of a typical user of the brands (Sirgy, Grewal, Mangleburg, & Park, 1997). Congruity with a brand reflects the degree of congruity between the consumer's self-image and the image of the brand (Sirgy, Lee, Johar, & Tidwell, 2008). In other words, customers intend to create meaningful and personal bonds with the brand by pairing the images of the brand with themselves.

Congruity is operationalized by a match between actual self-image with the corresponding affective images of a coffee shop brand (e.g., a pleasant and enjoyable experience, a sense of escapism and discovery, and relaxation). The match between self-image and affective brand image has been referred to as self-congruity (Sirgy, 2015). High self-congruity occurs when a consumer's own self-image matches suitably with the brand image. Therefore, the greater the congruity between the actual and ideal self-image, coupled with the image of the coffee shop, the greater the possibility that the customer will be motivated to continue patronizing the coffee shop (Beerli et al., 2007). In addition, congruity with a coffee shop franchise helps create a favorable attitude toward that brand's individual stores among customers, and these positive feelings are associated with the franchisor of the coffee shop. Such feelings are more easily transferred to the coffee franchisor when the consumer recognizes having previously transacted with a brand (i.e., being a customer of that firm) versus visiting other coffee franchisors for the first time (Gwinner, 1997; Gwinner & Eaton, 1999).

Congruity has been widely recognized as an important construct in explaining consumer behavior (Lee & Back, 2009). Although most prior studies have empirically tested the effects on behavior, such as motivation, choice, and intention (Back, 2005), hospitality literature says that congruity favorably affects customer satisfaction. For instance, Chon (1992) studied the direct effects of congruity on customer satisfaction and found a significant relationship between congruity and customer satisfaction. In their study on brand loyalty, Bonsnjak, Sirgy, Hellriegel, and Maurer (2011) found that the greater the match between customer self-image and brand name, the greater the satisfaction. As Sirgy and Su (2000) stated, individuals have need for self-consistency and often behave in ways consistent with their personal identity. As a result, congruity will influence customers' overall evaluation of the coffee shop during and after consumption.

Congruity is one of many factors that determine brand loyalty and has been proven to be an antecedent of customer attitudes toward products and behavior (Lee & Hyman, 2008). This causal relationship can be applied to other contexts. For instance, Sirgy et al. (2008) have extended self-image congruence research to a corporate sponsorship context by demonstrating that congruity with a sponsorship event is a mediating role in the relationship between corporate sponsorship and brand loyalty. As a result, customers of a certain brand are likely to develop feelings of brand loyalty when they recognize that they can experience self-congruity with the brand (Kressmann et al., 2006). Based on the discussion above, our hypotheses are proposed below:

H4. Congruity has a positive effect on customer satisfaction.

H5. Congruity has a positive effect on brand loyalty.

Customer Satisfaction

Customer satisfaction, a fundamental marketing concept, is defined as the notion of satisfying the needs and desires of consumers (Spreng, MacKenzie, & Olshavsky, 1996). Rodriguez del Bosque and San Martin (2008) suggest that consumer satisfaction is cognitive as well as emotional, meaning that satisfaction arises from both logical points of reference (i.e., value) and/or feeling-based points of reference (i.e., nostalgia). Customer satisfaction results when customers either confirm their pre-purchase expectations for a purchased service or positively disconfirm (exceed) their expectations regarding a purchased service, resulting in some level of post-purchase affect toward the experience (Back & Parks, 2003). While the literature includes significant differences in the definition of satisfaction, there are two common types of satisfaction. The first type of satisfaction, known as transaction-specific satisfaction, is an immediate post-purchase evaluative judgment and is an affective reaction to the most recent experience with a firm (Oliver, 1993). The transaction-specific approach suggests that satisfaction occurs at the post-consumption stage following a single encounter with the service provider (Jones & Suh, 2000).

Overall satisfaction is the second type of satisfaction. This type uses an evaluative judgment with the last purchase occasion and is based on all encounters with the service provider (Bitner & Hubbert, 1994). Therefore, overall satisfaction is an aggregation of all transaction-specific satisfaction with service encounters (Veloutsou, Gilbert, Moutinho, & Goode, 2005). Transaction-specific satisfaction is likely to vary from experience to experience while overall satisfaction is a moving average that is relatively stable and most similar to an overall attitude toward purchasing a brand (Auh, Salisbury, & Johnson, 2003). This conceptualization is notable because overall satisfaction is a better indicator of future loyalty and business performance (Johnson, Gustafsson, Andreassen, Lervik, & Cha, 2001). Therefore, we view consumer satisfaction as a consumer's overall emotional response to the entire brand experience following the most recent purchase.

Satisfaction has been found to lead to a long-term combination of relationships (Sahin, Zahir, & Kitapçı, 2011). The satisfaction derived and the attitude formed as part of a prior experience (Ganesan, 1994) then impact subsequent purchases (Oliver, 1993), creating a cyclical pattern (Bennett, Hartel, & Mccoll-Kennedy, 2005). Brand relationship quality can be defined as the degree to which the consumer views the brand as a satisfactory partner in an ongoing relationship; it is the consumer's overall assessment of the strength of his or her relationship with the brand (Algesheimer, Dholakia, & Herrmann, 2005).

Many consumer researchers have found a significant causal relationship between customer satisfaction and behavioral intention. Satisfaction is an antecedent of brand loyalty, with increases in satisfaction leading to increases in brand loyalty (Bennett et al., 2005; Jones & Suh, 2000). Satisfaction is found to increase loyalty when brand loyalty is measured in a number of successive purchases of the same brand (Ha & Park, 2012). Fornell, Johnson, Anderson, Cha, and Beyant (1996) stated that increased customer satisfaction increases brand loyalty in terms of repurchase likelihood and price tolerance. Oliver (1999) argued that customer satisfaction is "the beginning of a transitioning sequence that culminates in a separate loyalty state" (p. 34). Customer satisfaction and brand loyalty are positively related, as proven in a number of studies

(Bloemer & Kasper, 1995). Satisfaction with the preferred brand is one of the determinants of brand loyalty (Sahin et al., 2011). Thus, the research hypothesis is proposed:

H6. Customer satisfaction has a positive effect on brand loyalty.

Brand Loyalty

The modeling of loyalty has a long history in academic literature, and articles within the marketing discipline dealing with the subject of brand loyalty can be traced back to the early 1920s (Homburg & Giering, 2001). In reference to brand marketing research, loyalty acts as a biased behavior expressed over time by an individual with respect to one or more alternatives and is a function of psychological processes (Jacoby & Kyner, 1973). The majority of early loyalty studies conceptualized loyalty with behavior, as a form of repeat purchasing of a particular product or service over time. Behavioral brand loyalty can be defined as a customer's overt behavior toward a specific brand in terms of repeat purchasing patterns (Back & Parks, 2003). Specifically, a repeat purchasing pattern can be determined as actual purchase frequency, and the proportion of occasions in which a specific brand is purchased as compared to the total number of purchased brands and/or the actual amount of purchase.

Brand loyalty can be defined as "a deeply held commitment to re-buy or re-patronize a preferred product/service consistently in the future, thereby causing repetitive same brand or same brand-set purchasing, despite situational influences and marketing efforts having the potential to cause switching behavior" (Oliver, 1999, p. 34). This definition emphasizes both behavioral and attitudinal perspectives on brand loyalty, which is considered as one of the most important factors affecting consumer choice (Ha & Park, 2012). The definition of behavioral brand loyalty is often considered to be synonymous with repeat purchase behavior (Kuikka & Laukkanen, 2012; Quester & Lim, 2003). The definition of attitudinal brand loyalty refers to repurchase intention and word-of-mouth or cross-buying potential (Sirdesmukh, Singh, & Sabol, 2002). Furthermore, authentic brand loyalty goes beyond repetitive purchasing behavior and implies a true commitment to a specific brand (Back & Parks, 2003; Quester & Lim, 2003) as well as share of wallet, the percentage of brand purchases in a product category for fast-moving consumer goods (Sirdesmukh et al., 2002).

Although some authors focused on the sequence in which brands were purchased (Caruana, 2002; Lau & Lee, 1999), others measured loyalty through the proportion of purchases devoted to a given brand (Yi & Jeon, 2003). Dick and Basu (1994) propose that customer loyalty is the result of psychological processes and has behavioral manifestations, and should therefore incorporate both attitudinal and behavioral components. In conclusion, most of the marketing literature defines brand loyalty as a result of the interplay between the consumer's attitude and repeat purchase behavior (Kuikka & Laukkanen, 2012; Ogba & Tan, 2009).

As the global rise in the purchase of hot beverages, which began over a decade ago, has become an industry of its own, both scholars and practitioners have tried to initiate various brand strategies and apply them to diverse global cultures. East Asian countries, including China, South Korea, Japan, Singapore, and Taiwan, have increased in economic power and are considered significant markets (Lee, Kim, Son, & Kim, 2015). However, relatively few studies have paid attention to how brand strategies should be practiced when global coffee shop companies move into East Asian markets. Though a plethora of studies have emphasized the linkages among personality traits, congruity, satisfaction, and brand loyalty on Western consumer populations, very little is known about whether those relationships, incorporating personality traits and congruity, hold true for East Asian coffee shop consumers. For example, the increased visits to branded coffee shops in East Asian countries reflect the nature of collectivistic cultures, in which similar patterns of purchasing behavior exist within a social group (Kang et al., 2012). This study proposes and tests relationships that are more characteristic of East Asia.

METHODS

Sample and Procedure

The data were collected using a cross-sectional survey on customers from both franchised and independent coffee shops located in South Korea. South Korea's coffee shop industry has seen a dramatic increase over the past 10 years in comparison to the global coffee shop industry (Kang et al., 2012). The total sales of South Korea's coffee shop industry have increased annually, breaking the annual sales goal of $4.5 billion in 2014. This study applies the trait and self-congruity theories to the understanding of the current trends of coffee consumption in East Asian countries with a collectivistic culture, such as Korea (House, Hanges, Javidan, Dorfman, & Gupta, 2004). From a practical perspective, several international coffee shop brands (e.g., Starbucks and The Coffee Bean & Tea Leaf Company) have already dominated the East Asian markets. For example, in Korea, 554 Starbucks locations have achieved overall sales of $369 million and round out net profits of $23 million (Global Coffee Report, 2013). Therefore, this study has significant implications for global coffee shop companies that either already operate in or plan to establish themselves in the East Asian coffee shop markets.

The questionnaire was first developed in English and then translated into Korean. The translation was discussed with two Korean−American bilinguals. Back-translation was used during the translation process. A pilot test was conducted with 60 customers from coffee shops in South Korea. After minor changes were made, the questionnaire was completed. Copies of the questionnaire were delivered to owners of coffee shops after they agreed to participate in the study. Owners distributed the questionnaires to their customers visiting their coffee shops. The participants were offered a free beverage or dessert menu item, along with a $10 gift certificate to be used in the coffee shop, to avoid non-response bias. A total of 780 questionnaires were collected in the month of March and April in 2014. Of the 780 returned responses, 743 samples were used for further analysis because 37 questionnaires were not usable due to missing information. Statistical Package for the Social Sciences 18.0 (SPSS) and AMOS 20.0 were used for data analysis.

Measures

All constructs were measured by using multiple items developed and tested in previous studies. Each item was measured on a seven-point Likert-type scale anchored by "strongly disagree" and "strongly agree." The personality trait dimension was measured with six items from Vazquez-Carrasco and Foxall (2006). This study drew on a comprehensive literature review in terms of personality traits for adapting those measures. As exhibited in Hultman et al.'s (2015) study, two academic researchers with a background in hospitality and consumer behavior evaluated the content validity of the measures by judging the extent to which each item precisely formulates the overall personality traits.

For congruity, five items were used (Kang et al., 2012). This study is the first to apply self-image congruity to specific consumer conditions pertaining to the coffee shop industry in the Korean cultural setting. For customer satisfaction, three items were used (Lee, Lee, & Yoo, 2000). Lastly, five items adapted from Olsen (2007) were used to measure the brand loyalty dimension. Each item for customer satisfaction and brand loyalty has arguably received the greatest support, and has been subjected to the greatest empirical scrutiny in the consumer behavior literature (Lee et al., 2000; Olsen, 2007).

Statistical Analysis

The measures used in the survey were subjected to reliability and validity analysis. confirmatory factor analysis (CFA) was employed to test the relationships between the observed and the latent variables and to examine the reliability and validity of the constructs using AMOS 20.0 (Hair, Black, Babin, Anderson, & Tatham, 2006). The internal consistency reliability was examined using Cronbach's alpha coefficients of each factor using the SPSS 18.0. Structural equation modeling (SEM) was carried out to test the hypothesized relationships in the proposed model. To adequately assess the goodness-of-fit and parsimony of the model, a series of indices, including chi-square values with related degrees of freedom (d.f.), the root mean square error of approximation (RMSEA), the comparative fit index (CFI), the adjusted goodness-of-fit index (AGFI), and the normed fit index (NFI), were examined.

RESULTS

As shown in Table 1, over half of the respondents were female (66.8%); 38.5% were 25–34 years of age and 24.4% were 35–44 years of age. More than two-thirds (67.2%) of the respondents graduated from or are currently attending a four-year college. Annual household income range in the category of "less than $49,999" was 56.3%, followed by "$80,000 or above" (28.7%).

Table 1.   Demographics of the Respondents.

Variables (N = 743)	Characteristics	Frequency
Gender	Male	247 (33.2%)
	Female	496 (66.8%)
Age	18−24	169 (22.7%)
	25−34	286 (38.5%)
	35−44	181 (24.4%)
	45−54	88 (11.8%)
	55−64	16 (2.2%)
	55 above	3 (0.4%)
Education	High school	144 (19.4%)
	2- or 4-year college	499 (67.2%)
	Graduate school	98 (13.2%)
	Missing	2 (0.3%)
Annual household income	Less than $49,999	418 (56.3%)
	$50,000−$59,999	33 (4.4%)
	$60,000−$69,999	47 (6.3%)
	$70,000−$79,999	2 (0.3%)
	$80,000 or above	213 (28.7%)
	Missing	4 (0.4%)

Based on the assessment of the adequacy of the measurement model (Table 2), the items that loaded poorly on the hypothesized factor were removed for purification of the measures. For example, two items each from the personality traits, congruity, and brand loyalty categories, along with one item from the customer satisfaction category, which had factor loadings lower than 0.50, were dropped for further analyses to maintain an acceptable level of convergent and discriminant validity (Kim, Kim, Han, & Holland, 2016). The CFA showed that all loadings exceeded 0.70 except for one item that had 0.68 (a personality traits item), and each indicator t-value exceeded 17.79 ($p < 0.001$), confirming convergent validity. The χ^2 fit statistics showed 249.761 with 48 d.f. ($\chi^2/\text{d.f.} = 5.203$) ($p < 0.001$). All measurement statistics support the overall quality given the number of indicators (Anderson & Gerbing, 1988): the RMSEA = 0.075; the CFI = 0.960; the goodness-of-fit index (GFI) = 0.949; the NFI = 0.952. The Cronbach's alpha values of all dimensions exceeded the recommended value of 0.70 (Nunnally & Bernstein, 1994), ranging from 0.815 (congruity) to 0.891 (customer satisfaction).

Table 2. Measurement Model Resulting from Confirmatory Factor Analysis.

Constructs and Variables[a]	Standardized Loading (t-Value)	CCR[b]	AVE[c]	Skew	Kurtosis
Personality traits (α = 0.827)		0.833	0.557		
I feel my favorite coffee shops offer a warm dining experience	0.746 (Fixed)			−0.807	0.249
I feel my favorite coffee shops offer a pleasant dining experience	0.800 (20.911)			−0.542	−0.010
I feel excited when I go to my favorite coffee shops	0.806 (21.060)			−0.354	−0.428
My favorite coffee shops offer a sophisticated servicescape[d]	—			—	—
My favorite coffee shops have higher drinking quality standards[d]	—			—	—
I feel my favorite coffee shops offer a hometown atmosphere	0.681 (17.794)			−0.378	−0.566
Congruity (α = 0.806)		0.825	0.612		
The typical customers at my favorite coffee shop have an image similar to how I see myself	0.782 (Fixed)			−0.625	0.035
The overall atmosphere of my favorite coffee shop reflects who I am	0.824 (21.076)			−0.388	−0.646
The typical customers at my favorite coffee shop have an image similar to how other people see me[d]	—			—	—
The typical customers at my favorite coffee shop have an image similar to how I would like other people to see me	0.711 (18.642)			0.046	−0.791
The menus of beverages as well as designs and layouts at my favorite coffee shops reflect what I prefer to have[d]	—			—	—

Table 2. (Continued)

Constructs and Variables[a]	Standardized Loading (t-Value)	CCR[b]	AVE[c]	Skew	Kurtosis
Satisfaction ($\alpha = 0.700$)		0.863	0.759		
Overall, satisfaction with my favorite coffee shop	0.902 (Fixed)			−0.903	0.089
Satisfaction with visiting my favorite coffee shop when compared with my expectations	0.892 (29.007)			−0.752	0.791
Satisfaction with visiting my favorite coffee shop considering my invested time and effort[d]	—			—	—
Brand loyalty ($\alpha = 0.911$)		0.800	0.570		
I consider myself a loyal customer at my favorite coffee shops[d]	—			—	—
I will continue to enjoy drinks at my favorite coffee shops	0.849 (Fixed)			−0.964	0.480
I would give positive recommendations to others about my favorite coffee shops	0.834 (26.106)			−0.755	0.069
Overall, I will continue to repurchase drinks at my favorite coffee shops[d]	—			—	—
Overall, I will continue to maintain a valued membership card if provided at my favorite coffee shop	0.798 (24.696)			−0.932	0.468

[a] $\chi^2 = 249.761$, d.f. = 48 (χ^2/d.f. = 5.203), $p = 0.000$, GFI = 0.949, AGFI = 0.917, RMSEA = 0.075, NFI = 0.952, CFI = 0.960.
[b] Composite construct reliability.
[c] Average variance extracted.
[d] Items were deleted during the confirmatory factor analysis.

Three measures, Cronbach's alpha coefficients, composite construct reliability (CCR), and average variance extracted (AVE), were examined to assess the reliability as well as the convergent and discriminant validity of the latent constructs. The CCR coefficients all exceeded 0.60, the cut off recommendation. Also, the AVE values indicated the discriminant validity since the AVE value of each construct was greater than the recommended value of 0.50 (Anderson & Gerbing, 1988). Therefore, the measurement models for personality traits, congruity, customer satisfaction, and brand loyalty constructs were well justified enough to be tested in the ensuing structural model (Fig. 2).

AMOS 20.0 was used to conduct SEM analyses. The testing of the hypotheses was based on the significance of the standardized path coefficients (Table 3). The χ^2 statistic was significant ($\chi^2 = 249.761$, d.f. $= 48$, $p < 0.001$), as would be expected for a model of this complexity with this sample size. The overall evaluation of model fit was completed using various indices: GFI $= 0.949$; AGFI $= 0.917$; NFI $= 0.952$; CFI $= 0.961$; RMSEA $= 0.075$. The squared multiple correlations (SMCs) among personality traits, congruity, customer satisfaction, and brand loyalty were found to be moderate. Over half of the variance (SMC $= 0.626$) in brand loyalty was explained by the direct effects of personality traits, congruity, and customer satisfaction. In addition, the direct effects of personality traits and congruity accounted for 37.0% of customer satisfaction. Lastly, the direct effect of personality traits accounted for 52.9% of congruity. Specific results of testing each hypothesis are as follows.

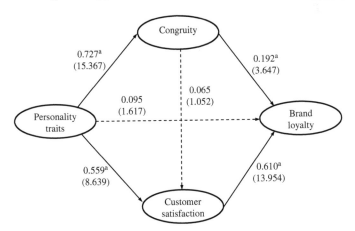

Fig. 2. Estimates of Structural Model. [a]$p < 0.01$, [b]$p < 0.05$. *Note*: Standardized coefficient (*t*-value), Solid line: significant path, Broken line: insignificant path.

H_1 addressed that the personality traits dimension positively affects congruity. Personality traits had a significant positive effect on congruity ($\beta = 0.727$, $t = 15.367$, $p < 0.001$), so H_1 was supported. H_2 stated that the personality trait construct is positively associated with customer satisfaction. The personality trait construct was positively associated with customer satisfaction ($\beta = 0.559$, $t = 8.639$, $p < 0.001$), supporting H_2. H_3 demonstrated that the personality trait dimension influences on brand loyalty; however, it is not supported ($\beta = 0.095$, $t = 1.617$, $p > 0.05$). H_4 showed that congruity has a positive effect on satisfaction; however, it is also not supported ($\beta = 0.065$, $t = 1.052$, $p > 0.05$). H_5 addressed that congruity positively affects brand loyalty. Congruity had a significant positive effect on brand loyalty ($\beta = 0.192$, $t = 3.647$, $p < 0.001$), so H_5 was supported. H_6 stated that customer satisfaction is positively associated with brand loyalty. Customer satisfaction was positively associated with brand loyalty ($\beta = 0.610$, $t = 13.954$, $p < 0.001$), supporting H_6.

Table 3. Standardized Parameter Estimates.

Path	Standardized Estimates	t-Value
Personality traits → Congruity	0.727	15.367[a]
Personality traits → Customer satisfaction	0.559	8.639[a]
Personality traits → Brand loyalty	0.095	1.617
Congruity → Customer satisfaction	0.065	1.052
Congruity → Brand loyalty	0.192	3.647[a]
Customer satisfaction → Brand loyalty	0.610	13.954[a]
Indirect effects		p-Value
Personality traits → Customer satisfaction	0.047	0.239
Personality traits → Brand loyalty	0.510	0.001[a]
Congruity → Brand loyalty	0.040	0.241
SMC (R^2)		
Congruity	0.529	
Customer satisfaction	0.370	
Brand loyalty	0.626	

[a]$p < 0.01$, [b]$p < 0.05$.
Note: $\chi^2 = 249.761$, d.f. = 48, $p = 0.000$, GFI = 0.949, AGFI = 0.917, NFI = 0.952, CFI = 0.961, RMSEA = 0.075.

DISCUSSION

The key objective of this study is to explore the role of personality traits and their importance on brand loyalty in the coffee shop context in Korea while focusing on the partial mediating variables of congruity and customer satisfaction. While scholars in the consumer behavior field have pointed out the importance of personality traits and self-congruity, research is scarce on the role of these variables in the East Asian coffee shop industry. To address this shortcoming, we empirically provide evidence that the personality trait construct has direct positive influences on congruity and customer satisfaction and an indirect influence on brand loyalty. If brand managers better understand the role of personality traits, their coffee shops can maximize the effect of personality in order to sustain its relationship with customers. This study extends the existing brand loyalty literature by studying the relationships among the personality trait dimension, congruity, customer satisfaction, and brand loyalty using trait theory and self-congruity theory. This application in the coffee shop context not only contributes to the body of knowledge on personality traits and self-congruity but also confirms the solidity of the theoretical framework. This study applies Korean culture to explore customers' branded coffee shop visit behavior, which offers a foundation for future research examining consumption in accordance with Asian culture.

Representing the potential of personality traits and congruity effects, this study provides empirical support that personality traits play a critical role in influencing congruity that affects customers' responses, such as customer satisfaction and brand loyalty. Therefore, coffee shop brand managers should study personality traits as well as the congruity of their brands from the consumer's point of view to develop a brand image consistent with the coffee shop consumer's ideal self-concept. As consumers choose coffee shops beyond satisfying their immediate needs, brand personality traits and congruity can be used for positioning coffee shop brands in competitive markets.

Implications

Brands have received much attention from many marketing researchers. These researchers also studied the effect of brand power on consumers (Aaker, 1997; Aaker et al., 2004; Freling, Crosno, & Henard, 2011; Malar, Krohmer, Hoyer, & Nyffenegger, 2011). When a brand is strong, it can enhance brand attitudes and the consumer–brand relationship as well as brand loyalty (Freling et al., 2011). To our knowledge, however, research about brand loyalty did not consider the effect of both the personality trait dimension and congruity on brand loyalty. Accordingly, this study examines the effect of the personality trait construct and congruity on customer satisfaction and brand loyalty in the context of the coffee shop industry in Korea.

The findings of this study provide theoretical and empirical evidence to support the proposed model. Primarily, this study revealed the significant role of personality traits on congruity, which increases customers' brand loyalty toward a coffee shop. Thus, personality traits can be used as a practical framework for Western marketers to understand Korean customers' motivations, recognition, and behaviors. By using various marketing approaches, a coffee shop conveys its personality to consumers and attracts consumers of varying personality traits. As a result, consumers can develop a relationship with the brand, which will further influence brand loyalty. The shaping of distinct personality traits can add value to a coffee shop's brand. Coffee shop brand managers should keep their brand personality traits distinct, lasting, and consistent to attract customers and cultivate their satisfaction with the specific coffee shop brand and to create loyal customers. Before customers enter, they should recognize the exterior design and brand logo of the coffee shop. The coffee shop should provide what customers seek and expect from the brand. As customers walk through the door, they should be welcomed by a familiar interior and greeted by a barista who wears a familiar uniform in the same branded coffee shop elsewhere in the country. The beverage and dessert names should also be the same. If customers recognize what they want, and if they get it from the coffee shop brand time and time again, they will feel fulfilled and satisfied with the brand. All these practices reflect brand image, avoid brand confusion, and enhance the standardized, yet satisfying, connection with the brand through consistency.

Congruity has significant effects on customer satisfaction and brand loyalty. Customers may have expectations of the coffee shop in regards to the quality of coffee, employee service, variety of menu items, interior design and decor, location, and price. A customer's desire for consistency suggests that brand managers can expect brand loyalty if they make an effort to meet the degrees of congruity their target customers pursue. Coffee shop brand managers must recognize the extent to which their target customers desire to express or enhance their self-image based on their coffee shop experience. This study demonstrates that brand managers' effort to match customers' self-image with the coffee shop image will result in an increase in customers' satisfaction as well as increased future purchases and recommendations. Therefore, brand managers can build a favorable coffee shop image by managing and marketing attributes of the coffee shop. The coffee shop brand managers are also advised to identify their target customers and design the coffee shop image based on their values. Finally, coffee shop brand managers should note that Korean customers seek the added experience of finding an image that is consistent with or enhances their own image. Furthermore, it is common for Koreans to look for a "Third Place" (i.e., home being the first and work being the second). Starbucks, one of the dominant brands in the Korean coffee shop market, has played a central role as the third place for its customers. Starbucks believes customers connect with its brand because they associate with what the brand stands for. It is the feeling of warmth and community that brings customers to a Starbucks. Starbucks continually emphasizes the importance of a healthy body and mind, brand image that fits a Korean consumer's self-image. Other coffee shop companies would benefit from developing their brand image based on the cultural assumptions and personality traits of their customers.

Another implication of this study is the need for more individual branding. This call is based on this study's finding that the effect of congruity on brand loyalty depends on the customer-specific context, which is consistent with the current trend in marketing of moving away from mass marketing to one-to-one marketing. The results of this study suggest that the one-to-one marketing approach should be applied to branding as well. New technologies in Web 2.0 allow individualized advertising based on consumers' self-image to be implemented. In addition, managers can develop innovative ways to combine the consumers' self-image with their branding efforts. Thus, coffee shop companies that seek to develop their connections with customers should not hesitate to express their emotions and feelings as well as show their facts or personal opinions on social network services. Such acts of displaying self-image can encourage emotional exchanges with consumers, ultimately creating a match between self-image and coffee shop brand. The trend toward collaborative branding (especially through social media), which enables marketing managers to give consumers the opportunity to contribute to a brand's image, may be a good way to create a brand congruent with consumers' self-image.

The study's findings indicate that increasing customer satisfaction increases customer brand loyalty. The close relationship between satisfaction and brand loyalty was confirmed in the context of the Korean coffee shop industry through SEM analysis. From the perspective of coffee shops, this finding implies that coffee shop brand managers should be encouraged to develop customer brand loyalty by investing in the satisfaction of their customers. In addition, the managers of coffee shop must do their best to understand the needs and wants of their customers. Moreover, the managers should ensure that personnel are completely oriented with regard to the level of the service that should be performed. A training program is recommended to improve the staff's qualifications. Coffee shop managers should also continuously monitor their customers' perception of products as well as customers' latest needs and wants in order to keep the company's marketing tools updated and keep customers more satisfied and delighted.

Limitations and Future Research

Although this study provides insightful findings, it has limitations. However, these limitations provide opportunities for future research. The limitations are as follows:

First, this study relied on a limited number of personality trait scales and examined a specific business model, coffee shops. Further research, with more extensive sets of personality traits and coffee shop brands, can be utilized to identify the degree of generalizability of these results. Second, the survey in this study was conducted in coffee shop franchises and independent coffee shops in South Korea. While this study did analyze differences between customers of franchising coffee shops and customers of independent coffee shops, there was no significant difference between the two customer groups. However, since customers in each type of coffee shop demonstrate similar characteristics, there may be other differences between the two customer groups. Future research should look for significant differences between the two types of coffee shops by conducting multi-group analyses with other determinants of brand loyalty. Third, the random sample investigated in the study included only Korean customers. Further work is necessary for explaining brand loyalty behaviors in other East Asian country contexts. Fourth, the practice of coffee shop owners distributing questionnaires to their customers might have skewed the findings because owners could have been selective in whom they gave the questionnaires to. Future research should increase the overall quality of the respondent to collect data from a random sample of customers and in the coffee shop context with wider samples and settings. Lastly, we recognize that there are several largely unexplored factors influencing brand loyalty, such as brand personality, perceived value, and brand involvement. Future research should also include these additional relevant variables to provide a more comprehensive picture of brand loyalty in this regard.

REFERENCES

Aaker, D. A. (1996). *Building strong brands*. New York: The Free Press.

Aaker, J. L. (1997). Dimensions of brand personality. *Journal of Marketing Research*, *34*(3), 347−356.

Aaker, J. L., Fournier, S., & Brasel, S. (2004). When good brands do bad. *Journal of Consumer Research*, *31*(1), 1−16.

Ahluwalia, R., & Gurhan-Canli, Z. (2000). The effects of extensions on the family brand name: An accessibility diagnosticity perspective. *Journal of Consumer Research*, *27*(3), 371−381.

Algesheimer, R., Dholakia, U. M., & Herrmann, A. (2005). The social influence of brand community: Evidence from European car clubs. *Journal of Marketing*, *69*(3), 19−34.

Allen, M. W., Gupta, R., & Monner, A. (2008). The interactive effect of cultural symbols and human values on taste evaluation. *Journal of Consumer Research*, *35*(2), 294−308.

Allport, G. W. (1937). *Personality: A psychological interpretation*. Oxford: Holt.

Allport, G. W. (1961). *Pattern and growth in personality*. Oxford: Holt, Reinhart & Winston.

Anderson, J. C., & Gerbing, D. W. (1988). Structural equation modeling in practice: A review and recommended two-step approach. *Psychological Bulletin*, *103*(3), 411−423.

Auh, S., Salisbury, L. C., & Johnson, M. (2003). Order effects in customer satisfaction modeling. *Journal of Marketing Management*, *19*(3−4), 379−400.

Back, K. (2005). The effects of image congruence on customers' brand loyalty in the upper middle-class hotel industry. *Journal of Hospitality & Tourism Research*, *29*(4), 448−467.

Back, K. J., & Park, S. C. (2003). A brand loyalty model involving cognitive, affective, and conative brand loyalty and customer satisfaction. *Journal of Hospitality & Tourism Research*, *27*(4), 419−435.

Batra, R., Lenk, P., & Wedel, M. (2010). Brand extension strategy planning: Empirical estimation of brand-category personality fit and atypicality. *Journal of Marketing Research*, *47*(2), 335−347.

Baumgartner, H. (2002). Toward a personology of the consumer. *Journal of Consumer Research*, *29*(2), 286−292.

Beerli, A., Meneses, G. D., & Gil, S. M. (2007). Self-congruity and destination choice. *Annals of Tourism Research*, *34*(3), 571−587.

Bennett, R., Hartel, C. J. H., & Mccoll-Kennedy, J. R. (2005). Experience as a moderator of involvement and satisfaction on brand loyalty in a business-to-business settings. *Industrial Marketing Management*, *34*(1), 97−107.

Bitner, M. J., & Hubbert, A. R. (1994). Encounter satisfaction versus overall satisfaction versus quality. In R. T. Rust & R. L. Oliver (Eds.), *Service quality: New directions in theory and practice* (pp. 72−94). London: Sage.

Bloemer, J. M., & Kasper, H. D. P. (1995). The complex relationship between consumer satisfaction and brand loyalty. *Journal of Economic Psychology*, *16*(2), 311−329.

Bloemer, J. M., & Oderkerken-Schroder, G. (2002). Store satisfaction and store loyalty explained by customer- and store-related factors. *Journal of Consumer Satisfaction, Dissatisfaction and Complaining Behavior, 15*, 68–80.

Bonsnjak, M., Sirgy, M. J., Hellriegel, S., & Maurer, O. (2011). Postvisit destination loyalty judgments: Developing and testing a comprehensive congruity model. *Journal of Travel Research, 50*(5), 496–508.

Brakus, J. J., Schmitt, B. H., & Zarantonello, L. (2009). Brand experience: What is it? How is it measured? Does it affect loyalty? *Journal of Marketing, 73*(3), 52–68.

Branaghan, R. J., & Hildebrand, E. A. (2011). Brand personality, self-congruity, and preference: A knowledge structures approach. *Journal of Consumer Behavior, 10*(5), 304–312.

Caruana, A. (2002). Service loyalty: The effects of service quality and the mediating role of customer satisfaction. *European Journal of Marketing, 36*(7–8), 811–828.

Cervone, D., & Pervin, L. A. (2010). *Personality theory and research*. New York, NY: Wiley.

Chen, C. F., & Phou, S. (2013). A closer look at destination: Image, personality, relationship and loyalty. *Tourism Management, 36*, 269–278.

Chon, K. S. (1992). Self-image/destination image congruity. *Annals of Tourism Research, 19*(2), 360–363.

Clark, L. A., & Watson, D. (1999). Temperament: A new paradigm for trait psychology. In L. A. Pervin & O. P. John (Eds.), *Handbook of personality: Theory and research* (pp. 399–423). New York: The Guilford Press.

Coffer, D. (2014, March). *The evolution of the coffee shop: Coffee brands around the world are staying relevant with food, alcoholic beverage*. Retrieved from http://nrn.com/opinions/evolution-coffee-shop

Das, G. (2014). Impacts of retail brand personality and self-congruity on store loyalty: The moderating role of gender. *Journal of Retailing and Consumer Services, 21*(2), 130–138.

D'Astous, A., & Gargouri, E. (2001). Consumer evaluations of brand imitations. *European Journal of Marketing, 35*(1–2), 153–160.

Dick, A. S., & Basu, K. (1994). Customer loyalty towards an integrated framework. *Journal of the Academy of Marketing Science, 22*(2), 99–113.

Ekinci, Y., Sirakaya-Turk, E., & Preciado, S. (2013). Symbolic consumption of tourism destination brands. *Journal of Business Research, 66*(6), 711–718.

Epstein, S. (1980). The self concept: A review and the proposal of an integrated theory of personality. In E. Staub (Ed.), *Personality basic issues and current research*. Englewood Cliffs, NJ: Prentice-Hall.

Fornell, C., Johnson, M. D., Anderson, E. W., Cha, J., & Beyant, B. E. (1996). The American customer satisfaction index: Nature, purpose, and findings. *Journal of Marketing, 60*(4), 7–18.

Freling, T. H., Crosno, J. L., & Henard, D. H. (2011). Brand personality appeal: Conceptualization and empirical validation. *Journal of the Academy of Marketing Science, 39*(3), 392–406.

Funder, D. C. (1997). *The personality puzzle*. New York, NY: W.W Norton.

Ganesan, S. (1994). Determinants of long-term orientation in buyer-seller relationships. *Journal of Marketing, 58*(2), 1–19.

Global Coffee Report. (2013, September). *Korean coffee, Gangnam style*. Retrieved from http://gcrmag.com/market-reports/view/coffee-gangnam-style

Govers, P. C. M., & Schoormans, J. P. L. (2005). Product personality and its influence on consumer preference. *Journal of Consumer Marketing, 22*(4), 189–197.

Graeff, T. R. (1996). Image congruence effects on product evaluations: The role of self-monitoring and public/private consumption. *Psychology & Marketing, 13*(5), 481−499.

Gwinner, K. (1997). A model of image creation and image transfer in event sponsorship. *International Marketing Review, 14*(3), 145−158.

Gwinner, K. P., & Eaton, J. (1999). Building brand image through event sponsorship: The role of image transfer. *Journal of Advertising, 28*(4), 47−57.

Ha, H. Y., & Park, K. H. (2012). Effects of perceived quality and satisfaction on brand loyalty in China: The moderating effect of customer orientation. *African Journal of Business Management, 6*(22), 6745−6753.

Hair, J., Black, W., Babin, B., Anderson, R., & Tatham, R. (2006). *Multivariate data analysis* (6th ed.). New Jersey, NY: Pearson Prentice Hall.

Han, H., & Back, K. J. (2008). Relationships among image congruence, consumption emotions, and customer loyalty in the lodging industry. *Journal of Hospitality & Tourism Research, 32*(4), 467−490.

He, H., & Mukherjee, A. (2007). I am, ergo I shop: Does store image congruity explain shopping behavior of Chinese consumers? *Journal of Marketing Management, 23*(5−6), 443−460.

Helgeson, J. G., & Supphellen, M. (2004). A conceptual and measurement comparison of self-congruity and brand personality. *International Journal of Marketing Research, 6*(1), 205−233.

Herstein, R., Tifferet, S., Abrantes, J. L., Lymperopoulos, C., Albayrak, T., & Caber, M. (2012). A cross-cultural study of Mediterranean countries. *Cross Cultural Management, 19*(2), 196−214.

Hogg, M. K., Cox, A. J., & Keeling, K. (2000). The impact of self-monitoring on image congruence and product/brand evaluation. *European Journal of Marketing, 34*(5−6), 641−667.

Homburg, C., & Giering, A. (2001). Moderators of the relationship between customer satisfaction and loyalty − An empirical analysis. *Psychology & Marketing, 18*(1), 43−66.

House, R. J., Hanges, P. J., Javidan, M., Dorfman, P. W., & Gupta, V. (2004). *Culture, leadership, and organizations: The GLOBE study of 62 societies.* CA: Sage.

Hsieh, M. H., Pan, S. L., & Setiono, R. (2004). Product-, corporate-, and country-image dimensions and purchase behavior: A multicountry analysis. *Journal of Academy of Marketing Science, 32*(3), 251−270.

Hu, H. H., Kandampully, J., & Juwaheer, T. D. (2009). Relationship and impacts of service quality, perceived value, customer satisfaction, and image: An empirical study. *The Service Industries Journal, 29*(2), 111−125.

Hultman, M., Skarmeas, D., Oghazi, P., & Beheshti, H. M. (2015). Achieving tourist loyalty through destination personality, satisfaction, and identification. *Journal of Business Research, 68*(11), 2227−2231. doi:10.1016/j.busres.2015.06.002

Jacoby, J., & Kyner, D. B. (1973). Brand loyalty vs. repeat purchasing behavior. *Journal of Marketing Research, 10*(1), 1−9.

Jamal, A., & Al-Marri, M. (2007). Exploring the effect of self-image congruence and brand preference on satisfaction: The role of expertise. *Journal of Marketing Management, 23*(7−8), 613−629.

Jamal, A., & Goode, M. M. H. (2001). Consumers and brands: A study of the impact of self-image congruence on brand preference and satisfaction. *Marketing Intelligence & Planning, 19*(7), 482−492.

Jang, Y. J., Kim, W. G., & Lee, H. Y. (2015). Coffee shop consumers' emotional attachment and loyalty to green stores: The moderating role of green consciousness. *International Journal of Hospitality Management, 44,* 146–156.

Johnson, M. D., Gustafsson, A., Andreassen, T. W., Lervik, L., & Cha, J. (2001). The evaluation and future of national customer satisfaction index models. *Journal of Economic Psychology, 22*(2), 217–245.

Jones, M. A., & Suh, J. (2000). Transaction-specific satisfaction and overall satisfaction: An empirical analysis. *Journal of Services Marketing, 14*(2), 147–159.

Kang, J., Tang, L., Lee, J. Y., & Bosselman, R. H. (2012). Understanding customer behavior in name-brand Korean coffee shops: The role of self-congruity and functional congruity. *International Journal of Hospitality Management, 31*(3), 809–818.

Karney, B. R., & Bradbury, T. N. (1995). The longitudinal course of marital quality and stability: A review of theory, method, and research. *Psychological Bulletin, 118*(1), 3–34.

Kim, S. H., Kim, M. S., Han, H. S., & Holland, S. (2016). The determinants of hospitality employees' pro-environmental behaviors: The moderating role of generational differences. *International Journal of Hospitality Management, 52,* 56–67.

Kim, Y. G., Suh, B. W., & Eves, A. (2010). The relationships between food-related personality traits, satisfaction, and loyalty among visitors attending food events and festivals. *International Journal of Hospitality Management, 29*(2), 216–226.

Kressmann, F., Sirgy, M. J., Herrmann, A., Huber, F., Huber, S., & Lee, D. J. (2006). Direct and indirect effects of self-image congruence on brand loyalty. *Journal of Business Research, 59*(9), 955–964.

Kuikka, A., & Laukkanen, T. (2012). Brand loyalty and the role of hedonic value. *Journal of Product & Brand Management, 21*(7), 529–537.

Kumar, R., Luthra, A., & Datta, G. (2006). Linkages between brand personality and brand loyalty: A qualitative study in an emerging market in the Indian context. *South Asian Journal of Management, 13*(2), 11–35.

Kwun, D. J., & Oh, H. (2006). Past experience and self-image in fine dining intentions. *Journal of Foodservice Business Research, 9*(4), 3–24.

Lai, F., Griffin, M., & Babin, B. J. (2009). How quality, value, image, and satisfaction create loyalty at a Chinese telecom. *Journal of Business Research, 62*(10), 980–986.

Lau, G. T., & Lee, S. H. (1999). Consumers' trust in a brand and the link to brand loyalty. *Journal of Market-Focused Management, 4*(4), 341–370.

Lee, D., & Hyman, M. R. (2008). Hedonic/functional congruity between stores and private label brands. *The Journal of Marketing Theory and Practice, 16*(3), 219–232.

Lee, H. S., Lee, Y. K., & Yoo, D. K. (2000). The determinants of perceived service quality and its relationship with satisfaction. *Journal of Services Marketing, 14*(3), 217–231.

Lee, J., & Back, K. (2009). Examining the effect of self-image congruence, relative to education and networking, on conference evaluation through its competing models and moderating effect. *Journal of Convention & Event Tourism, 10*(4), 256–275.

Lee, S. H., & Yeu, M. S. (2010). Factors influencing the intention to redeem coffee shop coupons in Korea. *International Journal of Business and Management, 5*(7), 92–98.

Lee, Y. K., Kim, S., Son, M. H., & Kim, M. S. (2015). Linking organizational justice to job performance: Evidence from the restaurant industry in East Asia. *Asia Pacific Journal of Tourism Research, 20*(1), 1527–1544. doi:10.1080/10941665.2015.1016052

Lin, L. Y. (2010). The relationship of consumer personality trait, brand personality and brand loyalty: An empirical study of toy and video games buyers. *Journal of Product & Brand Management, 19*(1), 4–17.

Liu, H. (2014). Personality, leisure satisfaction, and subjective well-being of serious leisure participants. *Social Behavior & Personality: An International Journal, 42*(7), 1117–1126.

Lounsbury, J. W., Foster, N., Carmody, P. C., Kim, J. Y., Gibson, L. W., & Drost, A. W. (2012). Key personality traits and career satisfaction of customer service workers. *Managing Service Quality: An International Journal, 22*(5), 517–536.

Malar, L., Krohmer, H., Hoyer, W. D., & Nyffenegger, B. (2011). Emotional brand attachment and brand personality: The relative importance of the actual and the ideal self. *Journal of Marketing, 75*(4), 35–52.

Matzler, K., Bidmon, S., & Grabner-Krauter, S. (2006). Individual determinants of brand affect: The role of the personality traits of extraversion and openness to experience. *Journal of Product & Brand Management, 15*(7), 427–434.

Mengxia, Z. (2007). Impact of brand personality on PALI: A comparative research between two different brands. *International Management Review, 3*(3), 36–46.

Mooradian, T. A., & Olver, J. M. (1997). "I can't get no satisfaction:" The impact of personality and emotion on postpurchase processes. *Psychology & Marketing, 14*(4), 379–393.

Nam, J. H., Ekinci, Y., & Whyatt, G. (2011). Brand equity, brand loyalty and consumer satisfaction. *Annals of Tourism Research, 38*(3), 1009–1030.

Nunnally, J., & Bernstein, I. (1994). *Psychometric theory* (3rd ed.). New York, NY: McGraw-Hill.

Ogba, I. E., & Tan, Z. (2009). Exploring the impact of brand image on customer loyalty and commitment in China. *Journal of Technology Management in China, 4*(2), 132–144.

Oliver, R. L. (1993). Cognitive, affective and attribute bases of the satisfaction response. *Journal of Consumer Research, 20*(3), 418–430.

Oliver, R. L. (1999). Whence consumer loyalty. *Journal of Marketing, 63*(4), 33–34.

Olsen, S. O. (2007). Repurchase loyalty: The role of involvement and satisfaction. *Psychology & Marketing, 24*(4), 315–341.

Pirog, S. F., & Roberts, J. A. (2007). Personality and credit card misuse among college student: The mediating role of impulsiveness. *Journal of Marketing Theory and Practice, 15*(1), 65–77.

Quester, P., & Lim, A. (2003). Product involvement/brand loyalty: Is there a link? *Journal of Product & Brand Management, 12*(1), 22–38.

Roberts, B. W., Kuncel, N. R., Shiner, R. L., Caspi, A., & Goldberg, L. R. (2007). The power of personality: The comparative validity of personality traits, socioeconomic status, and cognitive ability for predicting important life outcomes. *Perspectives on Psychological Science, 2*(4), 313–345.

Roberts, B. W., Walton, K. E., & Viechtbauer, W. (2006). Patterns of mean-level change in personality traits across the life course: A meta-analysis of longitudinal studies. *Psychological Bulletin, 132*(1), 1–25.

Rodriguez del Bosque, I., & San Martin, H. (2008). Tourist satisfaction a cognitive-affective model. *Annals of Tourism Research, 35*(2), 551–573.

Romaniuk, J. (2008). Comparing methods of measuring brand personality traits. *The Journal of Marketing Theory and Practice, 16*(2), 153–161.

Rosowsky, E., & Sega, D. L. (2012). Marital satisfaction and personality traits in long-term marriages: An exploratory study. *Clinical Gerontologist, 35*(2), 77–87.

Sahin, A., Zahir, C., & Kitapçı, H. (2011). The effects of brand experiences, trust and satisfaction on building brand loyalty: An empirical research on global brands. *Procedia-Social and Behavioral Sciences, 24*, 1288–1301.

Seimiene, E. (2012). Emotional connection of consumer personality traits with brand personality traits: Theoretical considerations. *Economics and Management, 17*(4), 1472–1478.

Sirdesmukh, D., Singh, J., & Sabol, B. (2002). Consumer trust, value, and loyalty in relational exchanges. *Journal of Marketing, 66*(1), 15–37.

Sirgy, M. J. (1986). *Self-congruity: Toward a theory of personality and cybernetics.* New York, NY: Praeger.

Sirgy, M. J. (2015). Self-image/product-image congruity and advertising strategy. In *Proceedings of the 1982 Academy of Marketing Science (AMS) annual conference* (pp. 129–133). Springer International Publishing.

Sirgy, M. J., Grewal, D., & Mangleburg, T. F. (2000). Retail environment, self-congruity, and retail patronage: An integrative model and a research agenda. *Journal of Business Research, 49*(2), 127–138.

Sirgy, M. J., Grewal, D., Mangleburg, T. F., & Park, J. O. K. (1997). Assessing the predictive validity of two methods of measuring self-image congruence. *Journal of the Academy of Marketing Science, 25*(3), 229–241.

Sirgy, M. J., Lee, D. J., Johar, J. S., & Tidwell, J. (2008). Effect of self-congruity with sponsorship on brand loyalty. *Journal of Business Research, 61*(10), 1091–1097.

Sirgy, M. J., & Su, C. (2000). Destination image, self-congruity, and travel behavior: Toward an integrative model. *Journal of Travel Research, 38*(4), 340–352.

Solomon, B. C., & Jackson, J. J. (2014). Why do personality traits predict divorce? Multiple pathways through satisfaction. *Journal of Personality and Social Psychology, 106*(6), 978–996.

Spreng, R. A., MacKenzie, S. C., & Olshavsky, S. W. (1996). A reexamination of the determinants of consumer satisfaction. *Journal of Marketing, 60*(3), 15–52.

Sternberg, R. J. (2000). *Handbook of intelligence.* New York, NY: Cambridge University Press.

Tett, R. P., Jackson, D. N., & Rothstein, M. (1991). Personality measures as predictors of job performance: A meta-analytic review. *Personnel Psychology, 44*(4), 703–742.

Vazquez-Carrasco, R., & Foxall, G. R. (2006). Influence of personality traits on satisfaction, perception of relational benefits, and loyalty in a personal service context. *Journal of Retailing and Consumer Services, 13*(3), 205–219.

Veloutsou, C., Gilbert, G. W., Moutinho, L. A., & Goode, M. M. H. (2005). Measuring transaction-specific satisfaction in services: Are the measures transferable across cultures? *European Journal of Marketing, 39*(5–6), 606–628.

Viktoria Rampl, L., & Kenning, P. (2014). Employer brand trust and affect: Linking brand personality to employer brand attractiveness. *European Journal of Marketing, 48*(1–2), 218–236.

Wang, X., Yang, Z., & Liu, N. R. (2009). The impacts of brand personality and congruity on purchase intention: Evidence from the Chinese mainland's automobile market. *Journal of Global Marketing, 22*(3), 199–215.

Westjohn, S. A., Singh, N., & Magnusson, P. (2012). Responsiveness to global and local consumer culture positioning: A personality and collective identity perspective. *Journal of International Marketing, 20*(1), 58–73.

Yi, Y., & Jeon, H. (2003). Effects of loyalty programs on value perception, program loyalty, and brand loyalty. *Journal of the Academy of Marketing Science, 31*(3), 229–240.

Zimmerman, R. D. (2008). Understanding the impact of personality traits on individuals' turnover decisions: A meta-analytic path model. *Personnel Psychology, 61*(2), 309–348.

THE EFFECT OF INTEGRATING NEED AND EXPECTATION'S FACTOR-COMMUNITY PARTICIPATION WITH MULTINATIONAL CORPORATIONS' TOURISM MARKET DEVELOPMENT STRATEGIES IN EMERGING AFRICAN MARKETS

Henry G. Iroegbu

ABSTRACT

An investigation of multinational corporations (MNCs) integration of the concept of community participation into the factors of needs and expectations revealed a significant difference amongst MNCs' strategic choice in their tourism market development in those African host countries. The findings identified only 16% of the participating MNCs

Advances in Hospitality and Leisure, Volume 12, 35–49
Copyright © 2017 by Emerald Group Publishing Limited
All rights of reproduction in any form reserved
ISSN: 1745-3542/doi:10.1108/S1745-354220160000012002

integrated the concept of community participation. The integrators increased in growth more than the non-integrators of concept of community participation. It is concluded that MNCs need to realize that strategy involves forecasting and understanding the business environmental factors, planning on which applicable strategy to choose and implementing a strategy that is rewarding to both the corporation and the host community with minimum risks.

Keywords: Multinational corporations; needs and expectations; African host countries; integration; community participation

INTRODUCTION

Dependency paradigm extrapolates the notion that the tourism and hospitality multinational corporations (MNCs) that operate in the peripheral regions are just as their manufacturing and mining counterparts who were labeled "dependent developers," for the fact that they encourage the use of expatriates and machinery from developed countries in their developing host countries. They lagged in introducing bases for training local staff and producing manufacturing and mining accessories in their host developing nations, and imported all their requirements, thereby inducing excessive foreign exchange leakage and little employment opportunities (Freitag, 1994).

Despite improving their *Gross national product* (GNP) and becoming more of market economies, the developing Third World countries also expect MNCs to be catalysts in bringing changes that would satisfy their needs. Such general needs that could be realized from MNCs' foreign investments in host countries are: participation through full or partial local ownership of an enterprise, the upgrading and transferring of technology from home country to host country, technical training of local staff, training and advancement opportunities for citizens of the host country, industrialization of the economy, opportunities for host country's middle men-suppliers, agents, contractors, and entrepreneurs, investment distribution to urban and suburban areas, generation of foreign exchange and export revenues, governmental revenues in forms of taxes and tariffs and offer of employment to host country's citizens (Stover, 1985). Armitt (2014) alluded the importance of inclusion of low-income residents in tourism development strategies whilst ensuring high level of the area's tourism demand could have tremendous positive economic outcomes in African destinations (African Tourism Monitor, 2014).

Needs and Expectations Theory

MNCs were considered to be companies that have equity interests in two or more countries (Dunning, 1992; Glynn, 1983). According to Glynn (1983), they are very powerful large organizations that pursue success worldwide by applying valid principles to their dynamic business operations. The earlier classical theory of international trade was based on companies that conduct exporting and importing transactions (Aharoni, 1967; Cyert, 1963; Simon, 1967). However, the new MNCs' concept (Kobrin, 1982) is now considered by researchers (Caves, 1974; Dunning, 1992; Dunning & McQueen, 1988; Dunning & Norman, 1983) and projected by Harvard Multinational Enterprise project team as large corporations that operate in different countries with access to "a common pool of financial resources, and controlling their widespread activities rather than serving as mere exporters and licensers of technology" (Turnbull, 1996, p. 26).

Tourism MNCs that operate in the Third world countries need to understand the development needs of host countries and their local residents. Kobrin (1988) stressed the importance of a good understanding of a host country's needs and expectations by MNCs. The 1980s and 1990s have seen an emergence of literature on the needs and expectations theory and the effect of national culture on MNCs' operating environment (Beamish, 1987; Kobrin, 1988; Kogut & Singh, 1988; Zhao, 1994). Iroegbu (2006) stated that the competitiveness of a tourist destination depends on its ability to attract the international tourism market which vastly depends on MNCs' market development strategies in developing countries in Africa. In 2014, the total tourist arrivals in Africa increased by 200,000 from tourist arrivals in 2013 (African Tourism Monitor, 2015). As Zhao (1994) portrayed, host countries usually welcome MNCs to their communities as apparent channels for economic development. Some of the host country's needs and expectations stated by Zhao (1994) are "finance, human resources, marketing development, management know-how, and political needs."

The five forms of benefits identified by Meleka (1985) that host countries expect from MNCs are national economic development, creation of jobs and employment, training of skilled labor and management development, creating opportunities for entrepreneurship and industrialization through joint ventures, and promoting political stability and good international relationships between host country and home country. From his series of pilot studies on the relationship between the need and commitment of partners and performance, Beamish (1987) also identified the following five categories of needs and expectations that could also be attributed to host countries: readily capitalized items such as capital assets, access to raw materials, and transfer of technology and equipment; human resources such as skilled and semi-skilled labor, management and technical personnel pool; access to international market such as exporting and distributing outlets; political needs such as political stability and inter-governmental relationships; and knowledge needs such as information and training systems.

MNCs' Tourism Market Development Strategies in African Countries

As Brohman (1996) stated, it is essential to assess tourism according to how it has been integrated into the broader development goals of existing local communities, and how investments and revenues that are associated with tourism have benefited those communities. The main goal of an MNC may be to maximize profit and minimize its cost, but the measure of successful tourism strategies in developing African countries should also be assessed on an MNC's community development effort. According to Iroegbu (2010), it is vital for tourism MNCs to enact ongoing market development strategies that should incorporate the needs and expectations of developing countries.

Hyma, Ojo, and Wall (1980) stated that the governments of the developing countries in Africa implement privatization policies as forms of checks and balances in some foreign investment sectors such as the tourism industry. It is a move to restrict foreign exchange leakage from those African countries to the MNCs' host countries. Some of the countries that privatize are Nigeria, which has rescinded its 50% indigene ownership (African News Service, 2000), Tanzania, which requires 50% of tourism operations in its national parks, and Uganda, which imposes 60% state ownership of all industrial sectors (Hyma et al., 1980).

Management contract is the prevailing mode of MNCs' development strategy and entry into African markets. As Ankomah (1991) stated, managerial contract accounted for 72% of all hotel rooms in sub-Saharan Africa. Foreign wholly owned and joint ventures accounted to only 18% of all hotel rooms in the region. Some of the major identified tourism firms that adopted the managerial contract strategy were Accor, which is a French multinational hotel chain (Ofei-Nkansah, 1988); Holiday Inns in Swaziland; and Hilton International in Lesotho (Crush & Wellings, 1983). Most of the MNCs are not known to be adopting the franchising development strategy in the African host countries. Hilton, Club Med, Holiday Inns, amongst others are so far not franchising in the region. Dunning and Norman (1983) stated that tourism MNCs adopt the managerial contract entry mode to enter this region's international tourism market and at the same time provide quality service with the image associated with the international chain.

Some other management contracts are in form of consultation and advisory. A Danish tourism advisory team of four consulted on Ghana's Tourism Master Plan for the 1975–1999 planning period (Teye, 1988); British advisory team consulted for Tanzania's tourism rejuvenation (Hancock, 1979); Technical experts from European Economic Community assisted in the rehabilitation of Uganda's tourism industry; Experts from Ireland, Spain, and Australia conjointly complemented the Nigerian Tourist Board in its effort to address the acute shortage of tourism skilled labor.

Many African countries' tourist activities such as Rawanda-national parks, Malawi-Michiru Mountain Conservation, and Botswana-Moremi Wildlife Reserve had expatriate managers (Almagor, 1985; Comfort & Comfort, 1984; van den Berghe, 1986). While MNCs have been criticized in the literature for adopting mostly managerial contract for the African market as a strategy to circumvent governments' privatization policies, McQueen (1983) argues that it is the element of power and control that induces MNCs not to offer franchising in the region. In referring to McQueen (1983), Brown (1996) stated:

> by supplying expertise only through long-term contracts, control transfers over operations to the multinational enterprise (in this case, the U.S. channel); by staffing key positions with its own personnel and combining this with a policy of appointing senior management posts only from within the organization, MNE hotels may be able to limit the rate of diffusion of knowledge. Thus they can "lock" employees into the organization and reduce the possibility of potential competitors obtaining access to proprietary knowledge through hiring from the organization. (Brown, 1996, p. 29)

Community Participation

Residents of tourist areas should be assimilated into the operations of tourism MNCs in the area. Tourism has been associated with various negative impacts such as environmental degradation, air-pollution, prostitution, increase in crime rate, and cultural-destruction (Ankomah, 1991; Brohman, 1996; Chow, 1980; Hyma et al., 1980; Zhao, Park & Zhou, 2014). Third World tourism has been marred with the above listed attributes and others with detrimental, economical impacts. The most prevailing detrimental factor in the Third World countries is "leakage." Brohman (1996) stated that the domination of foreign ownership contributes to residents' loss of control over their own local resources, excessive overseas leakage of locally generated tourism earnings, and lack of articulation with other domestic economic sectors. He stipulated that these negative weak multiplier effects outside of tourism enclave as well as possible reintroduction of socio-economic inequality with spatial uneven distribution are the ailments of insensitivity of foreign owners in their tourism planning.

An anticipatory and visionary tourism planning should adopt proactive measures that could curb environmental destruction, resistance, and rising alienation among the local residents. Lack of adequate and proactive tourism development planning attributed to tourism related negative issues, such as "increasing crime, overcrowding and overloading infrastructure, pollution and other environmental damage, conflicts over access to scarce resources, and the perceived loss of cultural identity and social control to outsiders" (Brohman, 1996, p. 53).

Tourism MNCs should control leakages and curb residents' resistance by employing local residents, training them to attain managerial positions, and purchasing most of their supplies from local purveyors. They should also make efforts in contributing to the development of the area's infrastructure, health clinics, and maintenance of schools that could produce graduates who could be their promising labor pool. Adopting strategies that enhance localization concepts (Fryxell, Butler, & Choi, 2004; Jamali, 2010) would be rewarding to MNC's operations in African host countries.

Globalization of Corporations

Firms indulge in worldwide expansion in order to explore potential markets that would enable them to maintain profitable operations. They do this by exerting their competitive advantages in different international markets. Ghoshal (1987) stipulates that a major goal to internationalize is to make profit. The firm does so by exploiting its strengths in technological know-how, brand name recognition, and management expertise in various international markets. Ghoshal (1987) also rationalizes the notion of "diversity of environments" in which tourism MNC operates. Thus by operating in different countries with different general environmental issues, the MNC would acquire diverse capabilities and achieve broader learning facets for successful global operations.

Porter (1986) asserts that a global firm is one that gains some elements of competitive advantage by integrating its worldwide activities. As some studies (Buckley & Casson, 1976; Cyert, 1963; Dunning, 1977; Kundu, 1994) posit, the globalization of the firm is an outcome of international trade imbalances or international interest differentials of equal or less risks. The product and market imperfection theory as projected by Hymer (1960) stipulates that product and factor imperfections that are created by protective governments and some corporations' limited operational technicalities influence the influx of firms' globalization. MNCs pursue international growth so that they could attain the following objectives: Follow Customers; Market Exposure; Resource Exploitation; Economic Hedge; and Profit Maximization (Ghoshal, 1987; Tse & West, 1992; Webster & Hudson, 1991).

Study Objective

With inference to the aforementioned MNCs' market development strategies in the emerging markets of Africa, this research was conducted to determine if there is any relationship between the integration of "Community Participation" as African host countries' Need and Expectations factor with MNCs' performance in those countries. It investigated the strategic choice of MNCs on their tourism market development in emerging African markets to accommodate the integration of "Community Participation." Four major market development strategies were analyzed, namely: wholly owned, joint venture, management contract, and franchising.

METHODS

A structured self-administered mail-in survey questionnaire was the instrument used to collect data from an exhaustive list of tourism MNCs in the emerging African market. Its sample population consisted of top management executives of tourism MNCs with operations in the African market. The unit of analysis was the corporation. The initial sample size was 106 tourism MNCs' executives. Thirty-seven of them responded to the mail in survey questionnaire. Two of the questionnaires were discarded due to numerous missing data. Thus, there were 35 usable questionnaires for data analysis, which is a response rate of 33%.

The statistical methods applied to this study were analysis of variance (ANOVA), factor analysis, bivariate regression analysis, and Turkey's multiple range post hoc test method. ANOVA was used to determine variability among strategic type dependable variables on emerged "Needs and Expectations" factor — "Community Participation" from a pre-test factor analysis, which was the independent variable. It had an eigen value of 2.59, explained 6.47% of the total variance and a standardized reliability alpha $(a) = .70$. Total variance explained by all factors was 72% (acceptable criteria for the study were: eigen value ≥ 1, variance explained $\geq 5\%$, a standardized reliability alpha $(a) \geq .50$, and total variance explained by all factors to be $\geq 50\%$).

The one-way ANOVA's F statistic had a p value is $\leq .05$ for the influence of the Need and Expectations factor on MNC's strategic choice to be deemed significant. Turkey's multiple range post hoc test method was also administered to determine variability within groups that show significant differences between groups. Descriptive data analyses (frequency distributions) were used to determine the distribution of data and their other characteristics.

RESULTS AND FINDINGS

Table 1 depicts the demographic characteristics of the responding MNCs. On the classification of the responding MNCs, 17.1% of them were in the Resort sector, 20% in the Hotel sector, 22.9% in the Airline sector, while 8.6% and 17.1% were in the Tour operators and Travel agencies sectors, respectively. Also, five MNCs in five different tourism sectors, namely Cruises; Tourism consulting groups; Amusement parks; Restaurants; and Car rentals (all grouped together as "other" in this study), represented 14.3% of the responding MNCs.

Sixty percent of the responding MNCs operated in 10 or more countries worldwide, 37.1% operated in between three and nine countries worldwide and only 2.9% operated in two countries worldwide. In the African market, 8.6% of the responding tourism MNCs had operations in only one country, 57.1% operated in between two and five countries while 34.3% had operations in more than five countries. Majority of the responding

Table 1.   Demographic Characteristics of Responding MNCs.

Demographic Characteristics	Percent Distribution	Demographic Characteristics	Percent Distribution
Classification of MNC		Respondent's corporate position	
Resort	17.1%	C.E.O.	5.7%
Hotel	20.0	Managing director	2.9
Airline	22.9	President	20.0
Tour operator	8.6	Vice president	31.4
Travel agency	17.1	Director	20.0
Other	14.3	GM	17.1
		Comptroller	2.9
Number of countries of operations worldwide		Respondent's gender	
1−2	2.9%	Male	82.9%
3−9	37.1	Female	17.1
10 or more	60.0		
Number of African host countries		Number of years in current position	
Only 1	8.6%	1−2	2.9%
2−5	57.1	3−5	34.2
More than 5	34.3	More than 5	62.9

MNCs' executives were the vice presidents of the corporations (31.4%) followed by presidents (20%) and directors (20%). General managers (GM) accounted for 17.1% of the respondents and Chief executive officers (C.E.O.) for 5.7%. Managing directors and comptrollers each accounted for 2.9% of the responses. Eighty three percent of the responding MNCs' executives were males and 17% were females. Most of the responding executives (62.9%) have held their current positions for more than five years. Thirty four percent of the executives have held their current positions as long as 3−5 years while only 2.9% of them have held their positions between one and two years.

The distribution of the 35 responding tourism MNCs' primary African market development strategic choice is depicted in Table 2. Approximately 29% ($n = 10$) of the respondents chose wholly owned development strategy (including business acquisitions and market segmentations). Approximately 23% ($n = 8$) of them chose joint ventures (including strategic alliance), 17% of them ($n = 6$) chose franchising, and 31% of them ($n = 11$) chose management contract.

Table 2.   Number of Respondents' Primary African Market
Strategic Choice.

MNCs' African Market Strategic Choice	Number	Percent Response
Wholly owned subsidiaries (acquisitions/market segmentation)	10	28.6
Joint ventures (strategic alliance)	8	22.9
Franchise	6	17.1
Management contract	11	31.4
Total	35	100

Table 3.   ANOVA of Tourism Market Development Strategies.

Needs and Expectations' Factors	Mkt. Development Strategies					
Community participation	Wholly owned subsidiaries	Joint venture	Franchising	Management contract	F	p
Mean	3.0333	2.0833[a]	3.6111[b]	3.3939[b]	5.477	.004
Std.	1.1161	.2955	.4907	.8409		

[a,b]Mean scores of those with different superscripts are statistically different.

Tourism MNCs' Market Development Strategic Choice

A one-way ANOVA ($p < .05$) statistical procedure was employed to determine the relationship between tourism MNCs' market development strategies and the factor of needs and expectations of African host countries. The results (see Table 3) show that significant differences exist among various MNCs' market development strategies in their bid to integrate the Need and Expectations factor – "Community Participation" with $p = .004$ ($a = .05$).

The findings determined that the MNCs that integrated the joint venture strategy were more interested in requesting the participation of the residents of their African host countries. They believed in the association of the host countries' residents in implementing the goals and objectives of their operations in those host countries. On the same token, the same joint ventures strategy implementers are more pruned to offering opportunities to host countries' residents to institute their own businesses. They may establish business relationships such as purchasing, subcontracting, training, sharing of amenities, etc., with the local entrepreneurs.

Table 4. Operational Growth of Tourism MNCs – Integrators/Non-integrators of African Host Countries' Need and Expectation with Market Development Strategies within the Past 3 Years.

	New operations (%)					Community Participation									
						Ave. revenue (US$ million) (%)					Ave. profit (US$ million) (%)				
	0	1	2	3	4	<$.5	.5–5	>5–15	>15–25	>25	<$.5	.5–5	>5–15	>15–25	>25
Integrators	27	36	18	9	10	3	6	9	9	73	6	12	6	30	46
Non-integrators	25	36	21	16	2	0	0	7	22	71	0	13	14	17	56

Notes: Percentages were rounded up to zero. Missing values were given for the mean value of the group response.

A multiple range comparison using Tukey's honestly significant differ-ence (HSD) post hoc comparison test was applied to the community parti-cipation factor and two significant groups emerged. Group 1 comprised of integrators of joint venture and franchise strategies with $p = .007$ and Group 2 comprised of joint venture and management strategies with $p = .007$ This would enable one to clearly understand the differences amongst MNCs' strategic choice within the identified significant factor.

Table 4 tabulated the growth of the responding MNCs' operations for the past three years in the African market. It was based on the integration or non-integration of their market development strategies with African host countries' Need and Expectations factor — community participation in the form of (1) number of new operations; (2) average revenue in mil-lions of US dollars; and (3) average profits in millions of US dollars. The percentages in Table 4 are across-row percentages with the specific number of integrators or non-integrators of a particular construct.

It was quite astonishing to notice that only 16% of the respondents inte-grated "Community Participation." Out of this 16% of integrators, 10% had up to four new operations in the past three years, 73% had average revenue of more than 25 million US dollars, and 46% had more than 25 million US dollars in profits. On the other hand, 84% of the respondents were non-integrators of community participation. Two percent of these non-integrators extended to four new operations within the past three years, 71% had average revenue of more than 25 million US dollars, and 56% had average profit of more than 25 million US dollars.

CONCLUSION

The findings of this study gave an insight into the variability of market development strategic choice with regard to the integration of African host countries Needs and Expectations factor — community participation with MNCs' tourism market development strategies in the emerging African markets. It is determined that MNCs can be equally successful in the operations by involving residents and local businesses in their host African countries in delivering and supplying essential services to the multinational chains. MNCs need to realize that strategy involves forecasting and under-standing the business environmental factors, planning on which applicable strategy to choose and implementing a strategy that is rewarding to both the corporation and the host community with minimum risks.

REFERENCES

African News Service. (2000). *Investment opportunity in tourism sub-sector of Nigeria's economy*. June 5, Comtex production.

African Tourism Monitor. (2014). *Social inclusion: Sustainable tourism development* (Vol. 2(1), pp. 28–29).

African Tourism Monitor. (2015). *African tourism monitor: The numbers* (Vol. 3(1), pp. 9–10).

Aharoni, Y. (1967). *The foreign investment decision process*. New York, NY: McMillian.

Almagor, U. (1985). A tourist's "vision quest" in an African reserve. *Annals of Tourism Research, 12*, 31–47.

Ankomah, P. K. (1991). Tourism skilled labor: The case of Sub-Saharan Africa. *Annals of Tourism Research, 18*, 433–442.

Armitt, T. (2014). African tourism monitor. *Social Inclusion: Sustainable Tourism Development, 2*(1), 28–29.

Beamish, P. W. (1987). Joint venture in LDCs: Partner selection and performance. *Management International Review, 27*(1), 23–37.

Brohman, J. (1996). New directions in tourism for third world development. *Annals of Tourism Research, 23*(1), 48–70.

Brown, D. O. (1996). *The effects of channel power, destination attractiveness and destination political risk events on U. S. tourism channel firm performance: The case of tourism destination in Africa*. Unpublished dissertation. Virginia Polytechnic Institute and State University, Blacksburg, VA.

Buckley, P. J., & Casson, M. C. (1976). *The future of the multinational enterprise*. London: Macmillan.

Caves, R. E. (1974). Multinational firms, competition and productivity in host country markets. *Economics, 41*, 176–193.

Chow, W. T. (1980). Integrating tourism with rural development. *Annals of Tourism Research, 7*(4), 584–607.

Comfort, A., & Comfort, N. (1984). Akagera: Rawanda's national park. *Parks, 8*(4), 8.

Crush, J. S., & Wellings, P. A. (1983). The Southern Africa pleasure periphery, 1966–1983. *Journal of African Studies, 21*(4), 673–698.

Cyert, R. M. (1963). *A behavioral theory of the firm*. Englewood Cliffs, NJ: Prentice-Hall.

Dunning, J. H. (1977). Trade, location of economic activity and the MNE: A search for an eclectic approach. In B. Ohlin, P. Hesselborn, & P. Wijkman (Eds.), *The international allocation of economic activity: Proceedings of a Nobel symposium held at Stockholm* (pp. 395–418). London, UK: Macmillan.

Dunning, J. H. (1992). *Multinational enterprises and the global economy*. Reading, MA: Addison-Weasley Publishing Co., Inc.

Dunning, J. M., & McQueen, M. (1988). The eclectic theory of international production: A case study of the international hotel industry. *Managerial and Decision Economics, 2*(4), 197–210.

Dunning, J. M., & Norman, G. (1983). The theory of the multinational enterprise: An application to the multinational office location. *Environment and Planning, 15*, 675–692.

Freitag, T. G. (1994). Enclave tourism development: For whom the benefits roll? *Annals of Tourism Research, 21*(3), 538–554.

Fryxell, G. E., Butler, J., & Choi, A. (2004). Successful localization programs in China: An important element in strategy implementation. *Journal of World Business*, *39*(3), 268–282.

Ghoshal, S. (1987). Global strategy: An organizing framework. *Strategic Management Journal*, *8*, 425–440.

Glynn, L. (1983). Multinationals in the third world of nations. In P. D. Grub, F. Ghadar, & D. Khambata (Eds.), *The multinational enterprise in transition, selected readings and essays* (3rd ed.). Princeton, NJ: The Darwin Press, Inc.

Hancock, G. (1979). *Packaged Africa*. Africa Report, pp. 38–42.

Hyma, B., Ojo, A., & Wall, G. (1980). Tourism in tropical Africa: A review of literature in English and agenda. *Annals of Tourism Research*, *7*(4), 525–553.

Hymer, S. (1960). *The international operations of national firms: A study of direct investment*. Published dissertation. MIT Press, Cambridge, MA.

Iroegbu, H. I. (2006). The effects of airfares and foreign exchange rates of global tourism. *Advances in Hospitality and Leisure*, *2*, 255–263.

Iroegbu, H. I. (2010). The influence of external environmental factors on tourism market strategies in Africa tourism. *Advances in Hospitality and Leisure*, *6*, 215–222.

Jamali, D. (2010). The CSR of MNC subsidiaries in developing countries: Global, local, substantive or diluted. *Journal of Business Ethics*, *93*, 181–200.

Kobrin, S. J. (1982). *Managing political risk assessment: Strategic response to environmental change*. Berkeley, CA: University of California Press.

Kobrin, S. J. (1988). Trends in ownership of American manufacturing subsidiaries in developing countries: An inter-industry analysis. *Management International Review*, [Special Issue], *28*, 73–83.

Kogut, B., & Singh, H. (1988). The effect of national culture on the choice of entry mode. *Journal of International Business Studies*, *19*(3), 411–432.

Kundu, S. K. (1994). *Explaining the globalization of service industries: The case of multinational hotels*. Unpublished doctoral dissertation. Rutgers State University, Newark, NJ.

McQueen, M. (1983). Appropriate policies towards multinational hotel corporations in developing countries. *World Development*, *11*(2), 141–152.

Meleka, A. H. (1985). The changing role of multinational corporations. *Management International Review*, *25*(4), 36–45.

Ofei-Nkansah, O. (1988). Luxury in Accra. *West Africa*, October, 17–23.

Porter, M. E. (1986). Changing patterns of international competition. *California Management Review*, *28*(2), 9–40.

Simon, H. A. (1967). The business school: A problem in organizational design. *Journal of Management Studies*, *4*, 1–6.

Stover, W. A. (1985). The stages of developing country policy toward foreign investment. *Columbia Journal of World Business*, *20*(3), 3.

Teye, V. B. (1988). Coups d'etat and African tourism: A study of Ghana. *Annals of Tourism Research*, *15*, 329–356.

Tse, E. C., & West, J. J. (1992). Development strategies for international hospitality markets. In R. Teare & M. D. Olsen (Eds.), *International tourism management* (pp. 118–134). New York, NY: Wiley.

Turnbull, D. R. (1996). *The influence of political risk events on the investment decisions of multinational hotel companies in Caribbean hotel projects*. Unpublished dissertation. Virginia Polytechnic Institute and State University, Blacksburg, VA.

van den Berghe, P. I. (1986). Colonialism, culture, and nature in Africa game reserves: Comment on Amalgor. *Annals of Tourism Research, 13*, 104–107.

Webster, M., & Hudson, T. (1991). Strategic management: A theoretical overview and its application to the hospitality industry. In R. Teare & A. Boer (Eds.), *Strategic hospitality management: Theory and practice for the 1990s.* London: Cassel Education Ltd.

Zhao, J. (1994). *The antecedent factors and entry mode choice of multinational lodging firms: The case of growth strategies into new international markets.* Unpublished doctoral dissertation. Virginia Polytechnic Institute and State University, Blacksburg, Virginia.

Zhao, M., Park, S. U., & Zhou, N. (2014). MNC strategy and social adaptation in emerging markets. *Journal of International Business Studies, 45*(7), 842–861.

DOMESTIC NATURE-BASED TOURISM IN JAPAN: SPIRITUALITY, NOVELTY AND COMMUNING

Christoffer Wanga Krag and Nina K. Prebensen

ABSTRACT

This paper explores why and how Japanese tourists travel in their home country. This work uses in-depth interviews and focus group interviews as its study design. Nature is an important aspect of Japanese life, and the meaning and use of nature include spiritual and bodily purification. Furthermore, Japanese domestic nature-based travels are strongly linked to self-identity and self-presentation, in that the Japanese travel not only for the sake of enjoyment, but also to a large extent as an instrument for learning, sharing and communing. The results are discussed in terms of theoretical contributions and practical applications.

Keywords: Japanese tourism; domestic; behaviour; spiritual; instrumental acts

Advances in Hospitality and Leisure, Volume 12, 51–64
ISSN: 1745-3542/doi:10.1108/S1745-354220160000012003

INTRODUCTION

The Japanese are depicted as having a unique, harmonious relationship with nature (Shove, Trentmann, & Wilk, 2009). In light of this, a relevant question would be how this relationship is demarcated in a tourism context. Although Japanese tourists are studied in outbound contexts and are seen as an attractive market for many countries (Lee, Han, & Lockyer, 2012; Reisinger & Turner, 2000), few have studied the Japanese domestic tourism market, although some exceptions do exist (Chon, Inagaki, & Ohashi, 2000; Graburn, 1983). Graburn discusses the seasonality of Japanese domestic tourism and the varieties of natural, historical, cultural, recreational, and sportive tourist sites. Graburn reports on the social environment of tourism and particularly the system of gift-giving that relates the traveller to the home environment. Additionally, the work outlines the history of Japanese travel and pilgrimage. Graburn (1983) concludes with a discussion of the place of tourism in the Japanese life cycle and in Japanese cultural conceptions of self, society and nationality. Chon et al. (2000) published a book with 12 papers on the Japanese domestic tourism market in terms of travel motivation, travel behaviour, satisfaction, souvenir-purchasing behaviour, and the characteristics of contemporary Japanese package tourism. Following the lead of these researchers and focusing on the Japanese domestic tourism market, this work aims to study the motivation and the behaviour of Japanese tourists travelling in their home country. Specifically, this work aims to study travel as an instrument to reach other goals, such as learning, socializing and expressing oneself in a social context, in addition to understanding the autotelic aspects of enjoying nature and socializing during precious moments.

Nature-based tourism as a concept is described in terms of tourists' preferences when it comes to partaking in nature-based activities during their vacation (Laarman & Durst, 1987). Tourists are often delineated as wanting to be in, and to enjoy nature (Bronsted, 1994; Cohen, 1972; Fredman & Tyrväinen, 2010; Vickerman, 1988). However, being in and enjoying nature may be performed in various ways and with different motivations.

This study will provide new knowledge in terms of understanding tourist practices in general, which should add to existing theoretical perspectives on tourist behaviour. Furthermore, it focuses on one particular market, the Japanese domestic market, providing the Japanese tourist industry with knowledge in terms of attracting the domestic market. The Japanese view of nature requires extensive research and is located beyond the exploratory boundaries of this study. However, acquiring a glimpse of understanding will undoubtedly make it easier for Japanese marketers to develop tours that attract the domestic market.

Japanese Structure and Purpose of Travelling

Tourists travel for a variety of reasons and do so in different ways (Holt, 1995). This paper utilises literature acknowledging how individuals delineate the meaning of nature, in addition to how the sense of self and self-presentation strategies are performed in a domestic tourism setting. In particular, the work of Belk (1988) concerning possessions and the extended self is embraced. Belk (1988) brought together a large body of literature to support the thesis that consumers use key possessions to extend, expand and strengthen their sense of self.

Japanese and the Perception of Nature

One of the characteristics of the Japanese is their gratitude and appreciation for nature. This feature is something they have long been famous for and is generally characterised by their not only being purely interested in the physical aspect of nature, but also take an interest in the spirituality that dwells in nature (Moeran, 1983). To understand their view of nature, one must examine their background and determine how nature is regarded according to the Japanese culture/religion as well as trying to understand how this view affects the daily life of the average Japanese. A very characteristic aspect in this matter is the Japanese connection to the biggest 'religion' in Japan, Shinto.

The Ise Grand Shrine is the most sacred Shinto shrine in Japan, with close ties to the Imperial Household. Shinto is delineated as the indigenous religion of Japan and its people (Jingu, 2013). Shinto is the inherent belief or way of life for the vast majority of Japanese and it is a way of living and thinking that has been integrated as a part of Japanese culture since ancient history (Jingu, 2013). Thus, one cannot directly classify Shinto with the word "religion" as traditionally comprehended by the Western world.

For the Japanese, Shinto, Christianity and Buddhism are mixed together (Gellner, 1997). However, it is Shinto that provides the foundation of Japanese society, in which pureness and honesty are important virtues. Shinto roots still define great parts of Japan's culture. Yet, there is great awe towards the might of nature and still one demonstrates gratitude for its generosity. Within Shinto, nature is viewed in connection with 神 (*Kami*), a concept that is often compared to God in the same way as God is portrayed within religions such as Christianity. However, *Kami* should perhaps rather be seen as an expression for the divine life force of the natural world (Jingu, 2013). The word *Kami* origins from nature itself and there exists *Kami* for wind, rain, lightning, rivers and so forth.

In the Shinto belief, nature itself is its own lord and does not necessarily adapt to the needs and desires of humans. For example, the sun gives us heat, but can on the contrary cause drought and hunger. A fresh breeze may in turn become a furious storm causing destruction and sorrow (Jingu, 2013). Natural landmarks such as the ocean, mountains or forests are seen as locations where *Kami* are present. During the ancient times such areas were sacred places, where no buildings of worship were needed as the 'Gods' (*Kami*) were present everywhere. Subsequently, residences for *Kami* were built in the forests, becoming the precursor to the so-called "神社" (*Jinja*), 'shrine' in English. Altogether, over 80,000 divine places are scattered around today's Japan (Jingu, 2013) and are associated with, and express, the appreciation the Japanese have for nature. The *Jinja* and its immediate surroundings are sacred locations and are kept clean and flawless. Given that the vast majority of *Jinja* are surrounded by trees or other natural landscape, the power of nature is all around them. In cities, they remind one of oases in the middle of Japan's busy streets. Not only are they used for rituals and prayers but they also function as a place where one can find serenity and achieve both mental and physical rejuvenation (Jingu, 2013).

Although these Shinto roots are greatly embedded in the Japanese culture, it does not necessarily mean that it has an effect on tourism. However, a number of researchers have noticed the unique fascination the Japanese have for nature. Moeran (1983) analyses the language used in Japanese travel brochures where nature is a very central topic. It is described as beautiful (美しい – utsukushii), grandeur (雄大 – yūdai), opulent (豊か – yutaka), and unpolluted (よごれの無い – yogore no nai). These words portray a focus on nature and the sceneries themselves more than focusing on activities that are enjoyed in natural surroundings. Visiting nature is also regarded as a means of "escaping" busy city life and participating in recreation that cannot take place at home (Watkins & Gnoth, 2011), but a trip to nature can also be considered as pilgrimage or be an appropriate atmosphere for prayer (Watkins, 2008). Indeed, nature is viewed as a sacred space of purity and brightness within Shinto (Nadeau, 1997). Additionally, nature is seen as a place where it is possible to cleanse the soul and mind. Nadeau (1997) writes that the Shinto separation between the inner/sacred/pure and the outer/profane/polluted defines Japanese cosmology just as it defines the Japanese character. This is not limited to the boundaries of Shinto shrines. Rather, 'the inner is the world of nature, in opposition to the cosmos and heavens' Nadeau (1997, p. 110).

Learning and Novelty Seeking

Learning in a tourism context is about using tourism and leisure settings as a means to obtain knowledge, ideas and visions for oneself and society (Falk, Ballantyne, Packer, & Benckendorff, 2012). Japanese travelling on vacation are depicted as being strongly affected by an intense 'regime', day by day, with activities and things that must be done, and the goal is to experience as much as possible in the shortest time possible (Ziff-Levine, 1990). However, others reveal that this type of travel has changed (Chon et al., 2000).

The search for novel experiences is about the need we all have to have variety in our lives (Faison, 1977). Within tourism this tendency is vast and deals with the tourists' need to experience something different from every-day life, but also for instrumental reasons such as learning and identity building (Chen, Prebensen, Chen, & Kim, 2013). A very widespread description of novelty is to say that it is the degree of contrast between our past experience and what we currently perceive (Lee & Crompton, 1992; Pearson, 1970). In other words, the degree of novelty is determined by the individual by comparing a stimulus with other stimuli encountered in the past, as well as stimuli present at that time (Greenberger, Woldman, & Yourshaw, 1967).

Since Japan is a society where hard work is highly valued, taking a holiday with the aim of pure relaxation can be a hard decision to make and a sense of guilt for pursuing pleasure can occur (Kajiwara, 1997). Based on this, Kajiwara states that education or learning, and other meaningful aspects that can be incorporated into the trip, still plays a crucial role in Japanese tourism (Kajiwara, 1997). Graburn (1983) argues that travel goals may vary according to cultural backgrounds and that a tourist's journey has to be morally justified by the home community. This means that one does not choose to travel in order to obtain leisure, but that there is an underlying and deeper intention for travel. Turner and Turner (1978) explain that in many societies throughout history, travelling has been justi-fied by pilgrimage. Travel in this respect is to carry out a duty as a pilgrim.

In Japan, the line between travelling as a pilgrim and travelling as a regular tourist has been unclear, but pilgrimage is often used to justify travelling (Watkins, 2008) and to get approval for travelling (Turner & Turner, 2011). In fact, a treatise on civil administration exists claiming 'no one of any class (should) travel without reason' (Kanzaki, 1992, p. 67). However, when going on pilgrimage an important component of the trip is the joy obtained by being able to see new things, people and places (Watkins, 2008). Research on elderly Japanese travellers also reveals that finding new relationships while travelling is of vast importance (Ryu, Sunghyup, & Changsup, 2014). According to Watkins, a pilgrimage today, however, may be enjoyed for the mere sake of novelty, having less moral restrictions on behaviour and intent, without losing its status as a 'pilgrimage' (Watkins, 2008).

The Search for, and Presentation of, Self

Consumers possess various lasting images or perceptions of themselves. The concept of self refers to what a person thinks of his or her own attributes and the way they are evaluated (Markus & Kitayama, 1991; Solomon, Bamossy, Askegaard, & Hogg, 2013). These self-images, or perceptions, of oneself are closely related with personality and the consumers' choice of products or services (Schiffman, Hansen, & Kanuk, 2008). People identify themselves through the use of specific products and services that have a symbolic value for them, or those that are consistent with the personal self-image of the particular individual. Belk (1988) terms the act of integrating consumption objects into one's identity as self-extension processes. In short, consumers attempt to describe themselves through their choice of products, services, or experiences that can strengthen their self-concept at the same time as avoiding those that weaken it (Schiffman et al., 2008). For example, if someone is very environmentally conscious, that person will choose, and surround themselves with, environmentally friendly products, services or experiences. Our social self-image is defined as how we want others to perceive us as a person (Markus & Kitayama, 1991; Schiffman et al., 2008). In different contexts, for example in tourism-related situations, individuals can choose to visit places in accordance with their self-image guiding their attitudes and behaviour. Whereas investing in "socially conspicuous" products or experiences, for example visiting places mainly to achieve a high social status or to impress others, one is guided by the desire of a better self-image, as viewed by others (Schiffman et al., 2008). One of the most distinctive behavioural characteristics of Japanese tourists is their dedication to buying souvenirs, or so-called おみやげ (*Omiyage*) (Guichard-Anguis & Moon, 2008; Park, 2000; Reisinger & Turner, 2000; Watkins, 2008). An explanation for this behaviour may be that Japan has a strong gift-giving culture and gifts are given at certain annual events, as well as throughout daily life (Park, 2000). Befu (1968, p. 445) goes as far as calling gift-giving a minor institution of Japan, encompassing strict rules and norms concerning how gift-giving should be carried out (Park, 2000). This indicates that when the Japanese are giving gifts, the gifts reflect their self-presentation and self-image (Schiffman et al., 2008). The importance of this 'gift-giving' can be explained by the concept of 義理 (*giri*), which is a moral, social obligation that requires people to perform one's duty towards other members of the group (Befu, 1968). Ziff-Levine (1990, p. 108) finds that the Japanese feel a strong sense of obligation to purchasing gifts for friends, family and other acquaintances. Keown (1989) shows that Japanese outbound travellers to Hawaii have a high frequency of shopping behaviour, particularly for gifts. Ziff-Levine (1990) reports that 25% of the time Japanese tourists spent on a standard four-day trip were on shopping.

METHODOLOGY

Given the lack of empirical research on Japanese domestic travel behaviour, this research is exploratory. In order to acquire new knowledge concerning why and how Japanese are vacationing in Japan, a study design using in-depth analysis and focus groups seems most suitable. This method is chosen because it acknowledges actors' constructions and interactions within their social world (Altheide & Jonson, 1994).

According to Morgan and Smircich (1980), qualitative research is an approach whose appropriateness is determined from the nature of the social phenomenon in question. The goal of this study is to explore the practices behind *how* Japanese consume travelling, and further, whether there are any particular reasons as to *why* these practices exist. In accordance with Yin (2014), how and why questions have a justifiable rationale for performing exploratory studies as well as explanatory studies. Accordingly, this study has chosen to apply an exploratory design using *qualitative* semi-structured interviews and one focus group as the research method.

The data collection was conducted in Kyoto and Osaka in Japan. Altogether, seven people, five women and two men, participated in the interviews. A focus group consisting of two men and one woman supplemented these interviews. The prepared questions were the same, but discussion was actively encouraged in the focus group. Before conducting the interviews, a test interview was performed in order to practice conversational flow. By doing so, it was possible to check the time needed as well as whether the questions were understandable or not. This process helped eliminate or alter confusing questions, which strengthens the internal validity (Saunders, Lewis, & Thornhill, 2012). Furthermore, performing a test interview develops the ability of the interviewer. Due to convenience, interviews were conducted at various locations throughout Kyoto, with one being conducted in Osaka. To create a comfortable setting, the interviewees were (if desired) given the freedom to choose themselves exactly where to hold the interview. If the informants feel comfortable, there is an increasing chance that they will be more willing to open up, increasing the probability of avoiding response bias (Saunders et al., 2012). Some of the informants were most comfortable in a quiet and private area, while others preferred public areas such as cafes or restaurants. To keep it manageable and to avoid bothering others, the focus group was held in a private and quiet environment. Before the interviews, the informants were informed that the interview would take ~50–60 minutes and the focus group ~75–90 minutes.

RESULTS AND DISCUSSION

Spiritual and Bodily Purifications in Nature

Japanese tourists demonstrate strong emotions connected to nature-based travels. Many responses align well with research, revealing that the Japanese might have a unique relation with nature as they indeed made ties to metaphysical or divine matters when asked about their feelings towards nature:

> The sea, the beauty, and blue sea. It is very calm and I feel something. Something holy, something special. (Watanabe)

The very young participants expressed themselves similarly when asked about their feelings towards nature.

> Yeah, relaxed, it makes me relaxed. (...) Comfortable. (Ono)

Additionally, when asked directly whether the informant had a scientific or supernatural-oriented mind in relation to nature he replied:

> Both. Usually scientific, but also something other than scientific. (Ono)

Moreover, Aoki also attempts to explain her profound feelings toward nature:

> When I'm in nature I'll be ... I'll be like dead, or small. So small small small compared to this earth and space. (...) if I have a small problem or worries (...), those small problems in my mind become gone if I see the big things, the great things. It's too human thinking. If I become too much concentrated on, focus on the small problems, like human thinking, it's gone when I see the greatest, God's creation. (...) It's more for cleansing my heart and thinking. That becomes a recovery for my heart, and mental health. (Aoki)

Even those informants expressing that they do not believe in any religion, or think of anything in relation to Shinto (such as *Kami*) when in nature, say that nature is a place for purification:

> (...) like pure. I think it's a kind of shower, I like clean myself. (Suzuki)

Cultural Interactions: Communing, Learning and Sharing
Learning seems very important for the informants. However, the term 'learning' did not carry a sense of serious learning, as in studying. Instead, many pointed out that they learned indirectly by doing activities, participating in the culture and talking to people. One of the informants even regards learning as a prerequisite for travelling.

Aoki said that she wanted to speak to other Japanese if she, for instance, spotted them looking at maps, asking them where in Japan they are from, etc. Tanaka always attempts to find new things to do and different foods to try out, but that he always tries to meet the same people every time.

For him, communing is a very important part of travelling:

> (...) it's very important for me to talk to people that I'm travelling with, about the trip. It gives me better feedback than travelling by myself. And I like discussing what we experience, what we ate, while travelling and after. (Tanaka)

It is evident that almost all of the participants of this study preferred travelling together with someone close to them, be it friends or family. Sharing the experience (communing) with others seems quite important. Aoki enjoys talking to the locals and deems it a necessary part of the trip. She illustrates this by saying that going shopping and not talking to anyone would invoke a feeling of actually never having been at the destination. The desire to learn may be related to the desire to extend the self-concept; however, separating self and learning in this context is difficult. Whether these actions are performed in order to strengthen the self-concept or to simply learn something is still unclear. Whatever the reason, these actions are by any means instrumental actions (a means to an end) and clearly important for individual Japanese travellers.

Japanese are notoriously known for both buying souvenirs and taking a great deal of photographs when they travel. Research discusses the meaning of such actions (Wallendorf & Arnould, 1988). In order to delineate why the *Omiyage* (souvenirs) is such an important aspect of travelling for the Japanese, the participants of this study were initially questioned about their general thoughts about this culture. Most of the interviewees (eight) were either neutral or positive towards the culture, whereas one thought it was unnecessary and one expressed strong hatred toward it. One of the more positive views of *Omiyage* was that it is a way of caring about others:

> *Omiyage*? It is great. (...) it's just how you care about, show how you care about a person, not being selfish (...) it's great to care about others for your journey, even if you're having fun, you can share it with others. (Aoki)

Whereas one of the participants utters his hate toward it:

> I hate it *[laughs]*. You do not know how much I hate it. It is one of the worst parts of our culture. I think it is a waste of time, just to take time buying souvenirs. In addition, people do not even appreciate it (...) and I do not get anything for *myself* either. Because I do not want things from trips, I just want to travel and I just want to eat good food. I enjoy the trip itself, not shopping. (Tanaka)

As displayed above, there are mixed feelings about the *Omiyage* culture. Nevertheless, they all participate in the culture. Additional discussions within the focus group included souvenir-giving to friends and family:

> We feel we can share the experience by giving souvenirs. (Yamamoto)

In Japan, the word お土産話 (*Omiyagebanashi*) means souvenir (*Omiyage*) combined with the word for story (*hanashi/banashi*). This means stories one has gathered from travelling that are meant to be shared (Jaffe, 2004). Serving as conversation pieces, souvenirs add context to stories. Having established the context, storytelling can further be used to highlight the quality of one's relationship towards the trip.

Park's (2000) study comparing the Japanese *Omiyage* culture with the Korean "*Sunmul*" culture indicates similar reasons as to why Japanese buy *Omiyage*. Park found evidence of the desire to share the experience with those unable to join the trip. Additionally, *Omiyage* provides evidence that one has been to a region or a country, at the same time it is proof that one knows something that is unknown to others (Park, 2000).

The concept of *giri* (social obligation) can be a reason for buying *Omiyage*. This is especially evident when observing those who have absolutely no desire to buy souvenirs, but for some reason still buy them. One of them felt a pressure to buy because his wife bought for her side of the family.

> Well, we're married and both have relatives. Moreover, they know we went on a vacation so we cannot help it. So we bought not that much, but pretty much and I think it's a waste of time (...) but if she buys something for her side I think I would have to buy for my side too right, to make it fair. (Tanaka)

Experience sharing seems important when explaining *Omiyage*-giving. Some Japanese might purchase *Omiyage* merely to share trip experiences with others in an act of solidarity (Park, 2000), such as Aoki, who describes the culture as 'great'.

Photos are also a great way of documenting one's attendance to something intangible such as travelling. The Japanese are widely known for taking many photos when they travel (Reisinger & Turner, 2000; Watkins, 2008). In the modern world, a great way of presenting oneself and to build identity is to use social networking sites actively by, for example, posting stories and pictures on Facebook (see, for instance, Krasnova, Wenninger, Widjaja, & Buxmann, 2013; Mehdizadeh, 2010). The interviewees, however, claim that they did not have such a goal, despite the fact that some of them possessed an impressive array of travel experience. All the participants except Yamamoto reported that they take many pictures when travelling, and most of the young participants (under 40 years old) reported that they regularly upload them to Facebook for their friends and family to see. They did so to share their experience with others or to keep pictures there as a memory for themselves, a modern way of photo arranging. Itou, Kobayashi and Aoki explain their reasons for sharing photos:

> This is how it was, to share either the joy or the beauty of the experience. (Itou)

> Because otherwise I just forget the views and things (...). That reminds me of beautiful days when I travelled. (Kobayashi)

> (...) when I see [the pictures] again I want to make the trigger to remember my memories from watching the photos, and I want to show my friends (...) I want to introduce the places that I've been experiencing. (Aoki)

CONCLUSION

This paper explores Japanese domestic tourist travels. The study finds two important lines of thoughts regarding how and why Japanese travel in their home country during their vacation, namely the importance of nature as a spiritual and bodily purification and the use of souvenirs and pictures as part of cultural interactions, such as communing, learning and sharing.

The informants described strong feelings when surrounded by nature and some indeed talked about spirituality and a God-like presence. Even the youngest of them described visiting nature as a way of spiritually cleaning. These findings align well with, for example Chen et al.'s (2013) motivation studies suggesting that novelty, learning and knowledge appear very frequently in relation to nature-based tourism and with those researchers highlighting the Japanese search for spirituality in nature (Moeran, 1983). It also fits well with the Japanese and their interest in learning (Kajiwara, 1997) together with the fact that new destinations and experiences are likely to be educational (Crompton, 1979).

Japanese use *Omiyage* (souvenirs) and pictures as a means to classify themselves and build their social self-image. Results from the interviews tell a two-fold story. It seems that some of the interviewees use *Omiyage* and pictures as a topic starter when returning home, enabling them to narrate their trip (so-called "*omiyagebanashi*"). Furthermore, some Japanese give others *Omiyage* in order to prove that they have been somewhere, thus differentiating themselves from others (building a distinction), that is self-presentation and classification. The findings in this study further point to the fact that research on Japanese tourist behaviour should implement aspects of self-identity strategies as well as communing behaviour. Additionally, research would gain from comparing tourists from different cultural backgrounds in order to acknowledge the various purposes and structures of tourist behaviour. The tourism industry may learn from the study results in that Japanese largely utilise nature to recover spiritually and physically. Furthermore, the industry may utilise and promote scenery and iconic places as sites to take pictures and buy souvenirs (*Omiyage*) as these acts are very important in the Japanese culture. As the interviews were relatively few and were performed in Kyoto and Osaka only, there may be limitations in terms of generalisation. However, the purpose of this study was to explore in-depth the Japanese way of travelling.

REFERENCES

Altheide, D. L., & Johnson, J. M. (1994). Criteria for assessing interpretive validity in qualitative research.

Befu, H. (1968). Gift-giving in a modernizing Japan. *Monumenta Nipponica, 23*, 445−456.

Belk, R. W. (1988). Possessions and the extended self. *Consumer Research, 15*, 139−168.

Bronsted, H. (1994). *Tourists' activities in Greenland.* Paper presented at the Tourism in Polar Regions Proceedings of the Symposium, Colmar, France, pp. 21–23.

Chen, J. S., Prebensen, N. K., Chen, Y. L., & Kim, H. (2013). Revelation of nature-minded travelers: A study of the Swedish. *Tourism Analysis, 18*(6), 651–661.

Chon, K. S., Inagaki, T., & Ohashi, T. (2000). *Japanese tourists: Socio-economic, marketing and psychological analysis.* Binghamton, NY: The Haworth Press.

Cohen, E. (1972). Towards a sociology of international tourism. *Social Research, 39*(2), 164–182.

Crompton, J. L. (1979). Motivations for pleasure vacation. *Annals of Tourism Research, 6*(4), 408–424.

Faison, E. W. (1977). The neglected variety drive: A useful concept for consumer behavior. *Journal of Consumer Research, 4,* 72–175.

Falk, J. H., Ballantyne, R., Packer, J., & Benckendorff, P. (2012). Travel and learning: A neglected tourism research area. *Annals of Tourism Research, 39*(2), 908–927.

Fredman, P., & Tyrväinen, L. (2010). Frontiers in nature-based tourism. *Scandinavian Journal of Hospitality and Tourism, 10*(3), 177–189.

Gellner, D. N. (1997). For syncretism. The position of Buddhism in Nepal and Japan compared. *Social Anthropology, 5,* 277–291. Reissued in Gellner, *The Anthropology of Buddhism and Hinduism. Weberian themes*: Delhi 2000.

Graburn, N. H. H. (1983). To pray, pay and play: The cultural structure of Japanese domestic tourism. In Graburn (Ed.), *Culture and the self: Implications for cognition, emotion, and motivation* (p. 89). Oxfordshire: CABI.

Greenberger, E., Woldman, J., & Yourshaw, S. W. (1967). Components of curiosity: Berlyne reconsidered. *British Journal of Psychology, 58*(3–4), 375–386.

Guichard-Anguis, S., & Moon, O. (Eds.). (2008). *Japanese tourism and travel culture.* Abingdon: Routledge. Online.

Holt, D. B. (1995). How consumers consume: A typology of consumption practices. *Journal of Consumer Research, 22,* 1–16.

Jaffe, J. C. (2004). Two views of Japan: The tower experience and the performance of cultural identity. *Current Issues in Tourism, 7*(6), 523–534.

Jingu, I. (2013). *Soul of Japan — An introduction to Shinto and Ise Jingu.* Retrieved from http://www.sengu.info/pdf/soul-of-japan.pdf

Kajiwara, K. (1997). Inward-bound, outward-bound: Japanese tourism reconsidered. In S. Yamashita, K. H. Din, & J.-S. Eades (Eds.), *Tourism and cultural development in Asia and Oceania* (pp. 164–177). Selangor: Penerbit Universiti Kebangsaan Malaysia.

Kanzaki, N. (1992). The travel loving tradition of the Japanese. *Japan Echo, 19*(4), 66–69.

Keown, C. F. (1989). A model of tourists' propensity to buy: The case of Japanese visitors to Hawaii. *Journal of Travel Research, 27*(3), 31–34.

Krasnova, H., Wenninger, H., Widjaja, T., & Buxmann, P. (2013). *Envy on Facebook: A hidden threat to users' life satisfaction?* 11th International Conference on Wirtschaftsinformatik (WI), Leipzig, Germany.

Laarman, J. G., & Durst, P. B. (1987). Nature travel in the tropics. *Journal of Forestry, 85*(5), 43–46.

Lee, M., Han, H., & Lockyer, T. (2012). Medical tourism: Attracting Japanese tourists for medical tourism experience. *Journal of Travel & Tourism Marketing, 29,* 69–86.

Lee, T. H., & Crompton, J. (1992). Measuring novelty seeking in tourism. *Annals of Tourism Research, 19*(4), 732–751.

Markus, H. R., & Kitayama, S. (1991). Culture and the self: Implications for cognition, emotion, and motivation. *Psychological Review*, *98*(2), 224−253.

Mehdizadeh, S. (2010). Self-presentation 2.0: Narcissism and self-esteem on Facebook. *Cyberpsychology, Behavior, and Social Networking*, *13*(4), 357−364.

Moeran, B. (1983). The language of Japanese tourism. *Annals of Tourism Research*, *10*(1), 93−108.

Morgan, G., & Smircich, L. (1980). The case for qualitative research. *Academy of Management Review*, *5*(4), 491−500.

Nadeau, R. L. (1997). Dimensions of sacred space in Japanese popular culture. *Intercultural Communication Studies*, *6*, 109−114.

Park, M. K. (2000). Social and cultural factors influencing tourists' souvenir-purchasing behavior: A comparative study on Japanese 'Omiyage' and Korean 'Sunmul'. *Journal of Travel & Tourism Marketing*, *9*(1−2), 81−91.

Pearson, P. H. (1970). Relationships between global and specified measures of novelty seeking. *Journal of Consulting and Clinical Psychology*, *34*(2), 199.

Reisinger, Y., & Turner, L. (2000). Japanese tourism satisfaction: Gold Coast versus Hawaii. *Journal of Vacation Marketing*, *6*(4), 299−317.

Ryu, E., Sunghyup, S. H., & Changsup, S. (2014). Creating new relationships through tourism: A qualitative analysis of tourist motivation of older individuals in Japan. *Journal of Travel & Tourism Marketing*, *32*, 325−338. doi:10.1080/10548408.2014.895478

Saunders, M., Lewis, P., & Thornhill, A. (2012). *Research methods for business students* (6th ed.). Harlow: Prentice Hall.

Schiffman, L. G., Hansen, H., & Kanuk, L. L. (2008). *Consumer behaviour: A European outlook*. London: Pearson Education.

Shove, E., Trentmann, F., & Wilk, R. (2009). *Time, consumption and everyday life*. Oxford: Berg.

Solomon, M., Bamossy, G., Askegaard, S., & Hogg, M. K. (2013). *Consumer behaviour: A European perspective*. Essex, England: Prentice Hall.

Turner, V. W., & Turner, E. (1978). *Image and pilgrimage in Christian culture: Anthropological perspective*. New York, NY: Columbia University Press.

Turner, V. W., & Turner, E. L. (2011). *Image and pilgrimage in Christian culture*. New York, NY: Columbia University Press.

Vickerman, S. (1988). *Stimulating tourism and economic growth by featuring new wildlife recreation opportunities*. Paper presented at the Transactions 53rd American Wildlife and Natural Resources Conference: Washington, D.C.

Wallendorf, M., & Arnould, E. J. (1988). 'My favorite things': A cross-cultural inquiry into object attachment, possessiveness, and social linkage. *Journal of Consumer Research*, *14*, 531−547.

Watkins, L. (2008). Japanese travel culture: An investigation of the links between early Japanese pilgrimage and modern Japanese travel behaviour. *New Zealand Journal of Asian Studies*, *10*(2), 93−110.

Watkins, L. J., & Gnoth, J. (2011). Japanese tourism values: A means−end investigation. *Journal of Travel Research*, *50*(6), 654−668.

Yin, R. K. (2014). *Case study research: Design and methods*. Singapore: Sage.

Ziff-Levine, W. (1990). The cultural logic gap: A Japanese tourism research experience. *Tourism Management*, *11*(2), 105−110.

IMPACT OF HOTEL EMPLOYEE'S GREEN AWARENESS, KNOWLEDGE, AND SKILL ON HOTEL'S OVERALL PERFORMANCE

Ming-Hsuan Wu, Weerapon Thongma, Winitra Leelapattana and Mei-Ling Huang

ABSTRACT

This study seeks to investigate issues transpiring in green hotels from a human resource perspective which is unlike most green-hotel studies centering on consumer behavioral subjects. It hypothesizes that the employees' green ability consisting of environmental awareness, environmental knowledge, and environmental skill creates a positive impact on hotels' green ability and ultimately on the overall performance of hotels. Using alumni from a tourism and hospitality program, this study collects 233 responses from a structured questionnaire survey. The findings indicate that hotel employees approximately contribute toward a fifth of the hotels' ability to implement greener practices.

Keywords: Green hotel; green image; environmental awareness; environmental knowledge; hotel performance

Advances in Hospitality and Leisure, Volume 12, 65–81
Copyright © 2017 by Emerald Group Publishing Limited
All rights of reproduction in any form reserved
ISSN: 1745-3542/doi:10.1108/S1745-354220160000012004

INTRODUCTION

Tourism scholars and industrial professionals have recently advocated an urgent need to adopt greener operations in the hotel industry (Han, 2015). It is attributed to the fact that an increasing number of consumers have embraced the idea of using eco-friendly products and services in the context of lodging operations (Kim & Han, 2010). This upcoming market has encouraged most if not all leading hotels to timely adopt greener practices to gain a competitive edge.

Nevertheless, in order to be successful, a hotel may need to consider barriers hindering the green practices before being committed to green practices. Chan (2008) underlined several pressing issues including lack of skills or knowledge to go green, lack of facilities, cost increase, and uncertain outcome.

Indeed, the employee is a critical actor significantly affecting the success of green operations of any kinds. Hotels, therefore, need to enhance their employees' environmental knowledge, awareness, and concern (Chan, Hon, Chan, & Okumus, 2014) to prevail upon the challenges of implementing green practices.

A growing amount of literature has recently taken on green-hotel issues and some pertain to guests' purchasing intention (Han, 2015; Han, Hsu, & Sheu, 2010; Yeh, Ma, & Huan, 2016) and some take hotel managers' perspectives regarding adopting green practice (Chan, 2008, 2013). However, as a contrast to consumer perspective, few studies (Chan et al., 2014) have assessed the issues relating to hotel work forces.

It has been suggested that hospitality employees resist complying with green practices (Hon & Chan, 2013) and consequently, the academia expresses a new interest in studying the motivation behind employees' devotion to green practice (Chan et al., 2014; Norton, Zacher, & Ashkanasy, 2014). However, to this day there is no empirical study measuring hotel employees' ability to help with a hotel's goal of achieving green practices.

To supply the above gap of research, this study is an attempt to assess the relationship between hotel employees' ability of green practice and their contribution to hotel's overall greenness. Specifically, the objectives of the study are (1) to investigate how hotel employees' environmental awareness, environmental participation, and environmental skills affect hotels' green ability in general; (2) to investigate how hotels' green ability affects overall performance of hotels; and (3) to determine the level of contribution of hotel employees' green ability in relation to hotels' overall green reputation.

The results of the study may shed some light on how hotel employees contribute to the growth of hotels with respect to their green operations. Meanwhile the findings may add pragmatic viewpoints concerning how hotel managers effectively assist their staffs to better to achieve the goals of green practices.

Green Hotels in Taiwan

The concept of green operations has recently been evoked among Taiwan's hotel operators. There are still many barriers to effective practices, such as a lack of financial incentive, undermining the effort of going green (Chang, Tsai, & Yeh, 2014; Yeh et al., 2016). In 2008, the Taiwan's central government and hotel practitioners initiated and sponsored a green-hotel award contest which intended to recognize and benchmark those hotels which have been diligently devoted toward green practices – even though many practices adopted may seem quite rudimentary, such as not providing the service for room cleaning unless requested.

Several studies (Teng, Horng, Hu, Chien, & Shen, 2012) find that hotels are able to implement a green practice without imposing excessive expenditures, financial incentives could have an impact on the hotel's willingness to practice green. Regardless, many hoteliers continue to remain reluctant to join the green movement beyond financial consideration (Chan, 2008; Wang, Chen, Lee, & Tsai, 2013).

The green-hospitality services have received less attention in Taiwan, compared to that in some other countries (Wang et al., 2013). The Taiwanese market is gradually showing a tendency to experience a greener product (Chang et al., 2014). Though the trend is upward, there are still barriers impacting customers' willingness to purchase green products. For example, since the official certification for green property is still in its infancy, customers' confusion and perceived risk are some problems coming in the way of customers accepting green products (Chen & Chang, 2013). This is particularly true after Taiwan's recent food scandal (Yang, Hauser, & Goldman, 2013) that destroyed many people's faith in certificated labels endorsed by the government. There is also a problem of greenwashing (Best & Thapa, 2013), which refers to using green marketing deceptively to promote products (Chen & Chang, 2013). In sum, despite those setbacks, Taiwan's green movement and the market for environment-friendly products are undoubtedly growing.

Hotel Employees' Practices toward Green

An environment-friendly operation could impact hotel employees in different ways. As soon as a hotel convers its current operations to be more environment-friendly, it is likely to put heavy pressure on its employees (Chan et al., 2014) who might not be familiar with green concepts and practices. The employees need to be properly trained to cope with green practices and services (Renwick, Redman, & Maguire, 2013). Resentment from various parts of employee groups may arise when a hotel considers these green opportunities. For example, implementing a new practice is a cost to the hotel and the new practice could also be seen as a source of stress for service staffs. Furthermore, when using green products or services, hotel guests may face challenges due to unfamiliarity that can quickly translate to a barrier for service staffs to deliver an excellent service that meets guest satisfaction (Chang et al., 2014). To remove the psychological barriers from employees, it is essential for hotel managers to provide service personnel with sufficient information regarding their role in and expected contributions to the hotel's green goals.

Hotel's Green Practices in Relation to Its Overall Performance

Environment management is thought to be complementary to quality management and both environment management and quality management can have positive effect on a firm's financial and marketing performance (Pereira-Moliner, Claver-Cortés, Molina-Azorín, & José Tarí, 2012). Environment-friendly and energy-saving technologies allow hotel firms to construct eco-friendly buildings with a reasonable cost that is no more than the cost of common buildings constructed today (Butler, 2008; Pereira-Moliner et al., 2012).

From a marketing point of view, delivering green products and services, such as servicing meals made by local produces and organic ingredients (Teng et al., 2012), is an effective way to appeal to environment-friendly customers (Miles & Covin, 2000) and might give hotels a competitive advantage over competition.

METHODOLOGY

Based on the literature, this study proposes a structural model (see Fig. 1) that contained eight hypotheses listed below.

H1. A hotel's green image positively affects its overall performance.

H2. A hotel's green image positively affects its green ability.

H3. An employee's green awareness positively affects his/her hotel's green ability.

H4. An employee's green knowledge positively affects his/her hotel's green ability.

H5. An employee's green skill positively affects his/her hotel's green ability.

H6. A hotel's green ability contribution is a significant portion of its overall performance.

H7. An employee's contribution accounts for a significant portion of hotel's green ability.

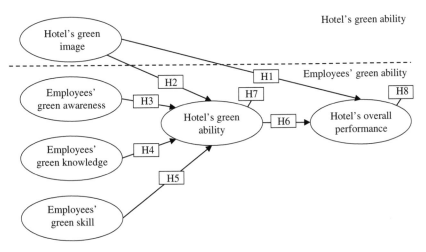

Fig. 1. Proposed Model and Hypotheses.

H8. An employee's contribution accounts for a significant portion of hotel's overall performance.

Based on past studies (Han, Hsu, & Lee, 2009; Han & Kim, 2010; Ko, Hwang, & Kim, 2013), this study posits that the green image of a hotel is able to affect the green ability and overall performance (H1 and H2) of the hotel. These two hypotheses were proposed to allow a comparison with an employee's contribution to a hotel's green ability and its overall performance. Further another hypothesis (H6) proposed a direct relationship between the above two variables that a hotel's green ability could positively affect its overall performance (Pereira-Moliner et al., 2012; Teng et al., 2012).

In the study model, H3, H4, and H5 were constructed according to a proposition that employees' environmental awareness, environmental knowledge, and environmental skill contribute to their intention to comply with their firm's green practices (Best & Thapa, 2013; Chan, 2008). Lastly, this study examines a hotel employee's contribution to a hotel's green ability and the hotel's overall performance which is represented by H7 and H8.

Sampling Method

Since the aim of this study was to examine hotel employees' green abilities and how they contributed to hotels' green and overall performance, the study population was junior, front-line hotel employees in Taiwan. This study used a convenient sample approach by inviting participants using an alumnus correspondence book as a sample frame. Once an alumnus was verified as a current front-line hotel employee and willing to join a follow-up questionnaire survey, the study sent an e-mail to her/him. Consequently, 250 questionnaires were sent out that resulted in 233 valid responses. The return rate was 93.2%.

Questionnaire Design

The questionnaire contained four parts which include nominal and ratio (e.g., measured by seven points) scales. The first part had three subsections and questions from these subsections were used to measure hotel employees' environmental awareness, environmental knowledge

(Chan et al., 2014), and environmental skill (Chan, 2008). Environmental awareness was represented by six items mirrored from past studies (Ballantyne, Packer, & Hughes, 2008; McCann, Sullivan, Erickson, & De Young, 1997). It assessed the perceptions of respondents and whether the respondents' action at work could lead to any negative impacts on the environment. Environmental knowledge, entailing four items, was to measure employees' level of environmental knowledge. Specifically, this scale measured employees' cognition of environment (e.g., how carbon dioxide could affect environment?), knowledge about the ways of helping to reduce potential environmental damage and their knowledge to assess which eco-friendly actions are most effective (Roczen, Kaiser, Bogner, & Wilson, 2014). Environmental skill questions evaluated whether respondent's job responsibility involved recycling and energy conservation (Wong, Lai, Shang, Lu, & Leung, 2012). These questions assessed the role of employees in relation to hotels' green practices and their work skills toward environmental protection.

The second part included seven items relating to the image of the hotel. Image, as a marketing term, describes how a firm (e.g., hotel) is perceived by the general public (Balmer & Greyser, 2006). Green image, on the other hand, is a term used to describe customers' perception of a firm's greenness. The concept of green image, proposed by a green hotel study (Han & Kim, 2010), was adopted by this study. However, instead of assessing customers' perception, this study measured the employees' evaluation of their hotel's green practices. *Albeit* past studies (Han & Kim, 2010) have mostly investigated customers' view of green practices, the green image inventory is applicable to a study focusing on employees' perception.

The third part contained five questions which were designed to assess employees' perception of their hotels' green certification (Peiró-Signes, Verma, & Miret-Pastor, 2012). The subjects covered in the question set included use of green suppliers (Wong et al., 2012) and level of hotel green practices in terms of energy conservation, waste management and material usage reduction (Chan & Hawkins, 2012).

The final part embodied four items in relation to employees' perceived overall performance of the hotel. In order to assess hotel performance, revenue per available room (RevPAR) is used. Although the front-line employees may not have an access to most financial information, RevPAR, which is calculated by combining average daily room rate (ADR) and occupancy rate, is most likely accessible to the employees. Thus, the RevPAR approach is generally used to measure financial performance in the hotel industry (Jorge, Xavier, Juan, Jose, Maria, & Eva, 2015; Shah, 2011).

Lastly, this study also queried the respondents to rate the reputation of their hotels (Benavides-Velasco, Quintana-García, & Marchante-Lara, 2014) and the level of perceived service quality they provide to their customers (Pereira-Moliner et al., 2012; Tarí, Claver-Cortés, Pereira-Moliner, & Molina-Azorín, 2010).

RESULTS

Respondents' Characteristics

Concerning the profile of respondents, this study included 38 males and 185 females and it was not surprising to see this result since in Taiwan the most junior-level hotel employees are females (Tsaur & Tang, 2012). As previously explained, this study focused on front-line employees and consequently the respondents were relatively young. For example, 121 out of 233 respondents were between 21 and 30 years of age and 102 respondents were between 31 and 36 years of age. Also because of being a junior staff, the monthly salary was relatively low. Salary ranged between NT$22K and NT$30K. Due to a young age and the work−family conflict (Karatepe & Karadas, 2014), it was also not surprising that only 12 respondents were married. The majority ($n = 122$) of the respondents worked in hotels in Northern Taiwan. The second large portion ($n = 75$) worked in Southern Taiwan. Some respondents ($n = 36$) also worked in Central Taiwan (36). The respondents worked in 52 different hotels with ranking ranging between four and five stars.

Reliability and Validity Test

When conducting a structural equation modeling (SEM), reliabilities and validities of scales were evaluated through different types of statistical tests including composite reliability (CR), average variance extracted (AVE), maximum shared squared variance (MSV), and average shared square variance (ASV). According to SEM literature (Fornell & Larcker, 1981; Hair, Black, Babin, & Anderson, 2009), it has been recommended that a CR value should exceed 0.7 to achieve adequate reliability. It has been recommended that an AVE value should exceed 0.5 and be greater than MSV and ASV to achieve acceptable discriminant validity. As shown in Table 1, the CR values ranged from 0.866 to 0.938, exceeding the suggested 0.7

threshold. The AVE values ranged from 0.615 to 0.834, exceeding the suggested 0.5 threshold and higher than their MSV counterparts and ASV, which ranged from 0.358 to 0.549 and from 0.229 to 0.315, respectively.

Convergent and discriminant validity are also important since an adequate convergent validity ensures that variables within the same factor correlate well with each other. For example, all the items under the factor "green image" is used to measure employees' perception of the firm's green image and not to measure other concept such as performance. Discriminant validity, on the other hand, is to ensure that variables do not correlate too highly with variables from other factors. This is to ensure that, for example, the green image and overall performance are measuring two different things.

Table 1. Reliability and Validity Tests and Correlations.

	CR	AVE	MSV	ASV	1	2	3	4	5	6
1. Green skill	0.938	0.834	0.476	0.284	0.913					
2. Hotel's performance	0.866	0.618	0.491	0.275	0.473	0.786				
3. Hotel's green ability	0.902	0.648	0.491	0.233	0.346	0.701	0.805			
4. Green awareness	0.929	0.688	0.549	0.242	0.659	0.313	0.199	0.829		
5. Green knowledge	0.873	0.635	0.549	0.315	0.690	0.459	0.397	0.741	0.797	
6. Green image	0.918	0.615	0.358	0.229	0.405	0.594	0.598	0.300	0.424	0.784

Hypothesis Testing

The purpose of using model fit indices is to determine if the observed data could fit into the proposed model. Model fit indices can be reviewed from different aspects. Several important fit indices were examined in this study including (1) chi-square to degrees of freedom (χ^2/df) and (2) goodness-of-fit index (GFI) (Doll & Xia, 1997). In addition, the root-mean-square error of approximation (RMSEA) and comparative fit index (CFI) (Jackson, Gillaspy Jr, & Purc-Stephenson, 2009). According to the literature (Hair et al., 2009; Hooper, Coughlan, & Mullen, 2008), GFI and CFI should exceed 0.8 (0.9 will be preferable) while RMSEA should be less than 0.08 (0.05 will be preferable), and χ^2/df should be in the range 1–3.

This study examined two models whose fit indices are shown in Figs. 2 and 3. Model 1 assessed the contribution of employees' green ability to hotel's green ability and overall performance compared to hotel's green image. The indices for Model 1 were GFI = 0.818, CFI = 0.927, $\chi^2/$df = 2.008, and RMSEA = 0.067. Model 2 removed hotel's green image from the first model and solely examined employees' contributions. The indices for Model 2 were GFI = 0.868, CFI = 0.951, $\chi^2/$df = 1.916, and RMSEA = 0.064.

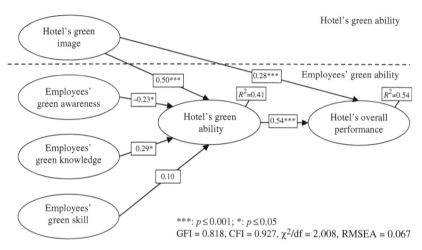

Fig. 2. Model 1.

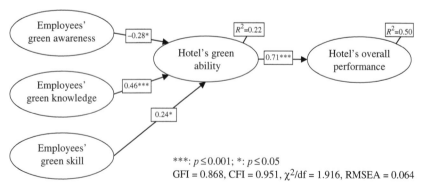

Fig. 3. Model 2.

Table 2 summarizes the result of the tests for models. Regarding the change of index values, model fit for the second model was slightly better than that of the first one. This was not unexpected since Model 2 had fewer constructs, making it easier to achieve a good model fit (Hair et al., 2009). Nevertheless, based on the values of indices, the model fit of both models were deemed to be acceptable.

As Table 2 indicates, the standardized regression weight ($\beta = 0.277$) of the path between green image and hotels' overall performance (H1) was statistically significant with $p < 0.0001$. The value ($\beta = 0.500$) for H2 regarding linkage between green image and hotels' green ability is also statistically significant at with $p < 0.0001$. From these two values, this study concluded that the green image of a hotel contributes significantly to its green ability and overall performance. The contribution to hotels' green ability was, however, stronger than the hotels' overall performance. Nevertheless, a hotel's green image played a vital role in the hotel's attempts to go green and earning bigger market share.

Hypotheses H3, H4, and H5 examined the impacts of employees' environmental awareness, environmental knowledge, and environmental skill, respectively, to hotels' green ability. In short, this section of hypotheses tested employees' contribution to a hotel's efforts to go green. The β values for the path H3 are -0.226 for Model 1 and -0.281 for Model 2. The p values were 0.026 and 0.014, respectively, indicating moderate significance. The β values for the path H4 were 0.289 for Model 1 and 0.458 for Model 2. The p values were 0.014 and 0.001, respectively. The causal links between employees' environmental knowledge and a hotel's green ability was clearly more pronounced when the hotel's green image was out of the picture. The β values for the path H5 were 0.105 for Model 1 and 0.236 for Model 2. The p values were 0.255 and 0.021, respectively. It was evident that when a hotel's green image is introduced to the equation, employees' green skill became less significant contributor to the hotel's green ability. The β values for the path H6 were 0.539 for Model 1 and 0.705 for Model 2. The p values are both less than 0.001. This indicated that a hotel's green ability does affect its overall performance in a positive way.

The hypotheses H7 and H8 were tested by examining the changes in R^2 between two different models. The R^2 of a hotel's green ability and overall performance of Model 1 were 0.41 and 0.54, respectively. When a hotel's green image was removed from the equation, the R^2 of the two constructs were dropped to 0.22 and 0.50. The R^2 changes were $\Delta R^2 = 0.19$ and $\Delta R^2 = 0.04$, respectively. It was clear that hotel's green image contribute significantly to its green ability, but less so to its overall performance.

Table 2.   Summary of Results.

	Path			Model 1		Model 2	
	Cause		Effect	β	p	β	p
H1	Green image	→	Hotel's performance	0.277	***		
H2	Green image	→	Hotel's green ability	0.5	***		
H3	Green awareness	→	Hotel's green ability	−0.226	0.026	−0.281	0.014
H4	Green knowledge	→	Hotel's green ability	0.289	0.014	0.458	***
H5	Green skill	→	Hotel's green ability	0.105	0.255	0.236	0.021
H6	Hotel's green ability	→	Hotel's performance	0.539	***	0.705	***
H7	Hotel's green ability	R^2		.41		.22	
H8	Hotel's performance	R^2		.54		.50	

***<0.001.

From the results, this study is able to draw some conclusive findings. For employees' green ability, an employee's environmental knowledge contributes the most to his/her hotel's green ability. Employees' green ability as a whole predicts approximately 22% of a hotel's green ability ($R^2 = 0.22$). It is over a fifth of a hotel's green ability. However, an employee's environmental awareness seems to have an adverse effect on his/her hotel's green ability. One can start to wonder why that is. From the literature (Chan et al., 2014), environmental awareness plays an important and positive role in implementing green practice. This particular finding is certainly confounding. One may argue that being aware of a problem and not being able to solve it is negative. And, although a study (Chan et al., 2014) showed that awareness promotes intention to act, junior employees rarely possess any autonomous decision-making opportunities and thus may be frustrated and be negative. There is also a study (Mathews, 1990) which asserts that sometimes awareness causes people to interpret a situation in a relatively threatening way. This situation may sabotage a hotel's green effort. One needs to keep in mind that Asian's environmental education is relatively rudimentary compared to that of the western societies (Chan, 2008). And awareness without proper knowledge may hinder the effort of coping with environmental problems.

A hotel's green ability accounts for 50% of the variance in its overall performance. The overall performance in this study is measured by RevPAR and by assessing an employee's perception of his/her hotel's quality of service and reputation. The 50% variance is thus a clear indication that green practices are able to create a positive effect not only on a firm's marketing effort, but also on its financial performance.

A hotel's green image improves the hotel's overall performance ($\Delta R^2 = .04$) slightly, but it mostly contributes to the performance indirectly through enhancing the hotel's green ability. Green image is, of course, just part of a hotel's brand image and to fully understand the role of image in a hotel's performance, further studies are required.

The change of R^2 values seems to be an interesting finding and the combination of a hotel's green image in conjunction with employees' green ability contributes 41% to a hotel's green ability. As noted earlier, an employee's green ability accounts for 22% his/her hotel's green ability.

Based on these results, this study concludes that an employee's green ability is very important to a hotel's green ability. It is therefore worthwhile for hotels to devote a certain amount of resources to train and educate their employees concerning how to further implement their green operations in eco-friendly ways.

CONCLUSION

Discussion

The paper may center on how to encourage hotel employees to gain new knowledge and skills of green operations. As previously discussed, an employee's green ability is very important factor adding to a hotel's green ability. Further examination reveals that an employee's environmental knowledge and skill contributes the most to his/her hotel's green ability, but an employee's environmental awareness seems to have an adverse effect on his/her hotel's green ability. This suggests that simply being aware of the problem does not give one the ability to solve it. It is thus important for hotels to commit a portion of their resources to train and educate their employees regarding the implementation of green operations.

Implication

Based on the findings, it is important to note that improving employees' environmental knowledge takes higher priority over improving environmental skill and environmental awareness. A special caution arises because environmental awareness may have an adverse effect on a hotel's green ability if employees do not have sufficient knowledge to interpret events correctly.

Green image contributes to a hotel's overall performance partly through direct influence and partly through improving a hotel's green ability. This is consistent with past studies (Han & Kim, 2010) that the image is a strong contributor to a hotel's success. This study only introduces an image construct to explore if an employee's green ability could foster his/her hotel's green ability.

A hotel's green ability, however, includes more than just image and employees' ability. Future study can incorporate constructs such as building's green function (Rashid, Spreckelmeyer, & Angrisano, 2012), environmental certification (Peiró-Signes, Verma, Mondéjar-Jiménez, & Vargas-Vargas, 2013), management level's leadership (Garrido-Moreno & Padilla-Meléndez, 2011), and green policy implementation (Chan, 2013) to fully understand the composition of a hotel's green ability.

Limitation

Given that the profile of all respondents is limited to a junior-level position at the hotel, it is important to note that the study implications could not be applied to all levels of employees. Further, each study hotel may possess a different level of greening ability. In other words, some hotels may devote a small portion of their effort to green operations whereas some may pursue green agendas extensively. However, as an exploratory study, this research is not designed for a comparative study that examines the differences of ability of employees from different types of green hotels. In this regard, there may be some variances in green ability among study hotels and thus it is important to recognize the above study limitation as readers interpret the resultant data. It is suggested that future research further investigates the ability of different levels of hotel employees and different types of hotels classified by the level of green engagement in relation to green awareness, knowledge, skills, and hotels' total performance.

REFERENCES

Ballantyne, R., Packer, J., & Hughes, K. (2008). Environmental awareness, interests and motives of botanic gardens visitors: Implications for interpretive practice. *Tourism Management*, 29(3), 439–444. doi:10.1016/j.tourman.2007.05.006

Balmer, J. M. T., & Greyser, S. A. (2006). Corporate marketing: Integrating corporate identity, corporate branding, corporate communications, corporate image and corporate reputation. *European Journal of Marketing, 40*(7/8), 730–741.

Benavides-Velasco, C. A., Quintana-García, C., & Marchante-Lara, M. (2014). Total quality management, corporate social responsibility and performance in the hotel industry. *International Journal of Hospitality Management, 41*, 77–87. doi:10.1016/j.ijhm.2014.05.003

Best, M. N., & Thapa, B. (2013). Motives, facilitators and constraints of environmental management in the Caribbean accommodations sector. *Journal of Cleaner Production, 52*, 165–175. doi:10.1016/j.jclepro.2013.03.005

Butler, J. (2008). The compelling "hard case" for "green" hotel development. *Cornell Hospitality Quarterly, 49*(3), 234–244.

Chan, E. S. W. (2008). Barriers to EMS in the hotel industry. *International Journal of Hospitality Management, 27*(2), 187–196. doi:10.1016/j.ijhm.2007.07.011

Chan, E. S. W. (2013). Managing green marketing: Hong Kong hotel managers' perspective. *International Journal of Hospitality Management, 34*, 442–461. doi:10.1016/j.ijhm.2012.12.007

Chan, E. S. W., & Hawkins, R. (2012). Application of EMSs in a hotel context: A case study. *International Journal of Hospitality Management, 31*(2), 405–418. doi:10.1016/j.ijhm.2011.06.016

Chan, E. S. W., Hon, A. H. Y., Chan, W., & Okumus, F. (2014). What drives employees' intentions to implement green practices in hotels? The role of knowledge, awareness, concern and ecological behaviour. *International Journal of Hospitality Management, 40*, 20–28. doi:10.1016/j.ijhm.2014.03.001

Chang, L.-H., Tsai, C.-H., & Yeh, S.-S. (2014). Evaluation of green hotel guests' behavioral intention. In J. S. Chen (Ed.), *Advances in hospitality and leisure* (Vol. 10, pp. 75–89). Bingley, UK: Emerald Group Publishing Limited.

Chen, Y.-S., & Chang, C.-H. (2013). Greenwash and green trust: The mediation effects of green consumer confusion and green perceived risk. *Journal of Business Ethics, 114*(3), 489–500. doi:10.1007/s10551-012-1360-0

Doll, W. J., & Xia, W. (1997). Confirmatory factor analysis of the end-user computing satisfaction instrument: A replication. *Journal of Organizational and End User Computing (JOEUC), 9*(2), 24–31.

Fornell, C., & Larcker, D. F. (1981). Structural equation models with unobservable variables and measurement error: Algebra and statistics. *Journal of Marketing Research, 18*(3), 382–388.

Garrido-Moreno, A., & Padilla-Meléndez, A. (2011). Analyzing the impact of knowledge management on CRM success: The mediating effects of organizational factors. *International Journal of Information Management, 31*(5), 437–444. doi:10.1016/j.ijinfomgt.2011.01.002

Hair, J. F., Black, W. C., Babin, B. J., & Anderson, R. E. (2009). *Multivariate data analysis* (7th ed.). Englewood Cliffs, NJ: Prentice Hall.

Han, H. (2015). Travelers' pro-environmental behavior in a green lodging context: Converging value-belief-norm theory and the theory of planned behavior. *Tourism Management, 47*, 164–177. doi:10.1016/j.tourman.2014.09.014

Han, H., Hsu, L.-T., & Lee, J.-S. (2009). Empirical investigation of the roles of attitudes toward green behaviors, overall image, gender, and age in hotel customers' eco-friendly decision-making process. *International Journal of Hospitality Management*, *28*(4), 519–528. doi:10.1016/j.ijhm.2009.02.004

Han, H., Hsu, L. T., & Sheu, C. (2010). Application of the theory of planned behavior to green hotel choice: Testing the effect of environmental friendly activities. *Tourism Management*, *31*(3), 325–334. doi:10.1016/j.tourman.2009.03.013

Han, H., & Kim, Y. (2010). An investigation of green hotel customers' decision formation: Developing an extended model of the theory of planned behavior. *International Journal of Hospitality Management*, *29*(4), 659–668. doi:10.1016/j.ijhm.2010.01.001

Hon, A. H. Y., & Chan, W. W. H. (2013). Team creative performance the roles of empowering leadership, creative-related motivation, and task interdependence. *Cornell Hospitality Quarterly*, *54*(2), 199–210. doi:10.1177/1938965512455859

Hooper, D., Coughlan, J., & Mullen, M. (2008). Structural equation modelling: Guidelines for determining model fit. *The Electronic Journal of Business Methods*, *6*(1), 53–60.

Jackson, D. L., Gillaspy, J. A., Jr., & Purc-Stephenson, R. (2009). Reporting practices in confirmatory factor analysis: An overview and some recommendations. *Psychological Methods*, *14*(1), 6–23.

Jorge, P. M., Xavier, F., Juan, J. T., Jose, F. M. A., Maria, D. L. G., & Eva, M. P. O. (2015). The Holy Grail: Environmental management, competitive advantage and business performance in the Spanish hotel industry. *International Journal of Contemporary Hospitality Management*, *27*(5), 714–738.

Karatepe, O. M., & Karadas, G. (2014). The effect of psychological capital on conflicts in the work–family interface, turnover and absence intentions. *International Journal of Hospitality Management*, *43*, 132–143. doi:10.1016/j.ijhm.2014.09.005

Kim, Y., & Han, H. (2010). Intention to pay conventional-hotel prices at a green hotel–a modification of the theory of planned behavior. *Journal of Sustainable Tourism*, *18*(8), 997–1014.

Ko, E., Hwang, Y. K., & Kim, E. Y. (2013). Green marketing' functions in building corporate image in the retail setting. *Journal of Business Research*, *66*(10), 1709–1715. doi:10.1016/j.jbusres.2012.11.007

Mathews, A. (1990). Why worry? The cognitive function of anxiety. *Behaviour Research and Therapy*, *28*(6), 455–468. doi:10.1016/0005-7967(90)90132-3

McCann, E., Sullivan, S., Erickson, D., & De Young, R. (1997). Environmental awareness, economic orientation, and farming practices: a comparison of organic and conventional farmers. *Environmental Management*, *21*(5), 747–758.

Miles, P. M., & Covin, J. G. (2000). Environmental marketing: A source of reputational, competitive and financial advantage. *Journal of Business Ethics*, *239*(3), 299–311.

Norton, T. A., Zacher, H., & Ashkanasy, N. M. (2014). Organisational sustainability policies and employee green behaviour: The mediating role of work climate perceptions. *Journal of Environmental Psychology*, *38*, 49–54. doi:10.1016/j.jenvp.2013.12.008

Peiró-Signes, Á., Verma, R., & Miret-Pastor, L. (2012). Does environmental certification help the economic performance of hotels? Evidence from the Spanish hotel industry. *Cornell Hospitality Quarterly*, *53*(3), 242–256. doi:10.1177/1938965512446417

Peiró-Signes, A., Verma, R., Mondéjar-Jiménez, J., & Vargas-Vargas, M. (2013). The impact of environmental certification on hotel guest ratings. *Cornell Hospitality Quarterly*, *55*(1), 40–51.

Pereira-Moliner, J., Claver-Cortés, E., Molina-Azorín, J. F., & José Tarí, J. (2012). Quality management, environmental management and firm performance: Direct and mediating effects in the hotel industry. *Journal of Cleaner Production, 37*, 82−92. doi:10.1016/j. jclepro.2012.06.010

Rashid, M., Spreckelmeyer, K., & Angrisano, N. J. (2012). Green buildings, environmental awareness, and organizational image. *Journal of Corporate Real Estate, 14*(1), 21−49.

Renwick, D. W. S., Redman, T., & Maguire, S. (2013). Green human resource management: A review and research agenda. *International Journal of Management Reviews, 15*(1), 1−14. doi:10.1111/j.1468-2370.2011.00328.x

Roczen, N., Kaiser, F. G., Bogner, F. X., & Wilson, M. (2014). A competence model for environmental education. *Environment and Behavior, 46*(8), 972−992. doi:10.1177/0013916513492416

Shah, K. U. (2011). Strategic organizational drivers for corporate environmental responsibility in the Caribbean hotel industry. *Policy Science, 44*(4), 321−344.

Tarí, J. J., Claver-Cortés, E., Pereira-Moliner, J., & Molina-Azorín, J. F. (2010). Levels of quality and environmental management in the hotel industry: Their joint influence on firm performance. *International Journal of Hospitality Management, 29*(3), 500−510. doi:10.1016/j.ijhm.2009.10.029

Teng, C.-C., Horng, J.-S., Hu, M.-L., Chien, L.-H., & Shen, Y.-C. (2012). Developing energy conservation and carbon reduction indicators for the hotel industry in Taiwan. *International Journal of Hospitality Management, 31*(1), 199−208. doi:10.1016/j. ijhm.2011.06.006

Tsaur, S.-H., & Tang, Y.-Y. (2012). Job stress and well-being of female employees in hospitality: The role of regulatory leisure coping styles. *International Journal of Hospitality Management, 31*(4), 1038−1044. doi:10.1016/j.ijhm.2011.12.009

Wang, Y.-F., Chen, S.-P., Lee, Y.-C., & Tsai, C.-T. (2013). Developing green management standards for restaurants: An application of green supply chain management. *International Journal of Hospitality Management, 34*, 263−273. doi:10.1016/j.ijhm. 2013.04.001

Wong, C. W. Y., Lai, K.-h., Shang, K.-C., Lu, C.-S., & Leung, T. K. P. (2012). Green operations and the moderating role of environmental management capability of suppliers on manufacturing firm performance. *International Journal of Production Economics, 140*(1), 283−294. doi:10.1016/j.ijpe.2011.08.031

Yang, J., Hauser, R., & Goldman, R. H. (2013). Taiwan food scandal: The illegal use of phthalates as a clouding agent and their contribution to maternal exposure. *Food and Chemical Toxicology, 58*, 362−368. doi:10.1016/j.fct.2013.05.010

Yeh, S.-S., Ma, T., & Huan, T.-C. (2016). Building social entrepreneurship for the hotel industry by promoting environmental education. *International Journal of Contemporary Hospitality Management, 28*(6), 1024−1224. doi:10.1108/IJCHM-03-2014-0122

AN INVESTIGATION OF RESTAURANT WEEK AS AN EFFECTIVE MARKETING STRATEGY

Yvette N. J. Green and John A. Williams

ABSTRACT

This paper investigated the effectiveness of using a Restaurant Week promotion to market a group of restaurants during a traditionally slow period in the calendar year for the city of New Orleans. A questionnaire was developed by the communications committee of the local restaurant association. The questionnaire included questions to ascertain why restaurants chose to participate in Restaurant Week. The results of the study showed that the Restaurant Week campaign was successful for the participating restaurants in several ways. Success was demonstrated in increase in sales, a better understanding of menu item sales, an awareness of the strongest days of promotion, and methods of making reservations. The majority of restaurants experienced an increase of sales up to 20%. For both lunch and dinner promotions, Friday ranked as the strongest day of the promotion. The use of Open Table increased as a means of making reservations during Restaurant Week.

Keywords: Restaurant Week; promotions; marketing

Advances in Hospitality and Leisure, Volume 12, 83–97
Copyright © 2017 by Emerald Group Publishing Limited
All rights of reproduction in any form reserved
ISSN: 1745-3542/doi:10.1108/S1745-354220160000012005

INTRODUCTION

In 2015, total restaurant industry sales nationally are expected to exceed $709 billion, a 3.8% increase over 2014. In addition, 2015 is projected to be the 16th straight year in which restaurant industry employment outpaced overall employment. Restaurants employ 14 million individuals as the nation's second-largest private-sector employer and in the next decade restaurants will add 1.7 million new positions (National Restaurant Association, 2015a, 2015b).

Restaurants represent 10% of the employment in the state of Louisiana. In 2013, there were 8,352 eating and drinking places in Louisiana. Every extra $1 million spent in Louisiana's restaurants generates an additional 24.6% jobs in the state, while every $1 spent in Louisiana's restaurants generates an additional $.87 in secondary spending. In 2015, Louisiana's restaurants are projected to register $7.3 billion in sales (National Restaurant Association, 2015a, 2015b).

With such impressive statistics, nationally and on the local level, it is important for operators to market themselves effectively both during peak seasons and during off-season to maintain the trend of growth. The purpose of this research is to investigate the effectiveness of using a Restaurant Week promotion to effectively market a group of restaurants during a traditionally slow period in the calendar year for the city of New Orleans.

LITERATURE REVIEW

The literature review explores the growth of foodies and food tourism as a catalyst for special dining events. Then the literature reviews general restaurant promotional strategies and finishes with Restaurant Week as a promotional strategy for restaurants.

Foodies and Food Tourism

In recent years, there has been an expansion in the number of foodies, a class of experienced and educated consumers who are looking for specialized products suited to their specific needs and interests and are prepared to travel to find these products and the culinary experiences connected with them. The result is a relatively new group of tourists who are acquainted with the traditions and culture of the destinations visited through food products and gastronomy. These diners visit restaurants in which they can enjoy traditional specialties or which offer an exceptional experience of exceptional food which is served in an exceptional way (Schwartzhoffová, 2014).

Getz, Andersson, Vujicic, and Robinson (2015) determined that planned food events were critical to the lifestyle and travel of food lovers and foodies. Active foodies enjoyed food events with high levels of involvement and translated into specialized benefits for the foodie. The study concluded with the importance of effective marketing of special food events to foodies and food tourists (Getz et al., 2015).

Getz and Robinson (2014) investigated the relationship between being a foodie and various food-related events. The study measured attendance at various types of food events and preferences for destination experiences including events. Ultimately, the research revealed that food events are a very important component in desired destination experiences and food-tourism planning and marketing (Getz & Robinson, 2014).

General Restaurant Promotion Strategies

Sales Promotions
Sales promotions can affect a customer's intention to consume or patronize the products or services of a restaurant. They also can be used to increase customers' interest and participation, build traffic, encourage visits, create an identity, and market themes or distinctive images. The effectiveness of sales promotions can be measured in terms of sales volume improvement, increased satisfaction, or improved perception on the part of the customers (Setthawiwat & Barth, 2002).

Sales promotions in restaurants can attract customers seeking bargains. However, customers may also patronize a restaurant because of familiarity, convenience, or product selection. Promotions can influence these two types of customers in several ways. For instance, promotions establish value for a product or service, affect the customers' decision to go or not, and influence a customer's decision to buy more once they have arrived. Sales promotions generally used in the restaurant business include coupon promotions and special event promotions (Setthawiwat & Barth, 2002).

Coupon Promotions as a Marketing Strategy
Coupon promotion is a commonly used sales promotional tool in the restaurant industry (Taylor, 2001). It is estimated that restaurants account for 10–15% of about six billion freestanding coupons distributed per year

in the United States (Perlik, 2002). In general, coupon promotion is often used to generate a short-term sales increase (Taylor, 2001), to increase customer traffic (Perlik, 2002), to attract new customers (Taylor & Long-Tolbert, 2002), and to encourage repeat purchase of a brand (Eunha, Barrash, & Feinstein, 2006). Marketers believe that a coupon is an effective promotional tool in generating a short-term sales increase and attracting new customers, but they still question the long-term effect of coupon promotion on repeat purchase. Marketers also expect that coupon promotion may drive new customers to switch brands, eventually converting them into repeat customers. Similarly, restaurateurs hope that new customers who redeem coupons will like the restaurants and will return even without coupons in the future and pay full price for those meals. Restaurants have found coupon promotion to be a more cost-effective method of increasing revenues than advertising (Eunha et al., 2006).

Special Events as a Marketing Strategy
Special events are another type of sales promotion. Special event promotions are powerful tools with direct and meaningful impact on customers and the decisions they make about products and services. Special events are promotions that command consumer attention and stimulate strong trade support. They provide restaurateurs with ways to create their own medium by which to deliver their message directly to their target consumers. They can call attention to a restaurant, create excitement, stimulate new interest among frequent users, and usually increase the average check (Setthawiwat & Barth, 2002).

Setthawiwat and Barth (2002) found that any kind of special event promotion increases the customer's propensity to spend. Personal special event promotions also increased the consumers' expectations of service quality and reduce perceived purchase risk. In the case of general special event promotions, customers felt that service quality was lower, and their purchase risk was greater. Setthawiwat and Barth (2002) concluded that special event promotions influenced consumers' behavior and perceptions in similar ways to coupons. Both coupons and special events appeared to increase purchase intentions and reduce perceived purchase risk in restaurant customers (Setthawiwat & Barth, 2002).

Restaurant Week Promotion Strategy

The concept of Restaurant Week is simple: local restaurants band together, often in conjunction with the area convention and visitors bureau and sometimes their local restaurant association to plan a week-long fixed-price meal. Participants pay a fee to cover promotional and advertising costs, and sponsors are often solicited for financial and additional promotional contributions. New York, Chicago, Boston, Denver, San Diego, Miami, Atlanta, and Philadelphia are a few of more than 26 major cities nationwide, plus a growing number of smaller communities, hosting Restaurant Weeks. In addition to showcasing a city's great dining options, Restaurant Weeks spur both local and out-of-town diners to revisit old favorites and, best of all, try new places (Hochwarth, 2005). The benefits are many and the costs are doable. Unlike "taste of" promotions that feature restaurants serving a signature dish off-site with a crowd of other restaurants, Restaurant Weeks let participating restaurants shine in their own place and show off their unique atmosphere and service (Hochwarth, 2005).

Restaurant Week offers an effective business strategy to attract customers through the adoption of Restaurant Week promotions. Enhanced quality of service, placing the priority on the existing customer, the offer of discounts, and the creation of upselling opportunities are keys to Restaurant Week success (Cavallaro, 2009). It has been shown that co-op groups of upscale-restaurant operators believe that rounds of set-price Restaurant Week promotions drive customer traffic despite recession conditions (Jennings, 2008). Shepherd (2007) reported that Restaurant Week promotions served as an initiative to boost business during slower months in the U.S. Restaurant Weeks are considered fixed-price promotions that are typically organized by local tourism board or restaurant association. They generate tens of millions of dollars in restaurant revenue annually as a result of popularity, as thousands of diners are attracted to visit restaurants (Shepherd, 2007). Lastly, Restaurant Week promotions not only promote dining out but generate funds for local food banks (Romeo, 2011).

We Live to Eat New Orleans
The We Live to Eat (WLTE) campaign of New Orleans was designed by the Greater New Orleans Chapter of the Louisiana Restaurant Association (LRA) to raise awareness of New Orleans' unique culinary industry, which is at the heart of the city's identity. In New Orleans, cuisine is a part of the culture. This movement's theme is therefore centered on supporting local restaurants and exploring the art and enjoyment of the city's dining scene. In New Orleans, the culinary industry is a cornerstone of the city's identity and is embraced by locals. The local community plays a vital role in supporting the city's restaurants, the culinary talent behind them and celebrating the way of life for which New Orleans is widely known. WLTE seeks to

keep all of the city's restaurants top-of-mind with consumers while also building an emotional connection with the local food-loving community. The result is a larger number of locals dining out more often and fueling the movement through referrals and word-of-mouth to increase patronage across every type of restaurant. The WeLiveToEatNOLA.com website is the home base for participation, allowing residents to join and take part in the movement. Participation is galvanized in other social networks, including Facebook and Twitter pages. The WLTE campaign was designed to market restaurants in the city of New Orleans during the month of September, a traditionally slow month for restaurants in the city. Restaurant Week, developed in 2011, is the signature event for We Live to Eat (WeLiveToEatNOLA.com, 2013).

The growth of foodies in the City of New Orleans along with the first-time diners willing to try a new restaurant provided a catalyst for the development of Restaurant Week. Because of an expressed interest by the Greater New Orleans Chapter of the Louisiana Restaurant Association to better understand the effectiveness of Restaurant Week, this research was undertaken.

METHODOLOGY

The purpose of the study was to investigate the effectiveness of using a restaurant promotional event to market a group of restaurants during a slow period in the year for the city of New Orleans. A questionnaire was developed by the communications committee of the Greater New Orleans Chapter of the Louisiana Restaurant Association. The survey included questions to ascertain why restaurants chose to participate in Restaurant Week. The survey also included questions to determine overall sales during Restaurant Week, menu item sales, restaurant advertisement, reservations, and satisfaction with the promotion campaign.

After Restaurant Week was completed, each participating restaurant was sent a link to the survey via Qualtrics. Restaurants were sent two reminder links to encourage survey completion.

RESULTS

The data were analyzed and the results reported to the Greater New Orleans Chapter of the Louisiana Restaurant Association.

In 2013, 17 of the 47 participating restaurants completed a post-event survey for a 36.2% response rate while in 2014, 16 of the 56 participating restaurants completed a post-event survey for a 28.5% response rate. The results of 2013 and 2014 will be presented and then comparisons will be made.

Sales Increase and Restaurant Week Advertisement

In 2013, 40% of the respondents experienced up to 10% increase in sales over the last year during the same week, 26.6% experienced an 11–20% increase, 6.7% experienced a 21–30% increase, 6.7% experienced a 31–40% increase, which was the highest increase. No one selected a higher percentage. There were 20% that experienced a decrease in sales over the last year during the same week. Based on the marketing provided by the LRA for 2013 Restaurant Week, restaurants expected 20% to be a reasonable percentage increase in sales over the last year during the same week. The pricing strategy for the 2013 Restaurant Week was flexible. Taking an average of the responses, the optimum price point for lunch was $19.70 while the best perceived price point for dinner was $34.50.

In 2013, 47% promoted Restaurant Week via their restaurant's email newsletter, while 88% promoted Restaurant Week via their restaurant's social media. In addition, 6% promoted Restaurant Week via their restaurant's paid advertising, while 53% promoted Restaurant Week via their restaurant's website and 6% promoted Restaurant Week via Open Table. For those who participated in both lunch and dinner during Restaurant Week, 92% responded that dinner produced higher sales during Restaurant Week and 8% responded that lunch produced higher sales. Table 1 shows the comparison of the percentage of sales increase during Restaurant Week for 2013 and 214 over the same week of the prior year.

In 2014, 57.2% experienced up to 10% increase in sales over the last year during the same week, 14.3% experienced an 11–20% increase, 7.1% experienced a 21–30%, and 7% experienced a 41–50% increase in sales, the highest percentage. There were 14.3% that experienced a decrease in sales over the last year during the same week. Based on the marketing provided by the LRA for 2014 Restaurant Week, restaurants expected on average 11.46% to be a reasonable percentage increase in sales over the last year during the same week.

Table 1. Percentage Sales Increase Over Same Week Prior Year.

	2013 (%)	2014 (%)
Up to 10% increase	40	57.2
11–20% increase	26.6	14.3
21–30% increase	6.7	7.1
31–40% increase	6.7	0
41–50% increase	0	7.1
More than 50% increase	0	0
Decrease in sales	20	14.3

In 2014, 50% promoted Restaurant Week via their restaurant's email newsletter and 94% promoted Restaurant Week via their restaurant's social media. Results showed that 6% promoted Restaurant Week via their restaurant's paid advertising, while 38% promoted Restaurant Week via their restaurant's website and 2% promoted Restaurant Week via in-house menus. For those who participated in both lunch and dinner during Restaurant Week, 100% responded that dinner produced higher sales during Restaurant Week. Table 2 shows Restaurant Week advertisement used by participating restaurants in 2013 and 2014.

Table 2. Restaurant Week Advertisement.

	2013 (%)[a]	2014 (%)[a]
Restaurant website	53	38
Restaurant email newsletter	47	50
Social media	88	94
Restaurant in-house promo	7	2
Restaurant paid advertising	6	6
Open Table	6	0

[a]May select "All That Apply."

Reservations, Strength of Day, Other Restaurant Promotions
In 2013, of the Restaurant Week menu sales, it is estimated on average that 19% of the sales came from Open Table Reservations, while 22% came from restaurant reservations (non-Open Table) and 59% were walk-in guests. While 65% found that Restaurant Week guests purchased additional menu items, 35% found that the Restaurant Week guests did not purchase additional menu items.

For restaurants who participated in lunch during Restaurant Week, Friday, September 13 ranked #1 as the strongest day for Restaurant Week participation, while Thursday, September 12 ranked as the second strongest day for Restaurant Week participation. For restaurants who participated in dinner during Restaurant Week, Friday, September 13 and Saturday, September 14 ranked #1 as the strongest day for Restaurant Week participation and Thursday, September 12 ranked #3 for the second strongest day for Restaurant Week participation.

In 2013, 88% participated in other restaurant promotions throughout the year. The other promotions included (restaurants were able to check all that applied): COOLinary (47%), Reveillon dinners (60%), Dine out for Life (33%), Dine out for the Arts (13%), OctoberFest (7%), and Wine dinners (47%). Results indicated that 88.2% were satisfied to very satisfied with the menu criteria required by the LRA, while 11.8% were neutral concerning the menu criteria. Table 3 shows the types of reservations and Table 4 shows the strongest day of participation and use of other promotions for participating restaurants for 2013 and 2014.

Table 3. Type of Reservations.

	2013 (%)	2014 (%)
Guest made reservations – Open Table	19	28
Guest made reservations – non-Open Table	22	24
Walk-in guests	59	48
Guests who purchased additional menu items	65	47

In 2014, of the Restaurant Week menu sales, it is estimated on average that 28% of the sales came from Open Table Reservations, while 24% came from restaurant reservations (non-Open Table) and 36% were walk-in guests. While 47% found that Restaurant Week guests purchased additional menu items, 35% found that the Restaurant Week guests did not purchase additional menu items.

Table 4. Strength of Day, Other Restaurant Promotions.

	2013	2014
Strongest lunch day	Friday	Friday
Strongest dinner day	Friday	Friday
Participated in other restaurant promotions	88%	79%

For restaurants who participated in the lunch during Restaurant Week, Friday, September 12 ranked #1 as the strongest day for Restaurant Week participation, while Monday, September 8 and Wednesday, September 10 ranked as the second strongest day for Restaurant Week participation. For restaurants who participated in dinner during Restaurant Week, Friday, September 12 ranked #1 as the strongest day for Restaurant Week participation and Saturday, September 13 ranked #2 for the second strongest day for Restaurant Week participation.

In 2014, 79% participate in other restaurant promotions throughout the year. The other promotions included (restaurants were able to check all that applied): COOLinary (82%), Reveillon dinners (82%), Dine out for Life (9%), City Eats (9%), OctoberFest (9%), and Wine dinners (64%). Results showed that 85.7% were satisfied to very satisfied with the menu criteria required by the LRA, while 14.3% were neutral concerning the menu criteria. Table 5 shows the other food and beverage promotional events for the participating restaurants during 2013 and 2014.

Table 5. Other Restaurant Promotions.[a]

	2013 (%)	2014 (%)
COOLinary	47	82
Reveillon dinners	60	82
Dine out for Life	33	9
Dine out for Arts	13	0
City Eats	0	9
OctoberFest	7	9
Wine dinners	47	64

[a]May select "All That Apply."

Program Satisfaction

In 2013, 68% were either satisfied or very satisfied with 2013 We Live to Eat − Restaurant Week; 13% were neutral and 19% were dissatisfied. While 71% decided to participate in Restaurant Week both to drive traffic during a traditionally slow period and to support the LRA's We Live to Eat campaign, 24% participated solely to drive traffic during a traditionally slow period and 1% participated solely to support the LRA's We Live to Eat campaign.

Results indicated that 76.4% were satisfied to very satisfied with the marketing plan developed by the LRA, 17.6% were neutral about the marketing plan, and 6% were dissatisfied with the marketing plan. As for promotional materials provided by the LRA, 82.2% were satisfied to very satisfied, 6% were neutral, and 11.8% were dissatisfied. Among the restaurants who participated in the 2013 Restaurant Week, 60% participated in the 2011 (Inaugural) Restaurant Week and 70% participated in the 2012 Restaurant Week. Of the restaurants, 88% plan to participate in Restaurant Week again, while 12% do not plan to participate in Restaurant Week again.

In 2014, 80% were either satisfied or very satisfied with 2014 We Live to Eat – Restaurant Week; while 20% were neutral. There were no participants who were dissatisfied with the 2014 Restaurant Week. Results indicated that 50% decided to participate in Restaurant Week both to drive traffic during a traditionally slow period and to support the LRA's We Live to Eat campaign; while 25% participated solely to drive traffic during a traditionally slow period and 25% participated solely to support the LRA's We Live to Eat campaign.

Results showed that 100% were satisfied to very satisfied with the marketing plan developed by the LRA for Restaurant Week, 85.7% were satisfied to very satisfied with the promotional materials provided by the LRA, and 14.2% were neutral about the promotional materials provided by the LRA. Of the restaurants who participated in the 2014 Restaurant Week, 71.4% also participated in the 2013 Restaurant Week. Of the restaurants, 93% plan to participate in Restaurant Week again, while 7% do not plan to participate in Restaurant Week again. Table 6 shows the level of satisfaction with the Restaurant Week event by participating restaurants.

Table 6. Satisfaction with Restaurant Week.

	2013 (%)	2014 (%)
Overall satisfaction with Restaurant Week	68	80
Satisfied with marketing plan developed by LRA	76.4	100
Satisfied with promotional materials provided by LRA	82.2	85.7
Will participate in Restaurant Week again	88	93

DISCUSSION

Sales Increase and Restaurant Week Advertisement

In 2013, the combined percentages up to 50% increase in sales for the same week prior year for Restaurant Week was 80% and in 2014 it was 85.7%. What this shows is that for two consecutive years, Restaurant Week grew sales in the same week for participating restaurants.

The participating restaurant's website and email newsletter were the most used and effective form of in-house advertising. However, in 2014, these advertising mediums took a slight dip. To the compliment, the use of Social Media grew from 88% of participating restaurants in 2013 to 94% in 2014. This spike in 2014 coincided with the slight dip in the use of websites and email newsletters. Social media proved to compliment and outpace traditional methods of promotions for the restaurants during Restaurant Week.

Reservations, Strength of Day, Other Restaurant Promotions

Open Table steadily increased as a means for making reservations during Restaurant Week. In 2013, Open Table became an official partner with We Live To Eat – Restaurant Week to help drive traffic for the promotion campaign.

Several restaurants participated in other promotions during the year. COOLinary was consistently the #1 additional promotion, followed by Reveillon dinners. COOLinary, produced by the Greater New Orleans Convention and Visitors Bureau, takes place during the month of August. Reveillon dinners coincides with Mardi Gras season, a generally high guest traffic time for New Orleans restaurants.

For those restaurants who participated in lunch during Restaurant Week, Friday was consistently the strongest day followed by Monday and Thursday. For those who participated in dinner, Friday was consistently the strongest day, followed by Saturday. Lastly, for those restaurants who participated in both lunch and dinner during Restaurant Week, the dinner shift proved to be the strongest meal period.

Satisfaction with Restaurant Week

In general, the participating restaurants were satisfied with Restaurant Week on a whole. However, there was some variation each year. The restaurants participated in order to drive traffic during a slow period and to support the local restaurant association. The restaurants were generally satisfied with the marketing plan and collateral materials for Restaurant Week. However, there was room for improvement of the advertising strategy. In general, restaurants planned to participate in future Restaurant Weeks.

Restaurant Week Campaign Event Improvements

In 2013, the We Live to Eat – Restaurant Week website received a significant upgrade. These improvements included the development of mobile website to compliment the full website. Links were added to participating restaurants directing the guest to the restaurant's website. Links were also added highlighting each restaurant's menu. A back office component was added to the website to allow participating restaurants the ability to update their respective information as opposed to a third party doing the updates. Other highlights included the development of a downloadable app for Smart Phones and increased presence on Facebook, Twitter, and other social media outlets.

In 2013 and 2014, the open-ended comments were consistent with prior years to combine with COOLinary, adjust the participation fee, and adjust the menu pricing structure. To that end, in 2013 and 2014, variable pricing for the Restaurant Week menus was introduced to participating restaurants. As a result, new moderate priced and casual themed restaurants joined the Restaurant Week campaign. In 2015, Restaurant Week was combined with COOLinary and if a restaurant participated in both events, the campaign was free to the restaurant. All the improvements to the structure of the Restaurant Week event were based on comments from participants.

CONCLUSION

The results of each year's Restaurant Week survey showed that there were increases in same week sales over prior years' sales. This was one of the goals of the We Live to Eat campaign. In general, participating restaurants were satisfied with the program details and execution. There is room for the restaurant association to improve the marketing and collateral for Restaurant week. Bolstering the various social media outlets will continue to prove effective as a marketing strategy for this event. The enormous growth in social media usage and the yearly website improvements are driving the grassroots effort for this marketing campaign.

The results of this study provide both academic and practical implications. The results showed that the Restaurant Week campaign was in fact successful for the participating restaurants. The increase in sales was one measure of success. In addition, understanding the menu item sales, the strongest days of the promotion, and how reservations are made are all practical implications. Tangible practical implications included, in 2015, as a result of suggestions from 2014, a separate restaurant promotion in the City of New Orleans, combining We Live To Eat — Restaurant Week and COOLinary. The academic implications included providing literature in the area of restaurant marketing promotions.

For future research, an investigation should be conducted on merging two separate yet equally successful restaurant promotions into one mega dining event spanning six weeks in the slow dining months in the City of New Orleans. Additional future research may include looking at Restaurant Week from the consumer perspective. Investigating things such as what menu items are ordered, which advertising strategies worked best, click statistics from the website from patrons looking for information on Restaurant Week, just to name a few. Lastly, best practices in Restaurant Week promotions across various cities will also increase the understanding of Restaurant Week.

In conclusion, this study investigated two years of research of Restaurant Week as an effective marketing strategy for restaurants during a slow period in a city's dining scene. The food culture of the city of New Orleans, along with the support of the locals during the traditionally slow period, was the key to success. The success of Restaurant Week in New Orleans can be used as a model for other cities. Other cities can use Restaurant Week as a guide for promoting local restaurants during a slow period within their city and developing a grassroots food culture that can be used to address seasonality in a particular locale. In New Orleans, the summer months are the slow dining months. In another city, perhaps it is the winter months that are the slow dining period and prove challenging to fill seats and increase revenue.

The Louisiana Restaurant Association is a very progressive state restaurant association and provides initiatives such as Restaurant Week as a service to the membership. Providing these types of services shows incredible support of the restaurant industry at the state and/or local level. It unifies the membership by working for a common cause which is the overall health of the restaurant industry. Rather than outsourcing the Restaurant Week promotion to an outside entity, by using Restaurant Week as an internal initiative, it shows collaboration of the members and a grassroots effort to promote the restaurant industry and varying dining options. This philosophy of service to the membership can be used as a model for other state restaurant associations as they consider membership benefits and services.

REFERENCES

Cavallaro, M. (2009). How to make restaurant week work better. *Restaurant Business, 108*(11), 22–26.

Eunha, M., Barrash, D., & Feinstein, A. (2006). The effects of coupon promotion on repeat visits in restaurants. *Journal of Foodservice Business Research, 9*(1), 55–75.

Getz, D., Andersson, T., Vujicic, S., & Robinson, R. (2015). Food events in lifestyle and tourism. *Event Management, 19*(3), 407–419.

Getz, D., & Robinson, R. N. S. (2014). Foodies and food events. *Scandinavian Journal of Hospitality & Tourism, 14*(3), 315–330.

Hochwarth. (2005). The genius of restaurant week. *Restaurant Hospitality, 89*(7), 6268.

Jennings, L. (2008). Recession-wary upscale operators eye restaurant weeks' traffic boosts. *Nation's Restaurant News, 42*(5), 4–49.

National Restaurant Association. (2015a). 2015 Restaurant Industry Forecast.

National Restaurant Association. (2015b). 2015 State Restaurant Industry Statistics.

Perlik, A. (2002). Let's make a deal. *Restaurant and Institutions, 112*(20), 57–61.

Romeo, P. (2011). A new week. *Restaurant Business, 110*(9), 16.

Schwartzhoffová, E. (2014). Selected events as a special product of gastrotourism in the Czech Republic. *Czech Hospitality & Tourism Papers, 10*(21), 62–72.

Setthawiwat, A., & Barth, J. (2002). The impact of special event promotions on full-service restaurant customers. *Journal of Foodservice Business Research, 5*(3), 37–49.

Shepherd, A. (2007). Restaurant week promotions, when properly executed, fill seats when business is slow. *Nation's Restaurant News, 41*(28), 26–39.

Taylor, G. A. (2001). Coupon response in service. *Journal of Retailing, 77*, 139–151.

Taylor, G. A., & Long-Tolbert, S. (2002). Coupon promotion in quick-service restaurants: Preaching to the converted? *The Cornell Hotel and Restaurant Administration Quarterly, 43*(4), 41–47.

WeLiveToEatNOLA.com. (2013). Accessed on August 15, 2013.

THE MARKETING VALUE OF CSR INITIATIVES AND POTENTIAL BRAND EQUITY, TASTE PERCEPTION, AND EMOTIONAL VALUE

Jeen Filz, Robert J. Blomme and
Arjan van Rheede

ABSTRACT

Corporations in all industries recognize the demand for responsible business behavior and have developed corporate social responsibility (CSR) programs accordingly. This paper examines to which extent sustainability practices − unrelated to the actual ingredients of a consumable product − affect brand equity, taste perceptions, and perceived emotional value. In an experimental setting, effects were determined of the presence or lack of a sustainability-marketing message within a beer brand's promotional material. The constructs were measured in a survey, and a PLS-SEM was used to analyze the results. In the factor model, all constructs proved to be sufficiently reliable and valid. The experiment's

Advances in Hospitality and Leisure, Volume 12, 99−117
Copyright © 2017 by Emerald Group Publishing Limited
All rights of reproduction in any form reserved
ISSN: 1745-3542/doi:10.1108/S1745-354220160000012006

results indicate that taste perception is positively influenced by the presence of a sustainability message.

Keywords: Corporate social responsibility; emotional value; brand value; taste perceptions

INTRODUCTION

As corporate social responsibility (CSR) programs become more prevalent across all industries, the marketing value of these initiatives becomes a more and more popular topic of discussion. Consumers are increasingly demonstrating a growing appreciation of, and in some cases even a demand for, responsible business behavior (Dowd & Burke, 2013). As a result, corporations are driven to seek appropriate responses to these shifting values, with an abundance of CSR programs proliferating in every sector in every industry (CSR News, 2007).

That consumers are sensitive to CSR messages has already been established (Hur, Kim, & Woo, 2013; Smith & Alcorn, 1991; Webb & Mohr, 1998), and recent studies have reinforced the notion that factors such as price and brand quality beliefs may influence consumers' consumption experience of food and beverage products and of alcoholic beverages (Plassmann & Weber, 2015). Most prominently conducted in the wine sector, research investigating the relationship between organic versus conventionally produced beverages and hedonic value attached to them has shown that differences are negligible (Pagliarini, Laureati, & Gaeta, 2013). This means that consumers did not conclusively indicate that they believed an organic wine to taste better than its conventionally developed counterpart. This being said, research is available that points toward the opposite (Theuer, 2006), making the value of marketing the organic nature of a product somewhat questionable.

However, sourcing ingredients organically is just one factor of being sustainable. Whether a message of sustainability that is unrelated to the actual ingredients of a consumable product has the potential to influence consumer taste perceptions, among other things, remains unanswered. Just as price can trigger certain unconscious expectations about a product's efficacy (Shiv, Camon, & Ariely, 2005), a phenomenon known as the marketing placebo effect, then perhaps so can a CSR message. For this reason, this study aims to examine to which extent sustainability practices that are marketed and integrated into the brand store affect brand equity, taste perceptions, and perceived emotional value, here defined as "the utility derived from the feelings or affective states that a product generates" (Sweeney & Soutar, 2001, p. 211). Emotional value is widely considered to be an important value dimension (Sweeney & Soutar, 2001).

With our study, we expect to contribute to theory in three ways. First, with a variety of studies pointing toward the notion that a CSR message may influence brand equity (Abdolvand & Charsetad, 2013; Torres, Bijmolt, Tribó, & Verhoef, 2012; Hsu, 2012), we seek to further solidify these findings. Second, and crucial to this paper, we investigate the effect of a CSR message on taste perceptions. As we broaden our understanding of flavor and how it is perceived, the influence of various extrinsic cues is becoming more prevalent (Okamoto & Dan, 2013; Poor, Duhachek, & Krishnan, 2013; Spence, 2015). In this case specifically, we examine what potential a content-focused message, a CSR message played over an image slideshow, holds with respect to influencing taste perception. Third, with the knowledge that CSR initiatives and the resulting value it generates in terms of corporate reputation (Hsu, 2012) have the ability to garner positive brand perceptions of a company's products (Brickley, Smith, & Zimmerman, 2002; Jones, 2005; Lai, Chiu, Yanf, & Pai, 2010; Smith & Higgins, 2000; Varadarajan & Menon, 1988), we explore the influence of a CSR message on perceived value. Building on Sweeney and Soutar's (2001) four-dimensional consumer perceived value scale, we focus on a single value construct: perceived emotional value.

LITERATURE STUDY

Flavor and the ways in which it is perceived are a complicated affair. While the sense of taste may be considered the driving force behind individual taste perceptions, other senses are also deeply entwined in the flavor perception process, something that is known as multisensory flavor perception. This relatively new area of study has developed rapidly in recent years (Poor et al., 2013; Prescott, 2015; Small, Gerber, Mak, & Hummel, 2005). Through the efforts of psychologists and cognitive neuroscientists, we are becoming increasingly aware not only of the integrated nature of all the human senses when it comes to taste perception, but also of the complexity of multisensory interactions associated with this process (Spence, 2015).

Traditionally, flavor is divided into gustatory (mouth) and olfactory (nose) stimuli. Through consumption of food and the subsequent experience of flavor, individuals experience a wide variety of sensations (Delwiche, 2004), and emotions (Desmet & Schifferstein, 2008). Olfactory cues have been shown to be exceedingly powerful in stimulating memory, a phenomenon known as autobiographical odor memory (Willander & Larsson, 2006). Furthermore, odor-evoked memories elicit a greater emotional response opposed to visual cues (Herz, Eliassen, Beland, & Souza, 2004). Hence, we can argue that the flavor perceived may influence the emotional value attributed to the consumed food product. In view of the above, we hypothesize the following:

H1. Flavor perception has a positive effect on emotional value.

Poor et al. (2013), on the other hand, have found strong support that certain imagery also has the potential to increase taste perceptions. For example, information that is communicated to the consumer outside of the physical food product or beverage itself, including information about the brand, may cause considerable bias toward the perception of taste and flavor, and may thus have a significant potential to influence taste perception. In fact, when researchers applied varying extrinsic cues, various significantly positive correlations were found in the primary taste cortex (Okamoto & Dan, 2013). A brand's ability to influence taste perception has been a subject of interest for researchers for many years, with experiments dating back to the 1960s (Allison & Uhl, 1964). Today, our understanding of the exact nature of this relationship is broadening still (Cavanagh, Kruja, & Forestell, 2014), as it is most commonly proposed that the effects of extrinsic cues, of which brand is one, are mediated by expectation (Okamoto & Dan, 2013). The use of CSR messages as part of brand equity has grown, particularly in the hospitality industry (cf. Hur et al., 2013) and research supports the effects on food and beverage consumption (see, e.g., Plassmann & Weber, 2015). Brand equity can be defined as the commercial value of a brand derived from the relevant consumer perceptions or the total value added to a product by the virtue of a brand (Yoo & Donth, 2001). Brand credibility as a first feature of brand equity can be defined as the extent to which consumers believe in the company's trustworthiness and expertise (Erdem, Swait, & Louviere, 2002). Brand credibility has been shown to positively influence brand purchase intentions via increasing perceived quality and increasing the information cost saved while lowering perceived risk (Baek, Kim, & Yu, 2010).

A company's reputation as a second characteristic of brand equity can function as a signal of company characteristics as well as a source of competitive advantage (Hur et al., 2013). Consumers will rely on their understanding of a company's corporate reputation when confronted with a shortage of information about a product or business (Schinietz & Epstein, 2005). A good reputation may also function as a preventative tool to guard against shifting consumer perceptions stemming from negative information (Lange, Lee, & Dai, 2011). As such, a known brand with a high brand credibility and a high reputation will create certain expectations among consumers as a result of witnessed advertising, familiarity with the brand and past experiences. As such, this will influence consumers' flavor perception. We may therefore formulate the following hypotheses:

H2a. Brand reputation has a positive effect on perceived emotional value.

H3a. Brand credibility has a positive effect on perceived emotional value.

H4. Flavor perception will mediate the relationship between brand reputation and perceived emotional value.

H5. Flavor perception will mediate the relationship between brand credibility and perceived emotional value.

Consumer attitudes toward companies' CSR efforts are generally positive (Webb & Mohr, 1998), with their willingness to purchase a company's product also being positively influenced (Smith & Alcorn, 1991). However, it is not entirely clear whether an advertisement with a CSR element will garner a significantly more positive consumer reaction compared to a similar advertisement devoid of such an element (Xialoi & Kwangjun, 2007). The relationship between CSR and brand equity has been made palpable by various publications, such as the works of Abdolvand and Charsetad (2013), who demonstrated that CSR positively affects brand equity in an industrial setting. Torres et al. (2012) argue that CSR aimed at various stakeholders has a positive effect on global, brand equity. Hsu (2012) established that CSR initiatives positively affect customer satisfaction, corporate reputation, and brand equity, the latter two being of most interest to this study. These research efforts were conducted in the life insurance sector. Various studies point toward the

notion that CSR and corporate reputation invoke positive brand perceptions of a company's products (Brickley et al., 2002; Jones, 2005; Lai
et al., 2010; Smith & Higgins, 2000; Varadarajan & Menon, 1988). In
view of the above, we hypothesize the following:

H2b. Brand reputation with CSR elements has a more positive effect on
perceived emotional value than brand reputation without CSR elements.

H3b. Brand credibility with CSR elements has a more positive effect on
perceived emotional value than brand credibility without CSR elements.

Fig. 1 depicts the study's conceptual model.

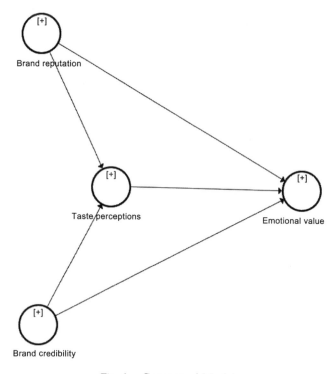

Fig. 1. Conceptual Model.

METHODS

Sample

A between-subjects experiment was conducted with one independent variable and containing the levels "Sustainability Message Present" and "Sustainability Message Not Present." The experiment aimed to determine the effects of the presence or absence of a sustainability-marketing message within a beer brand's promotional material on consumer taste perceptions (representing consumer perception), purchase intentions, perceived value, and brand equity.

Table 1. Descriptive Statistics ($N = 48$).

		Experimental Tasting (2015)
N		48
Gender	Male	25
	Female	23
Education	Bachelor	38
	Master	10
Age	Mean	25.4
	SD	6.33

The sample consisted of 52 participants, who were recruited on the basis of availability via face-to-face interactions, email, and/or social media messages. One of the reasons why these participants were invited was based on the fact that they enjoyed the taste of beer and were of legal drinking age. Overall, a total of the questionnaires of 48 respondents were found to be suitable for further processing: none of these had any missing data. From this sample, 52% of the respondents were male and 48% were female, with ages ranging from 20 to 48. Participants indicated whether they were familiar with the brand used in the promotional material. Additionally, they indicated how important sustainability was to them, not only in general, but also more specifically in relation to a beer brand or brewery. Finally, we evaluated the relative importance they placed on individual sustainability initiatives.

Experimental Set-Up

First, potential participants were asked about their willingness to participate in the experiment. These participants received a uniform message
pertaining to the purpose of the experiment as well as a guarantee of
confidentiality. They were told that there would be two separate sessions.
Those who agreed to participate in the study and were present on the
day it was held were then randomly assigned to one of the two conditions, with Group A containing a total of 27 participants and Group B
containing a total of 25 participants. Due to late arrivals, the ultimate
number of participants was determined to be 25 for Group A and 23 for
Group B.

Next, the participants were given a brief explanation of how the event
would proceed and they were then shown one of the two versions of
Sharp's Brewery's brand story video, differing only in terms of containing
or not containing a sustainability-marketing message. Group A was shown
a version of the video that contained a sustainability message, whereas the
version of the video shown to Group B did not contain such a message.
After the video had been shown, participants were asked to taste a beer
sample which they presumed to be Sharp's beer.

Finally, participants were asked to complete a questionnaire on the basis
of the video that they had viewed and the beer that they had tasted. Upon
completion of the questionnaire, participants were asked to answer up to
three semi-structured interview questions in groups of one or two participants per interview session.

Materials

The promotional video that was used consisted of two parts, and both
parts centered on the brewery's location. This particular brewery was
selected for a number of reasons: it produces a pilsener-style beer which is
commonly liked by a majority of beer drinking consumers, the video and
image materials were available online, and it was considered unlikely that
the Dutch participants would be familiar with the brand. The most
suitable beer product to be consumed by participants was determined after
taste testing a dozen local beers. Budget concerns and availability also
played a role.

First, a video was shown illustrating the general brewing process; this
video was the same for both groups. The process was followed by a picture

slideshow elaborating the brand story in which the history and values of the brewer were delineated via text that appeared on screen, accompanied by a voice-over recorded by a professional voice actor. The content of this information was taken directly from the brewer's website. In the material viewed by Group A, each of the five slides shown in the brand story picture slideshow contained one or two additional phrases that conveyed the brand's sustainability values. These values did not include anything related to organically sourcing the ingredients that are necessary to brew beer, but instead were limited to values associated with brewery sustainability. The sustainability marketing included in the brand story video for Group A mentioned levels of energy and water conservation, reducing CO_2 emissions, repurposing brewery waste, community mindfulness, and overall environmentally friendly brewing practices. Group B viewed material that was characterized by a lack of sustainability elements in the marketing video, which focused primarily on product quality and which made no mention of environmental or societal initiatives.

Measures

In this study, we used measures for brand equity, taste perceptions, and emotional value. The items for *brand equity* were adapted from Abdolvand and Charsetad (2013) and answered on the basis of five-point Likert scales ranging from "strongly disagree" to "strongly agree." Two different dimensions were explored, including "Corporate Brand Credibility" (three items), and "Corporate Reputation" (three items). Examples include *"The company product claims are believable"* and *"The Brewery is a company I can admire and respect."*

Taste perceptions were adapted from Stevens (1995), with one item on "taste pleasantness/unpleasantness," which was answered with a seven-point Likert scale option.

Emotional value was adapted from Sweeney and Soutar (2001) and measured with five items on a seven-point Likert scale, with options ranging from "strongly disagree" to "strongly agree." Examples from each dimension include *"This item is well made," "This item would make me feel good," "This item is a good product for the price,"* and *"This item would make a good impression on other people."*

Control variables consisted of demographic characteristics including age, gender, and education level. All questions were answered through a "fill in the blank" answer option with the exception of gender, which had a male and female multiple-choice option.

Analysis

For this study, a partial least squares structural equation modeling method (PLS-SEM) was used; this was done by means of the 3.2.3 SmartPLS version as discussed by Ringle, Wende, and Will (2015). PLS-SEM was considered the best possible option to analyze the data results, as our sample was too small ($N = 48$) for a standard multiple regression analysis to have enough predicting power (see, e.g., Knofczynski & Mundfrom, 2008). For this reason, we decided to use the ordinary least squares (OLS) to perform regressions as they are used in PLS-SEM, also because this method uses bootstrapping as a way to develop greater predictive power amongst small samples (Hair, Sarstedt, Ringle, & Mena, 2012). For the partial least square algorithm, we used the path weighting scheme, and we set the maximum number of iterations at 300. We used 10^{-5} as our stop criterion. We used a uniform value of 1 as the initial value for each of the outer weights (Henseler & Fassott, 2010). The items of the constructs used for this study are based on a $1-5$ Likert scale, and since these items are considered to be continuous variables, they also agree with the OLS principles (Table 1).

RESULTS

This section presents the results of the PLS-SEM analysis of the factor model and the path model.

Table 2. Reliability and Convergent Validity.

Construct	Actual Range	Mean	SD	Reliability	AVE
Brand reputation	1.00–5.00	3.28	0.68	0.70	0.62
Brand credibility	1.00–5.00	3.57	0.88	0.84	0.75
Taste intensity	1.00–7.00	4.93	1.07	1	1
Emotional value	1.00–7.00	4.67	1.68	0.96	0.68

Factor Model

For the evaluation of the constructs, we first examined the reliability of the measures used to measure brand reputation, brand credibility, and emotional value. As a first step, for all three constructs, we examined indicator reliability. All factor loadings were above 0.6 and therefore acceptable (Hair, Hult, Ringle, & Sarstedt, 2014). Subsequently, we checked convergent validity and reliability for all the constructs, as depicted in Table 2.

Brand reputation showed sufficient convergent validity as the average variance extracted (AVE) was 0.62, thus meeting the requirement of a score higher than 0.50 (Fornell & Larcker, 1981). In addition, our analyses showed sufficient reliability: composite reliability was 0.70, which is in line with the recommended value higher than 0.7 (Hair et al., 2014). Furthermore, *brand credibility* showed enough convergent validity: the AVE was 0.75, which is sufficient (Fornell & Larcker, 1981). Reliability was also sufficient, as Cronbach's alpha was 0.84. The last construct, *emotional value*, showed sufficient convergent validity (AVE = 0.68) as well as sufficient reliability (Cronbach alpha = 0.96).

Finally, we checked for discriminant validity, comparing the AVEs of the constructs with the inter-construct correlations determining whether each latent variable shared greater variance with its own measurement variables or with other constructs (Chin, 1998; Fornell & Larcker, 1981). We compared the square root of the AVE for each construct with the correlations with all other constructs in the model (Table 3). A correlation between constructs exceeding the square roots of their AVEs indicates that they may not be sufficiently discriminable. For each construct, we found that the absolute correlations did not exceed the square roots of the AVE. Hence, we may conclude that all constructs show sufficient reliability and validity.

Table 3. Discriminant Validity.

	Brand Credibility	Brand Reputation	Taste Perceptions	Emotional Value
Brand credibility	0.864			
Brand reputation	0.414	0.783		
Taste perceptions	0.330	0.365	1	
Emotional value	0.292	0.366	0.517	0.929

Model Estimations

Regarding the inner model evaluation and estimates, we analyzed the path coefficients by using bootstrap t-statistics for their significance (Anderson & Gerbing, 1988). For this bootstrapping, we used 5,000 subsamples, with a bias-corrected bootstrap, testing for a two-tailed significance of 95%. We first controlled for gender, age, and previous education, which was found to have no significant effect on emotional value ($\gamma = 0.104$, $p = 0.46$ for gender; $\gamma = -0.064$, $p = 0.72$ for age; $\gamma = -0.060$, $p = 0.74$ for previous education) and a low explained variance ($R^2 = 0.02$).

Subsequently, to test H1, H2a, H3a, H4, and H5, we estimated the relationships between the precursors and emotional value as hypothesized in the literature section; this was done for the whole group and we found that the model had an explained variance (R^2) of 0.31. In addition, the model proved to have a fit which fulfilled the norms as stated by Hu and Bentler (1998). The standardized root mean square residual (SRMR) was 0.07, which is in line with Hu and Bentler's recommended criterion threshold of lower than 0.08. H1 was supported, as taste perceptions were found to have a significant relation with emotional value ($\gamma = 0.43$, $p = 0.000$). H2a and H2b were not supported: the relation between brand reputation and emotional value ($\gamma = 0.08$, $p = 0.52$), and the relation between brand credibility and emotional value ($\gamma = 0.18$, $p = 0.38$) were not significant. H4 and H5 were supported as brand reputation ($\gamma = 0.46$, $p = 0.000$) as well as brand credibility ($\gamma = 0.32$, $p = 0.000$) were found to have significant relations with taste perception.

For testing H2b and H3b, we conducted a multi-group analysis in which we compared group A, which viewed material with a CSR message, with group B, which did not view CSR material. We found differences in the model for both groups. For group A, taste perception on emotional value ($\gamma = 0.69$, $p = 0.020$), brand reputation on taste perception ($\gamma = 0.38$, $p = 0.050$), and brand credibility on taste perception ($\gamma = 0.45$, $p = 0.018$) remained significant, while the direct relations between brand credibility ($\gamma = -0.13$, $p = 0.958$) and brand credibility ($\gamma = -0.24$, $p = 0.473$) on emotional value remained not significant. For group B, we found that taste perception on emotional value ($\gamma = 0.68$, $p = 0.000$) and brand credibility on taste perception ($\gamma = 0.50$, $p = 0.018$) remained significant. However, the relationship between brand reputation on taste perception became non-significant ($\gamma = 0.36$, $p = 0.123$) but the relation between brand reputation and emotional value became significant ($\gamma = 0.40$, $p = 0.013$), indicating that the mediating role of taste perception in this relation disappeared. These results provide support for H2b and no support for H3b.

DISCUSSION

This research study set out to determine the effects of a sustainability message on consumer attitudes in relation to a beer product. Specifically, the presence of a sustainability element in a marketing video was expected to positively influence perceived brand equity, taste perception, and perceived product value. Overall, our analyses yielded several results that supported some of the proposed hypotheses as well as some unexpected results, which may very well open the path for future research.

With respect to the difficulties that are generally associated with creating or maintaining corporate reputation or credibility, providing competitive advantage is viewed as one of the most important resources (Hur et al., 2013). While perceived credibility was higher among participants who viewed a sustainability message compared to those who were not presented with this message, the ultimate difference was relatively modest. Brand credibility is more forthcoming when the consumer is familiar with a brand (Wang & Yang, 2010). Thus, the unexpected slight difference that was found in this dimension may be explained by the fact that, in this case, it was necessary to employ a brand that was unknown to the participants.

By far the most thought-provoking results of the study are those in the field of taste perceptions. Taste perception was proven to be positively influenced by the presence of a sustainability message. Put simply, the presence of a sustainability message led participants to rate their beverage as tasting better and as more flavor intense, despite the fact that all participants were given the same product. These results are corroborated by the findings reported by Lotz, Fabian, and Fetchenhauer (2013), who found similar results under comparable circumstances. Interestingly, it would appear that a message focusing on environmental sustainability as opposed to a beverage's organic or conventionally produced nature might have a higher potential of positively influencing taste perceptions. While a beverage product with organically sourced ingredients would logically be expected to have a more direct influence on taste, this was disproven by Pagliarini et al. (2013). In sum, research is available that asserts the opposite, namely that organic produce is considered to taste better (Theuer,

2006). That being said, it must be borne in mind that this type of study is most commonly conducted using fruit and vegetables.

In the case of this research, a message of environmental sustainability, which would logically have no effect on taste, did in fact result in more positive taste perceptions. This certainly adds to our understanding of taste perceptions, their complexity, and the apparent fact that the primary taste cortex can be influenced subconsciously. If we take into account that in our relatively small sample all but one of the tested variables were rated higher after viewing a sustainability message, we may hypothesize that more significant findings may be found with larger sample sizes. For this reason, we recommend that more extensive research be conducted to deepen our understanding of the way in which a sustainability message may influence consumer perceptions and attitudes.

LIMITATIONS

The first limitation of our study concerns the possible presence of social desirability bias. Considering that the experiment was noticeably recorded on film, participants may have felt the need to answer in ways that are socially desirable, thus inflating the ratings of the product associated with the sustainable brand story. Still, while it may have affected responses in the video interviews, this should be balanced out by participants' responses in the paper questionnaires, which were relatively anonymous. Second, the sample selection for the experiment was limited in the sense that it was reduced to participants of a young age. As a result, our study ignored any existing segmentation of a potential client's customers of a higher age, but a client will most likely already have a segmentation of their current customer base. This could, however, in turn be linked to the characteristics of the experiment's participants, so that a statistical analysis may be conducted to determine the differing degrees of influence of a sustainability message on specific customer segments. Third, while it was generally established that none of the participants had an aversion to beer, individual biases toward beer in general may have affected the research results. Put simply, some individuals may simply like beer better than others, and this may have caused them to report the product as tasting better, regardless of the message they viewed. The experiment attempted to prevent existing biases such as these through random sampling. As a final limitation, we need to mention the issue of one single test product: this may have negatively impacted our results. Since only one type of beer was used, a pilsener, existing biases toward this particular kind of beer may have influenced outcomes. We therefore recommend that if similar experiments are conducted, several other types of beer should also be included, such as IPAs and Doubles.

RESEARCH IMPLICATIONS

Our research has confirmed the potential of the impact of sustainability messages on consumer perceptions and attitudes. However, we need to further explore the underlying principles, because our analysis showed some unexpected results.

First, the low effect of brand reputation needs to be explored in greater detail, because both H2a and H2b were not supported. A suggestion for an additional research is the expansion of the research model with the other value perceptions as suggested by Sweeney and Soutar (2001) and the effects on purchase intention and loyalty. Second, as the sample was small, there is a need to conduct this research with larger samples, as argued above, so that better results may be found between the variables. Also, larger samples will minimize the probability of errors and increase generalizability for the results.

Lastly, additional research is needed on the question if the impact can also be found in product groups where flavor and taste are not considered important. One would expect that in these products, too, unconscious processes influence the perceived quality of an important feature or characteristic of that product. We need to investigate what the effect of sustainable messages would be on the perception of other product groups and companies that do not work with taste as an important product characteristic.

PRACTICAL IMPLICATIONS

With a deeper understanding of the relationship between perceived sustainability and consumer perceptions, and most notably taste perceptions of a beer product, a discussion is justified of the implications for brands and the industry as a whole. Once we realize that every major brewer in the Netherlands is already active in the field of sustainability (Rank a Brand, 2014), it is a matter of developing methods to effectively communicate these values to the consumer. Still, this in itself may prove to be the most difficult task. Considering that beer is, essentially, a hedonic good as opposed to a utilitarian one, it can be theorized that over-emphasizing sustainability in a brand's primary marketing efforts may lead to alienation of existing customers. Having said that, we also know that some forms of green marketing are more effective than others when it comes to marketing hedonic products such as beer (Strahilevitz & Meyers, 1998). This realization, combined with the fact that such marketing efforts generally gain more traction in liberal societies (Watkins, Aitken, & Mather, 2016), points toward the merits involved in making consumers aware of a brand's sustainability efforts, especially in the Netherlands and countries similar to it.

Another consideration is a more practical one: does a better tasting product, or a product perceived as such, actually sell better? This may not always be the case: in many cases, it is the brand itself, and the subsequent value attached to it by consumers, that influences purchase intent (Cobb-Walgren, Ruble, & Donthu, 1995). Therefore, it might be better to focus on the influence of a sustainability message on brand equity, which was only partially proven by this research.

It is clear that consumer appreciation, and in some cases demand, for businesses to behave responsibly is spreading rapidly (Dowd & Burke, 2013), especially in the food and beverages industries. Responding to these shifting values is in the best interests of every company or organization that wishes to retain the loyalty of its customers. This rings true for the beer industry just as it does for any other industry. No longer is a "green beer" obligated to be brewed from organically sourced ingredients for it to prompt positive taste perceptions. With research reporting conflicting evidence that both proves and disproves the idea that organic foods positively influence taste (Pagliarini et al., 2013; Theuer, 2006), the marketing value attributed to using organic ingredients in alcoholic beverages is not as clear as we might logically assume. This assertion is further supported by the fact that the participants of this study indicated that the use of organic ingredients is the least important factor in comparison with other sustainability practices. Conversely, our experiment does conclusively prove that a sustainability message, unrelated to the actual beverage ingredients, has the ability to influence consumer perceptions. This opens up the door for marketers to start leveraging their brand's sustainability in any number of creative ways. Illustrative examples include consciously recycled beer coasters (CoasterKings, 2015), brewing beer with wastewater (Oregon Brewers, 2015) and online brand story campaigns (Koninklijke Grolsch, 2014).

REFERENCES

Abdolvand, M., & Charsetad, P. (2013). Corporate social responsibility and brand equity in industrial marketing. *International Journal of Academic Research in Business and Social Sciences, 3*(9), 273–284.

Allison, R. I., & Uhl, K. (1964). Influence of beer brand identification on taste perception. *Journal of Marketing Research, 1*(3), 36–39.

Anderson, J. C., & Gerbing, D. W. (1988). Structural equation modeling in practice: A review and recommended two-step approach. *Psychological Bulletin, 103*(3), 411–423.

Baek, T. H., Kim, J., & Yu, J. H. (2010). The differential roles of brand credibility and brand prestige in consumer brand choice. *Psychology and Marketing, 27*(7), 662–678.

Brickley, J., Smith, C., & Zimmerman, J. (2002). *Business ethics and organizational architecture.* Social Science Network Electronic Paper Collection, 250947.

Cavanagh, K. V., Kruja, B., & Forestell, C. A. (2014). The effect of brand and caloric information on flavor perception and food consumption in restrained and unrestrained eaters. *Appetite, 82,* 1–7.

Chin, W. W. (1998). The partial least squares approach to structural equation modeling. *Modern Methods for Business Research, 295*(2), 295–336.

CoasterKings. (2015). Retrieved from http://www.coasterkings.com.au/green-print.html. Accessed on September 3, 2015.

Cobb-Walgren, C. J., Ruble, C. A., & Donthu, N. (1995). Brand equity, brand preference, and purchase intent. *Journal of Advertising, 24*(3), 25–40.

CSR News. (2007). Retrieved from www.csrwire.com/press_releases/15922-%20Landmark-Study-Finds-Global-Spread-of-Corporate-Social-Responsibility. Accessed on September 9, 2015.

Delwiche, J. (2004). The impact of perceptual interactions on perceived flavor. *Food Quality and Preference, 15,* 137–146.

Desmet, P. M. A., & Schifferstein, H. N. J. (2008). Sources of positive and negative emotions in food experience. *Appetite, 50,* 290–301.

Dowd, K., & Burke, K. J. (2013). The influence of ethical values and food choice motivations on intentions to purchase sustainably sourced foods. *Appetite, 69,* 137–144.

Erdem, T., Swait, J., & Louviere, J. (2002). The impact of brand credibility on consumer price sensitivity. *International Journal of Research in Marketing, 19,* 1–19.

Fornell, C., & Larcker, D. F. (1981). Structural equation models with unobservable variables and measurement error: Algebra and statistics. *Journal of Marketing Research, 18*(3), 382–388.

Hair, J. F., Hult, G. T., Ringle, C. M., & Sarstedt, M. (2014). *A primer on partial least squares structural equation modeling (PLS-SEM).* Thousand Oaks, CA: Sage.

Hair, J. F., Sarstedt, M., Ringle, C. M., & Mena, J. A. (2012). An assessment of the use of partial least squares structural equation modeling in marketing research. *Journal of the Academy of Marketing Science, 40*(3), 414–433.

Henseler, J., & Fassott, G. (2010). Testing moderating effects in PLS path models: An illustration of available procedures. In V. Esposito Vinzi, W. W. Chin, J. Henseler, & H. Wang (Eds.), *Handbook of partial least squares* (pp. 713–735). Heidelberg: Springer Berlin.

Herz, R. S., Eliassen, J., Beland, S., & Souza, T. (2004). Neuroimaging evidence for the emotional potency of odor-evoked memory. *Neuropsychologia, 42*(3), 371–378.

Hsu, K. (2012). The advertising effects of corporate social responsibility on corporate reputa-
    tion and brand equity: Evidence from the life insurance industry in Taiwan. *Journal of
    Business Ethics, 109*, 189−201.
Hu, L. T., & Bentler, P. M. (1998). Fit indices in covariance structure modeling: Sensitivity to
    underparameterized model misspecification. *Psychological Methods, 3*(4), 424.
Hur, W., Kim, H., & Woo, J. (2013). How CSR leads to corporate brand equity: Mediating
    mechanisms of corporate brand credibility and reputation. *Journal of Business Ethics,
    125*, 75−86.
Jones, R. (2005). Finding sources of brand value: Developing a stakeholder model of brand
    equity. *Brand Management, 13*(1), 10−32.
Knofczynski, G. T., & Mundfrom, D. (2008). Sample sizes when using multiple linear regres-
    sion for prediction. *Educational and Psychological Measurement, 68*(3), 431−442.
Koninklijke Grolsch. (2014). *Grolsch duurzaam en verantwoord ondernemen.* Retrieved
    from https://www.youtube.com/watch?v = nEWdKQqP5HY. Accessed on September
    3, 2015.
Lai, C., Chiu, C., Yanf, C., & Pai, D. (2010). The effects of corporate social responsibility on
    brand performance: The mediating effect of industrial brand equity and corporate repu-
    tation. *Journal of Business Ethics, 95*(3), 457−469.
Lange, D., Lee, P. M., & Dai, Y. (2011). Organizational reputation: An overview. *Journal of
    Management, 37*, 153−184.
Lotz, S., Fabian, C., & Fetchenhauer, D. (2013). What is fair is good: Evidence of consumers'
    taste for fairness. *Food Quality and Preference, 30*, 139−144.
Okamoto, M., & Dan, I. (2013). Extrinsic information influences taste and flavor perception:
    A review from psychological and neuroimaging perspectives. *Seminars in Cell &
    Developmental Biology, 24*, 247−355.
Oregon Brewers. (2015). *Oregon brewers use purified recycled wastewater to make beer.*
    Retrieved   from   http://sanfrancisco.cbslocal.com/2015/04/29/oregon-brewers-use-
    purified-recycled-wastewater-to-make-beer/. Accessed on September 3, 2015.
Pagliarini, E., Laureati, M., & Gaeta, D. (2013). Sensory descriptors, hedonic perception and
    consumer's attitudes towards sangiovese red wine deriving from organically and con-
    ventionally grown grapes. *Frontiers in Psychology, 4*(896), 1−7.
Plassmann, H., & Weber, B. (2015). Individual differences in marketing placebo effects:
    Evidence from brain imaging and behavioral experiments. *Journal of Marketing
    Research, 52*(4), 493−510.
Poor, M., Duhachek, A., & Krishnan, H. S. (2013). How images of other consumers influence
    subsequent taste perceptions. *Journal of Marketing, 77*, 124−139.
Prescott, J. (2015). Multisensory processes in flavour perception and their influence on food
    choice. *Current Opinion in Food Science, 3*, 47−52.
Rank a Brand. (2014). *Grolsch voor het derde jaar de duurzaamste van Nederland.* Retrieved
    from   https://mvobierblog.wordpress.com/2014/10/09/grolsch-voor-het-derde-jaar-de-
    duurzaamste-van-nederland/. Accessed on September 3, 2015.
Ringle, C. M., Wende, S., & Will, A. (2015). *SmartPLS 2.* Hamburg: SmartPLS.
Schinietz, K. E., & Epstein, M. J. (2005). Exploring the financial value of a reputation
    for corporate social responsibility during a crisis. *Corporate Reputation Review,
    47*, 327−345.
Shiv, B., Camon, Z., & Ariely, D. (2005). Placebo effects of marketing actions: Consumers
    may get what they pay for. *Journal of Marketing Research, 11*, 383−393.

Small, D. M., Gerber, J. C., Mak, Y. E., & Hummel, T. (2005). Differential neural responses evoked by orthonasal versus retronasal odorant perception in humans. *Neuron, 47*(4), 593–605.

Smith, S. M., & Alcorn, D. S. (1991). Cause marketing: A new direction in the marketing of social responsibility. *Journal of Consumer Marketing, 8*(3), 19–34.

Smith, W., & Higgins, M. (2000). Cause related marketing: Ethics and the ecstatic. *Business and Society, 39*(3), 304–322.

Spence, C. (2015). Multisensory flavor perception. *Cell Magazine, 161*, 24–35.

Stevens, D. A. (1995). Individual differences in taste perception. *Food Chemistry, 56*(3), 303–311.

Strahilevitz, M., & Meyers, J. G. (1998). Donations to charity as purchase incentives, how well they work may depend on what you are trying to sell. *Journal of Consumer Research, 24*(4), 434–446.

Sweeney, J. C., & Soutar, G. N. (2001). Consumer perceived value, the development of a multiple item scale. *Journal of Retailing, 77*, 203–220.

Theuer, R. C. (2006). Do organic fruits and vegetables taste better than conventional fruits and vegetables. *State of Science Review: Taste of Organic View*, The Organic Center. Retrieved from https://organic-center.org/reportfiles/TasteReport.pdf

Torres, A., Bijmolt, T., Tribó, J., & Verhoef, P. (2012). Generating global brand equity through corporate social responsibility to key stakeholders. *International Journal of Research in Marketing, 29*(1), 13–24.

Varadarajan, P. R., & Menon, A. (1988). Cause-related marketing: A coalignment of marketing strategy and corporate philanthropy. *Journal of Marketing, 52*(3), 58–74.

Wang, X., & Yang, Z. (2010). The effect of brand credibility on consumers brand purchase intention in emerging economies: The moderating role of brand awareness and brand image. *Journal of Global Marketing, 23*(3), 177–188.

Watkins, L., Aitken, R., & Mather, D. (2016). Conscientious consumers: A relationship between moral foundations, political orientation and sustainable consumption. *Journal of Cleaner Production, 134*, 137–146.

Webb, D. J., & Mohr, L. A. (1998). A typology of consumer responses to cause- related marketing: From skeptics to socially concerned. *Journal of Public Policy and Marketing, 17*(2), 226–238.

Willander, J., & Larsson, M. (2006). Smell your way back to childhood: Autobiographical odor memory. *Psychonomic Bulletin and Review, 13*(2), 240–244.

Xialoi, N. X., & Kwangjun, H. K. (2007). Consumer responses to corporate social responsibility (CSR) initiatives: Examining the role of brand-cause fit in cause-related marketing. *Journal of Advertising, 36*(2), 63–74.

Yoo, B., & Donth, N. (2001). Developing and validating a multidimensional consumer-based brand equity scale. *Journal of Business Research, 52*, 1–14.

USING TOURISM AS A MECHANISM TO REDUCE POACHING AND HUNTING: A CASE STUDY OF THE TIDONG COMMUNITY, SABAH

Fiffy Hanisdah Saikim, Bruce Prideaux, Maryati Mohamed and Zulhazman Hamzah

ABSTRACT

In Sabah, Malaysia, illegal hunting has increased in recent years putting considerable pressure on large mammal populations. The causes for this phenomenon lie in increasing rural poverty, ineffective policies to regulate hunting, as well as a ready market for many wildlife products in the Chinese medicine markets. This paper examines how Community-Based Ecotourism has some potential to be used as a tool to reducing poaching using the Tidong community in Sabah as a case study. The key finding is that successful conservation outcomes for Community-Based Ecotourism projects are only sustainable over the long run if projects are structured to ensure that the local community is able to continue effective management once sponsoring organizations hand over control and that revenue from tourism does not decline. If tourist revenue declines communities

Advances in Hospitality and Leisure, Volume 12, 119–144
Copyright © 2017 by Emerald Group Publishing Limited
ISSN: 1745-3542/doi:10.1108/S1745-354220160000012010

may be forced to revert to previous practices reversing any initial conservation gains.

Keywords: Wildlife; poaching; hunting; Tabin wildlife reserve; Borneo; community-based ecotourism

INTRODUCTION

This paper examines how tourism may be used as a tool for developing a Community-Based Ecotourism (CBET) project designed to enhance local livelihoods while at the same time reducing illegal hunting activity including poaching. Despite the growing popularity of studies on aspects of sustainable tourism development, the issue of poaching and illegal hunting, a major enemy of sustainability, has been largely ignored in the tourism literature. In recent years wildlife poaching and illegal hunting have become a growing problem particularly in Africa and parts of Asia. In Asia, poaching has put considerable pressure on large mammal populations. In Borneo, many of the island's vertebrates and some specifically targeted species such as turtles, crocodiles, and certain birds, have already been hunted to virtual extinction (Bennett & Robinson, 2000). Continued illegal hunting in Sabah, a Malaysian state located in Borneo, has the potential to discriminate many large mammal populations, damage healthy, productive ecosystems and have an adverse impact on the welfare of the human communities that depend the natural ecosystem for their livelihoods.

The aim of this paper is to explore the potential offered by tourism as an alternative to poaching. To achieve this aim the paper first examines the positive effects on a local rainforest community when a tourism project based in part on wildlife viewing was established. One outcome was giving live animals in a nearby protected area a greater market value than poached animals. The paper then reports on the impact on wildlife and the community's economic situation when NGO support for the CBET project ceased.

Poaching is defined as the illegal hunting of wildlife in protected areas, hunting is defined as the permitted killing of wildlife while illegal hunting is defined as the illegal hunting of wildlife in unprotected areas (Eliason, 2003). Illegal hunting, which for the purposes of this paper includes poaching, poses a greater threat to large forest fauna than timber harvesting in many areas of the humid tropics (Auzel & Wilkie, 2000; Bennett et al., 2002; Linkie et al., 2003). In some regions illegal hunting may even be a greater threat to wildlife than habitat loss (Bennett et al., 2002; Kinnaird, Sanderson, O'Brien, Wibisono, & Woolmer, 2003; Robertson & van Schaik, 2001).

Literature Review

Several themes have emerged in the wider literature related to poaching including the threat from hunting (Kaltenborn, Nyahongo, & Tingstad, 2005; Magige, Holmern, Stokke, Mlingwa, & Røskaft, 2008), impacts from subsistence farming (Bulte & Horan, 2003), construction of roads (Ament, Clevenger, Yu, & Hardy, 2008; Trombulack & Frissell, 2000), the growing demand for wildlife products (Aryal, 2002; Moyle, 2003; Nijman, 2005) and issues related to enforcement (Broad, Mulliken, & Roe, 2003; Leader-Williams & Milner-Gulland, 1993). The aim of this review is to identify specific areas of research that relate to issues associated with illegal hunting including poaching and a role for tourism activities in communities engaged in poaching.

The most important international treaty prohibiting the trade of endangered species is the Convention on International Trade in Endangered Species (CITES) that came into force in 1975. Unfortunately, it is difficult to enforce such treaties and anti-poaching laws as demonstrated by the major poaching crisis that swept through Africa and Asia in the 1970s and 1980s, and again in the current decade, decimating the population of African and Asian elephants, rhinoceroses, and tigers. A paper by Wyler and Sheikh (2008) gave some indication of the value of illegally traded wildlife (see Table 1).

One major initiative of the CITES was the banning of the ivory trade in 1989. Along with this ban, the US Congress passed the African Elephant Conservation Act of 1988 to provide grants to help African countries preserve their endangered elephant population. In 1994, the Rhinoceros and Tiger Conservation Act was enacted by the Senate and House of Representatives of the United States of America and was, in part, responsible for a steady improvement in the status of endangered animal populations in Africa and Russia (Ellis, 2005; Walker, Brower, Stephens, & Lee, 2009). Unfortunately, this legislation seemed to have little effect on poaching in Asia. Rhinoceros and tigers are especially at risk with the reemergence of ivory markets and growth in demand for traditional Chinese medicines.

In Asia, poaching has focused on a number of species including Rhinoceros and Elephants for their tusks, bears for body parts, and in

Table 1. Selected Illicit Wildlife Trade and Estimated Retail Value.

Illegally Trade Wildlife	Estimated Retail Value
Elephants	$121–$900 per kilogram of ivory
Rhinos	$945–$50,000 per kilogram of rhino horn
Tibetan Antelopes	$1,200–$20,000 per shahtoosh shawl
Big Cats	$1,300–$20,000 per tiger, snow leopard, or jaguar skin; $3,300–$7,000 per set of tiger bones
Bears	$250–$8,500 per gall bladder
Sturgeon	$4,450–$6,000 per kilogram of caviar
Reptiles and Insects (often live)	$30,000 per python; $30,000 per komodo dragon; $5,000–$30,000 per plowshare tortoise; $15,000 per Chinese alligator; $20,000 per monitor lizard; $20,000 per shingle back skink; $8,500 per pair of birdwing butterflies
Exotic Birds (often live)	$10,000 per black palm cockatoo egg ($25,000–$80,000 per mature breeding pair); $5,000–$12,000 per hyacinth macaw; $60,000–$90,000 per Lear macaw; $20,000 per Mongolian falcon
Great Apes (often live)	$50,000 per Orangutan

Source: Wyler and Sheikh (2008).

many areas primates for bush food as well as the pet market. In Vietnam, for example, 90% of the country's 19 primate taxa are endangered, with eight critically endangered, primarily from deforestation, the wildlife trade, and poaching (Mittermeier, 2010). Currently there seems to be no effective solution to reducing poaching in Asia (Wang, 2010) although the potential to use tourism offers one approach that is worth investigating.

Over-poaching alters wildlife population densities, their distribution, and demography. This in turn may lead to shifts in seed dispersal, browsing, competition, predation, and other community dynamics in protected areas. Cumulatively, the loss of a key species can have significant knock-on effects throughout an ecosystem leading to changes in the abundance and distribution of key flora and fauna communities and in some cases encouraging invasive species to fill positions in the ecosystem previously occupied by threatened species.

Illegal Hunting in Borneo

Borneo, a recognized ecological hotspot with an enormous diversity of flora and fauna (Krupnich & Kress, 2003; Myers, Mittermeier,

Mittermeier, Da Fonseca, & Kent, 2000), is governed by Malaysia (the Malaysian states of Sabah and Sarawak), Indonesia (five provinces), and Brunei Darussalam, an independent nation. Tourism promotion of the island has consistently employed pictures of endemic species such as the orangutan as a key selling point yet poaching continues to reduce the populations of many of its major species. Despite protected areas being established in regions where forests remain largely untouched by logging, illegal hunting has the capacity to create "empty forests" devoid of higher order fauna (Redford, 1992). One study (Buckland, 2005) of poaching in the Kayan Mentarang National Park (North Kalimantan Province, Indonesia Borneo) found that after several years of uncontrolled poaching, primate populations had declined locally despite the forest remaining virtually untouched by illegal logging. Developing a sustainable wildlife tourism sector in such circumstances is difficult.

If wildlife populations decline significantly as a consequence of poaching and hunting, members of the communities who rely on these activities for food will eventually be forced to purchase food (Ferraro & Kiss, 2002; Gibson & Marks, 1995). A clear understanding of the financial implications of having to pay for food when animal populations crash may provide a positive incentive to encourage communities to work towards adopting sustainable hunting techniques. Traditional hunting is often nonselective and animals may be killed irrespective of their condition, fat or thin, with litter, pregnant or not; and hunting is sometimes wasteful, with only part of the animal taken (Meijaard et al., 2005). In Borneo, other factors increasing the impact of hunting include: increased access to forests; improved transport into remote areas using cars, motor bikes, motorized boats, and helicopters; ready access to guns and ammunition; the erosion of traditional prohibitions on killing and eating certain animals; increased immigration by nonindigenous people into the interior areas; and, a growing market for wildlife products either as food, trophies, or medicine (Bennett et al., 2002; Davies, Heydon, Leader-Williams, MacKinnon, & Newing, 2001; Fischer, 2010). Together, these factors often result in hunting being transformed from a subsistence to a commercialized activity.

Illegal hunting in Borneo appears to have been relatively sustainable at least until the 1970s, with the exception of the Sumatran Rhinoceros which was already in decline by the 1930s (Bosi, 2003). In the 1970s, the global demand for ivory increased due to the dramatic increase in the value of ivory leading to a significant increase in illegal hunting pressure and population declines (Messer, 2000). In Borneo, illegal hunting and poaching activities include harvesting rhinoceros horn (*Dicerorhinus sumatrensis harrissoni*), ivory from the Bornean pygmy elephant (*Elephas maximus borneensis*), for bushmeat, and for ingredients for traditional medicine. There is also an illegal pet trade. Other animals that are targeted by illegal hunters and poachers include the Bornean yellow muntjac (*Muntiacus atherodes*), red muntjac (*Muntiacus muntjak*), Sambar deer (*Cervus unicolor*), binturong (*Arctictis binturong*), bearded pigs (*Sus barbatus*), rhinoceros hornbills (*Buceros rhinoceros*), some primates including the Bornean orangutan (*Pongo pygmaeus*), Malayan sun bears (*Helarctos malayanus*), and clouded leopards (*Neofelis nebulosa*) (Bennett, Nyaoi, & Sompud, 1999; Bernard, Husson, Page, & Rieley, 2003).

Illegal hunting pressure varies between different areas of Borneo, although no comprehensive studies are available. In Sabah, there appears to be a significant difference between the rich eastern forests where many large mammals occur in higher densities including Bornean Pygmy elephants, Sumatran rhinoceros, Bornean orangutan, and banteng (*Bos javanicus*), whereas these species are rare or absent in the state's west. Because of cultural and religious reasons, poaching pressure in eastern forests is low compared with the state's west where indigenous hunting cultures predominate (Ancrenaz, Calaque, & Lackman-Ancrenaz, 2004; Alfred, Abdul Hamid, Payne, Williams, & Ambu, 2010).

While it is apparent that there is substantial research on the impact of poaching and illegal hunting on community livelihoods and its impact on ecosystems in the scientific literature, this issue has yet to receive attention in the tourism literature. Given that many forest communities in Asia, Africa, Central America, and South America continue to practice traditional hunting, fishing and agricultural practices, often in areas of potential high tourist value, research that can identify a role for tourism in mitigating the impact of these practices is required.

A Role for Tourism

A number of authors (Cottrell, Vaske, Shen, & Ritter, 2007; Dixon & Sherman, 1990; Goodwin, 2002; Kiss, 2004; Rodrigues & Prideaux, 2012; Saarinen, 2006; Sekhar, 2003; Tosun, 2006; Wallace, 1993) have argued that various forms of tourism are able to assist conservation by providing employment to local communities. In one of many examples, Rodrigues and Prideaux (2012) found that there was a reduction in hunting and the incidence of slash and burn agriculture when members of a river, local community they investigated in the Brazilian Amazon found long-term employment in a tourism enterprise. In Botswana, Snyman (2014) observed that for CBT projects to be successful, particularly where the venture is a partnership between a local community and an outside agency, there must be a clear connection between the benefits from tourism and the need for conservation.

The form of tourism required to achieve positive environmental outcomes has been subject to significant debate however there is a growing view that top-down, conservation first approaches are less likely to show long-term success than with community first approaches. A growing number of researchers (Adams & Hulme, 2001; Honey, 2008; Kiss, 2004; Kontogeorgopoulos, 2005; Tosun, 2006) advocate Community-Based Tourism (CBT) and CBET as strategies able to minimize harmful environmental practices such as poaching and slash and burn agriculture by providing communities with opportunities to generate alternative incomes. CBT aims to promote the social and economic sustainability of host communities while CBET emphasizes environmental objectives. In this way, CBET in theory offers host communities the opportunity to develop their capacity to control ecotourism development and its management (Walter & Regmi, 2016). As Sakata and Prideaux (2012) argue however, there is a propensity for many CBET projects to place the environment ahead of the community and for this reason the long-term success rates of many CBET projects are questionable.

A number of authors (de Haas 2002; Vincent & Thompson, 2002) see CBET as a tool for conservation which at the same time is able to generate benefits for local communities. In their investigation of a small scale CBET project in Belize (Timothy & White, 1999) found even very small projects located in peripheral areas had the ability to improve the lives of local communities as well as protecting the natural and cultural environments. As an approach to development Kontogeorgopoulos (2005) describes CBET as a method of distributing economic benefits widely with the potential to enhance social cohesion, harmony, and cooperation. Adams and Hulme (2001, p. 13) state that CBET should "emphasize the role of local residents in decision making about natural resources." Kiss (2004) extends this view by stating that the natural environment should pay for itself by generating economic benefits for local people. If successful, this will in turn foster proenvironmental attitudes (Sakata & Prideaux, 2012).

However, protection of the environment is a social issue as well as an ecological issue (Lele, Wilshusen, Brockington, Seidler, & Bawa, 2010) and where this element has been neglected, projects have failed (Honey, 2008). As Kontogeorgopoulos (2005) noted, CBET in theory places considerable importance on the social sustainability of local communities. However, economic aspects are just as important and if neglected, local communities that see little or no improvements to their livelihoods are likely to have less propensity to support CBET projects.

Sponsoring organizations generally fund CBET projects to achieve specific conservation outcomes. The apparent benefits of CBET has attracted significant attention from NGOs and government-aid agencies and according to Harrison (2010) the United Nations Development Program funded over 700 community-based and ecotourism projects between 1990 and 2007. Unfortunately, as a number of authors have noted (Harrison, 2010; Kiss, 2004; Wearing, McDonald, & Ponting, 2005), there are a number of problems related to the operationalizing of CBET projects including inequitable power relations between outside funding bodies and local communities and conflicting objectives between aid organizations and local communities. For these reasons, the track record of many CBET projects is poor. In part, this has been a result of the top-down approach taken in many CBET projects (Butcher, 2007; Erb, 2005; Harrison, 2010; Kiss, 2004). For example, Manyara and Jones (2007) in a study of six Kenyan CBET projects found that "outsiders" tend to reinforce dependency and enforce Western views on environmentalism. Burns and Barrei (2009) noted that problems of dependence might also arise. Insufficient training (Salazar, 2012; West, 2006) and the absence of adequate exit strategies (Manyara & Jones, 2007; Salazar, 2012) have also been identified as a problem that has led to poor CBET results.

Some of the characteristics of successful projects include their location in areas where tourism is already established (Kontogeorgopoulos, 2005; Matarrita-Cascante, Brennan, & Luloff, 2010; Mehta & Heinen, 2001; Stronza & Gordillo, 2008) and the local community being able to see visible improvements to their standard of living. Given the problems encountered in developing successful CBET and building on the observations of a number of authors (Kiss, 2004; Wearing et al., 2005) on the lack of understanding of why many CBET projects do not succeed, the failure of the CBET project discussed later in this paper is not surprising.

Tourism in Sabah

In 2012, Sabah hosted 3.4 million tourists, 1.1 million of whom were internationals (Sabah Tourism Board, 2014). Based on research conducted by the Sabah Tourism Board (2014) in 2011 at Kota Kinabalu International

Airport, Free Independent Tourists accounted for 54.7% of all arrivals; the remainder purchased a package tour product. Repeat visitors (47.2%) are a significant segment and 25.5% of visitors hold technical or professional jobs. Marketing by the Sabah Tourism Board emphasizes nature-based tourism experiences including wildlife viewing.

METHODS

This paper reports on local community attitudes to wildlife utilization in the Tabin Wildlife Reserve (TWR), Sabah, and examines how the degree of success of tourism activities is related to increases and decreases in poaching and hunting. The research focused on three kampongs (Dagat, Parit, and Kampung Tidong) located just outside the TWR.

In exploring local community attitudes to wildlife utilization, it is important to elicit local people's views of *their* world, in an effort to understand the environment and changes happening to or around them as *they* have experienced them (Eyler et al., 1999). With this need in mind the researchers adopted a mixed methods approach that combined qualitative and quantitative data collection. Given the lack of previous research into possible relationships between poaching and tourism, this research first adopted an inductive approach to identify major issues that were then quantified by adopting a deductive approach. Based on this approach four stages were identified as being required to meet the aim of the research with stages one to three using an inductive approach and stage four using a deductive approach. Stage one was based on an extensive literature review to develop a detailed understanding of the impacts of hunting and the society and culture of the villages (Kampong) that were the subject of this research. Stage two entailed the principle researcher undertaking ethnographic research by living in Kampong Dagat and Kampong Parit for an extended period of time. This allowed the researcher to observe firsthand the routine of village life and to understand the pressures faced by the community particularly in relation to food supply. The results of observations during this stage were used in the construction of the questionnaire used later in the research. During the third stage the principle researcher conducted informal conversations with community members including discussions about the value of tourism as an alternative livelihood to traditional hunting and poaching. These conversations were hand recorded in a field diary for later evaluation.

The fourth step entailed the construction and conduct of a survey to identify the views of various sections of the community on both poaching and tourism. A pilot survey was undertaken to pre-test the short question-naire that was developed for the purposes of this research. Specific ques-tions were designed to measure the attitude of local community members to wildlife utilization, their views on sustainable wildlife management in the TWR, and on tourism as an alternative livelihood. The items used in the questionnaire were derived from the outcomes of stages one, two, and three. The language used in the questionnaire was Malay which is spoken by respondents as either a first or second language. A five-point Likert scale was used with one being least likely and five being the most likely. The survey was conducted after the handover of the wildlife project to the community and in a period when tourism numbers had declined significantly.

As with any research of this type a number of limitations were encoun-tered that may affect the generalization of results. Primarily, the circum-stances that specific communities find themselves in are not uniform and what may be important to one community may be of little importance to another target community. For example, culture, governance, traditions, and the degree to which communities are undergoing change may vary from region to region. For these reasons the results of this research may not be able to be applied in whole to communities in other countries.

Study Area

The study was undertaken among the Tidong community located near the boundaries of the TWR (see Fig. 1). At the time the research was underta-ken there were 518 people including children, living in the three kampongs (Malaysian term for village), the majority of whom have Tidong (Dyak) ethnicity and adhere to the Muslim faith. The forest both inside and out-side of the TWR provides important sources of medicine, water, timber, rattan cane, and food, including fish and animals for the community (Majail, 1996). While not permitted within the protected area, some hunt-ing for species such as wild boar is permitted in a surrounding buffer zone although permits are required. Buffer zones were introduced to provide an added layer of protection to the protected area while providing an opportu-nity for neighboring rural communities to continue traditional hunting for food.

The TWR was established as a wildlife reserve in 1984 and covers an area of over 120,521 hectares (Fig. 1). The protected area is an important breeding ground for wildlife some of which are threatened by logging

Fig. 1.   Tidong Community Located near the Boundaries of the TWR.

activities outside the protected area. It also serves as a refugee for animals from nearby palm oil plantations (Bosi, 2003). The area has a rich assemblage of flora and fauna including 87 species of mammals. As a comparison, Sabah as a whole has 222 recorded species (Noraini, 2005; Yasuma & Andau, 2000). The most significant species in the TWR include Bornean pygmy elephant, orangutan, banteng, proboscis monkey, sun bear, clouded leopard, and bearded pig, as well as one internationally rare species, the Sumatran rhinoceros (Yasuma & Andau, 2000). Most large mammals live in the deep, dense forest, which is uninhabited by humans and in many areas penetrable only by foot. The Sabah Wildlife Department is responsible for enforcement of regulations protecting wildlife while the Sabah Forestry Department ensures the protection of the forest habitat.

In 2002, an outreach project funded by the Bornean Biodiversity and Ecosystem Conservation (BBEC) program was introduced to educate communities about the value of biodiversity and ecosystems and the importance of conserving them (Maryati, Suleiman, & Hashimoto, 2006). The implementation phase was based on a top-down approach and designed to achieve specific conservation outcomes for the TWR. Funding for the program came from a consortium comprising the Malaysian government and the Japanese International Cooperation Agency (JICA). An associated aim of the project was to fund a nature-tourism project to provide employment and encourage community members to give up traditional activities such as poaching and hunting. As one of its objectives the program funded the establishment of a home-stay style tourism venture in Kampong Dagat and employed external professional staff from Sabah Wildlife Department for a five-year period (2002−2007) to undertake training of community members in management and marketing. External professional staff were employed to manage the project. During this period the main target market was Japan with guests usually traveling in groups, staying for 3−4 nights in local family houses that had been refurbished with program funding to bring them up to a standard suitable for foreign visitors. Activities offered included cultural shows, fishing expeditions, wildlife viewing, and handicraft making. The product that was offered differed considerably from that offered by the Tabin Wildlife Lodge, a commercial venture located in the TWR that focuses specifically on wildlife viewing experiences. The Tabin Wildlife Lodge can be described as a high-end ecotourism product that offers accommodation in detached units set in the forest and connected by an elevated walkway to a central dining and recreation area. The Lodge has developed a tourism product that aims at a different segment to that which the CBET product was designed for.

During the five years that the project was externally funded the community experienced a significant improvement in their standard of living. The major selling point of the project was the opportunity to experience local culture in a "kampong lifestyle." During each year of the project more than 2,000 Japanese tourists visited the community generating sufficient income for the families involved to enable them to meet their monthly cost of food. When operating at capacity the project employed a significant number of community members as drivers, cooks, gardeners, housekeepers, and in a few instances in managerial roles such as temporary wildlife rangers (game wardens) managing the forest around the villages.

At the conclusion of the project in 2007 responsibility for managing the project was handed over to the community and funding for marketing previously provided by the consortium was withdrawn. The withdrawal of funding for professional managers in particular created a major crisis for the project in part because of inadequate training of the community to run a project of this nature and their lack of knowledge of the global tourism market where their product was sold. As a consequence the community was unable to continue funding promotional activities leading to a steep decline in visitors to an average of 100–200 per year by 2010 when this research was undertaken. Income to the community and the individuals involved rapidly declined, most tourism-related jobs were lost, and the number of homestays supporting the enterprise fell by three quarters. The loss of income from tourism led to many community members opting to return to traditional fishing activities and in some cases poaching and illegal hunting in an attempt to make up for the lost income.

RESULTS

Results are presented in two parts, the first of which reports on the verbal responses made by members of the community during stage three. Results of the community survey undertaken in stage four are then reported. During stage three informal conversations were held with 15 senior community members over an extended period of time and recorded in a field diary. Informants were advised that they would not be mentioned by name in any subsequent reporting to preserve confidentially.

Most respondents reported a decline in poaching during the period that the tourism venture was supported by external funding. Respondents generally understood animals were a major tourism draw card and needed to be protected to continue attracting tourists. This view was common throughout the kampongs. Respondents also commented that tourism provided them with an income that allowed them to purchase food from commercial outlets. Not all families participated in the tourism venture particularly those from Kampong Dagat whose main livelihood was based on fishing. Some respondents reported that they could not see how giving up fishing to work in a tourism business would generate sufficient income to feed their families which in some cases had up to 14 children.

As income from the tourism venture declined many respondents felt pressured to resume hunting. While aware of the damage caused by poaching and expressing regret that this situation existed, most respondents reported they felt they had little alternative but to resume poaching. As informant A observed *"the community is badly educated — it's just because the life is hard and the prices of things are high."* While conscious of the adverse impacts of poaching respondents expressed a fear that if they failed to take advantage of the resources in the present they will miss out because others will take all the available animals. This is aggravated by illegal hunting by people outside of the community who, as respondent B stated, *"don't care"* about the future as they will move on when the resource is finished. This was a common view amongst all respondents. As respondent E noted *"Every month, there's always sound of gunshots heard in TWR with findings of animal traps and snares in the reserve. However, it is not sure whether the poaching done by community alone or by other people who lived outside the reserve. Nevertheless, the hunting amongst community always occurred during festival seasons such as the Hari Raya Festival."* Based on the results of the interviews it was apparent that hunting is most prevalent amongst older community members however young men may be also asked to participate in hunting for special occasions such as weddings and the Hari Raya festival.

Because of the problems faced by the tourism business, many community members discouraged their children from continuing to work and train for tourism-related activities believing that further training was a waste of time and resources and unlikely to solve their economic problems. Nevertheless, the community continued to play an active role in many wildlife and forest conservation programs within the adjacent reserve, possibly because this was one of the few sources of paid work available to them. The communities also encouraged their teenagers who had finished school but have not found employment to participate in wildlife protection courses. By 2010, about 20 young school leavers have been awarded a wildlife protection ranger badge in part for their help as volunteers in monitoring wildlife species vulnerable to poaching. As some participants observed, this did cause some problems particularly when the younger members of the community were directed by the elders to hunt for big community occasions.

Interviews with community members indicated that species of particular value were wild boar (for meat), sun bear (for many products, but particularly gall bladder and paws), Bornean pygmy elephant (tusk), and the Sumatran rhinoceros (for its horn). The results also revealed that some wildlife species such as deer and wild boar and to a lesser extent pangolin was used for household consumption.

Many respondents expressed an opinion that the competition for resources has resulted in *"everyone going to the forest"* (respondent C) and *"using it in a 'disorderly' way"* (respondent H) (i.e., in a careless or disrespectful way), which they realized was not sustainable in the long term. It was explained by respondent M that *"in the forest there are long trees and short trees,"* that is, that everyone is different, and uses nature in different ways and for different purposes. The discussions revealed that while some families were almost completely reliant on natural resources for survival, for most the forest provides a supplementary food source and for a small number of respondents it was seen as a hobby that provided extra money. Discussions with community members indicated that where hunting was for cash it often occurred in response to orders from outsiders for specific products such as exotic meats (i.e., pangolins).

Most respondents expressed empathy with nature, despite the fact that they might also be using it in a disrespectful or destructive way; that is taking animals for purposes other than food, such as the Chinese medicine sector or for pets. However, while aware of the impacts they could not see a workable way out of the problem. Having a market value for exotic animals has clearly affected how people use the resource. Most respondents were aware that natural resources such as animals are important for their livelihoods but were being poached at a rate that is not sustainable in the long term.

The fourth stage consisted of a short verbally administrated questionnaire. The heads of families were specifically targeted because they are able to speak for the family and the community. If the head of the family was not available the wife or the eldest child aged 18 years old and above was asked to complete survey. Participants were asked to respond to a series of eight key statements related to their views on poaching, hunting, and involvement in tourism by describing the current situation in their community. A five-point Likert scale was used. Because of community sensitivities the only sociodemographic data collected was gender. Results are shown visually in the spider-web configuration in Fig. 2. The eight key statements of the survey are:

1. Became a poacher to earn extra money
2. Became a poacher to obtain food for my family
3. I am willing to give up poaching for a successful tourism business
4. I am actively involvement in tourism development
5. I encourage other members of the community to become involved in tourism

Level of Participation

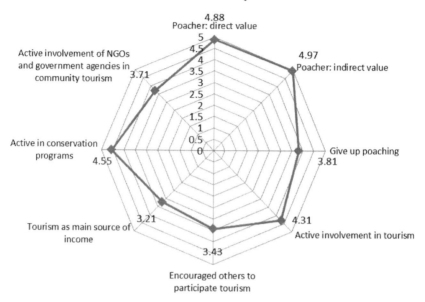

Fig. 2. Community Participation in Poaching and Wildlife-Forest Resources Conservation for Tourism Development.

6. I see tourism as the main source of my income
7. I actively participate in wildlife and forest conservation programs
8. I am actively involved in NGOs and government agencies supporting tourism development in the community.

The aim of statements 1 and 2 was to determine the level of support for poaching and why it was participated in. The aim of statements 3–8 was to test the level of support for continuing involvement in tourism including training and other tourism-related aid given by NGOs. Because a number of participants had poor literacy the principle investigator completed all surveys on behalf of the respondents. The survey was completed by 185 including 89 males and 96 females.

Table 2 shows the responses to the eight statements about views on poaching, conservation, and tourism. Responses indicate that the importance of hunting for personal consumption (mean = 4.9) is very high, as is hunting for on-sale (mean = 4.9). The statement "see tourism as a main source of income" recorded the lowest mean, a reflection of the significant

Table 2. Distributions of Mean of Indicators of Community Participation in Tourism Development.

Indicators	N	Mean (Max = 5)
1. Become poacher to earn money	185	4.9
2. Become poacher to obtain food for my family	185	4.9
3. I am willing to give up poaching for a successful tourism business	185	3.8
4. I was actively involved in tourism development	185	4.3
5. I encouraged other members of the community to become involved in the tourism business	185	3.4
6. I see tourism as the main source of my income	185	3.2
7. I actively participate in wildlife and forest conservation programs	185	4.6
8. I am actively involved with NGOs and government agencies supporting tourism development in the community	185	3.7

decline in tourism by the time the research was undertaken. At the time the survey was conducted, there were less than 100 visitors per year. Some of the remaining tourists were supported by the SOS Rhino Borneo Bhd, a nonprofit organization that works for the conservation and preservation of Borneo Sumatran rhinoceros in the TWR.

Results from statements 1 (Became a poacher to earn extra money) and 2 (Become poacher to obtain food for my family) show that while many respondents claim to have actively participated in wildlife and forest conservation programs (see statements 7 and 8) including working as wildlife rangers with Sabah Wildlife Department and rhino protection rangers with the SOS Rhino Borneo Bhd, most continued to be involved in poaching activities. The responses to key statements 1 (Became a poacher to earn extra money) and 2 (Become poacher to obtain food for my family) indicate the main reasons for continued involvement in poaching. Interestingly, the response to statement 3 (I am willing to give up poaching for a successful tourism business) does indicate a willingness to give up poaching if tourism is able to provide a better level of income.

The Tidong community gave the lowest rating (mean = 3.2) to making the tourism industry their main source of income. The reason for this response has to do with the failure of the tourism project, remoteness of the community, and the difficulty this causes for tourists seeking to visit that part of reserve for wildlife viewing. In addition to remoteness the community also has to compete for tourists with a commercial lodge that has been established within the reserve in a location that is more accessible.

Results appear contradictory in that respondents show a high level of support for conservation (statement 3 results) but are also actively involved in hunting. This situation is the result of several cultural and economic factors. At the time of the survey the village was suffering an economic crisis as a result of the fall in tourism income. When tourism income was high, village elders supported tourism and a reduction in poaching based on an understanding that live animals were a valuable tourism resource. When tourism income fell the village elders were confronted with a shortfall in income that was in part overcome by hunting and working for NGOs and the government. While working for conservation agencies and poaching appears contradictory it was, in the mind of the village elders, the only solution to providing adequate income for the community which in their view as their primary responsibility. For example, Respondent D stated *"Without money from tourism we had to go back to the forest to hunt even though we did not really want to."*

Fig. 2 shows the level of participation of the Tidong community in terms of tourism, participation in conservation, and poaching activity. Results appear as a spider's web configuration and illustrate how each variable is interconnected with other variables. These results, together with the responses given during the interviews with community members, indicate a strong relationship between the success of tourism and the propensity for poaching. Given that the community has few other sources of income the removal of one income source (in this case tourism) will force community members to look for alternative income sources. Another factor that needs to be considered is that prior to the establishment of the TWR the community had a long tradition of hunting to supplement fishing and farming as the community's major food source. In effect the declaration of the TWR overturned a century's long tradition of using areas such as this for traditional hunting.

DISCUSSION

The aim of this paper was to investigate how tourism may be used as a tool for reducing illegal hunting activity including poaching. The Tidong community is an example of a community that has yet to see permanent long-term benefits accruing from conservation in terms of improved personal and community income. They were willing to support tourism and curb hunting because they were able to see the benefits it provided, however when their tourism business faltered they were quite willing to return to hunting. This contradictory view of hunting can also be seen in the manner that the Kampong elders encouraged the young generation to work for NGOs or government agencies if there is an opportunity for them to receive income, but continued to request them to hunt particularly for ceremonial occasions.

It is difficult for traditional peoples such as the Tidong community to resist pressures to engage in illegal hunting particularly when food is required for consumption and occasionally for ceremonial purposes and where there is a commercial market willing to pay for poached animal products. The findings of this research show that when CBET projects are able to generate viable alternative incomes, communities have an incentive to place the environment above alternatives such as poaching. In effect tourism is able to create a different form of value to that created by poaching. The value created by tourism is ongoing with animals producing income over a long period of time. Illegal hunting however produces only short-term returns for once the animal is gone income ceases. The question of value and its definition is therefore important and one that has not been explored in the literature. Findings from this research indicate that strategies based on the concept of value may be a useful tool in demonstrating to target communities the benefits of conservation of animals versus their hunting.

Analysis of the project and its outcomes illustrates many of the factors that can cause a CBET to fail including:

- The period of support by sponsoring organizations was not sufficient to train the community to a standard where they were able to deal with the global tourism supply chain at a level that gave the project a capacity to achieve long-term economic sustainability. This is not surprising as the transition from an inward focused community that lived a semi-subsistence lifestyle to a community that had the capacity to engage with the global supply chain can be difficult.
- Training to enable the community to develop appropriate managerial capacity was inadequate. Previous research (Salazar, 2012; West, 2006) has identified similar failings in other projects leading to the view that this must be a key criteria for success in future projects of this type.
- The single market approach, in this case based on Japan, lacked wisdom given the propensity for markets to make rapid changes in the style of

product desired. Without sufficient training of the type discussed above this problem can be expected to be one that will be faced by other CBET projects where sponsors show a bias towards marketing to either a specific country or consumer segment.

- The exit strategy was time and budget based. A more appropriate strategy would be to base the exit strategy on the demonstrated capacity of the community to continue the project on a long-term commercial basis. The issue of exit strategies has been raised previously (Manyara & Jones, 2007; Salazar, 2012) and for some NGOs may be a matter of concern particularly when donors have expectations of outcomes within a timeframe that was negotiated prior to the realities of the on-ground situation becoming evident and where there are other worthwhile projects in the funding pipeline. From the perspective of the literature (Kiss, 2004), this is a further example of conflicting objectives between the aid organization and the local community. The top-down project administration and governance approach adopted by the project sponsors, while administratively efficient, may be less effective in the long run if target communities become alienated with the process.

- It is difficult to overturn centuries of tradition in a relatively short period of time. In the case of the Tidong community the use of certain types of meat at community special events is based on hunter gatherers traditions that in a sense define the community and the way in which it sees the world. Redefining traditions is a slow process that in some cases even legislative prohibitions are unable to overturn. This observation parallels the work by Manyara and Jones (2007) who identified issues that may occur when "outsiders" either overtly or inadvertently project their own views of society and the need for conservation on local communities.

- Unless a CBET project is able to demonstrate that the economic benefits of tourism provide a superior and sustainable standard of living over the long term it is difficult to overcome resistance to change both at the individual and community levels. In a sense CBET projects of this nature introduce a high level of rapid innovation-based change into the community and as previous experience has shown, it is difficult for some sectors of communities to accept change despite demonstrated benefits (Mendoza-Ramos & Prideaux, 2014). This finding also supports Honey's (2008) earlier discussion on the need to consider social as well as ecological aspects of CBET projects.

- One important finding of this research is the value of animals to the local community. The direct value of the animals at a particular point in time and the economic conditions prevalent at that time is important. When the tourism business was viable, the community was able to see that live animals produced far greater income than poached animals and poaching declined. Once the contribution of tourism fell the value of the animals to those who were no longer able to derive income from tourism was greater as a food source or a sellable commodity than as a live animal.

Many of these observations parallel those suggested by Snyman (2014) in relation to CBET.

CONCLUSION

The Tidong community is an example of how a community outreach approach to conservation based on wildlife focused (CBET) tourism business can successfully integrate conservation and development objectives so that each could be promoted without detriment apparently supporting earlier work by de Haas (2002) and Vincent and Thompson (2002). However, the Tidong community also provides a warning of what can go wrong when aid agencies leave too early and the community is unable to maintain the tourism enterprise that was gifted to them. It is apparent that the assisted community was willing to give up hunting and poaching when other sources of income became available but despite understanding that heavy hunting and poaching is not sustainable, were prepared to resume these activities when income from the tourism business declined. It is apparent that for hunting and poaching to cease the income earned from tourism must be sustainable over the long term. If the income stream is reduced, as in the case of the Tidong community, many community members will revert to hunting and poaching to supplement their daily food requirements. The warning that the findings highlight is central to many of the debates about aid: to what extent is success dependent on the successful matching of the objectives of aid givers with those of the receivers of aid?

In CBET projects that specifically target problems related to illegal hunting it is apparent that for past hunting practices to change, tourism must generate an acceptable level of income over the long term. This points to the need for NGOs and other aid agencies to accept the need for long-term monitoring of the viability of CBET businesses they assisted and the realization that further assistance may be required in the future if conservation gains are not to be lost.

It is also apparent that it may be difficult to change long-term cultural practices based on hunting. Education is one strategy but as the previous discussion highlights, it is difficult for young community members to defy direction given by community elders even where they are employed to prevent the poaching practices they may be directed to engage in. This observation also highlights the futility of banning traditional hunting activity by declaring them to be illegal without providing alternative income sources. As with any community that is asked to radically change traditional lifestyles the outcome of change must be seen by those asked to change to be better than the lifestyle they had prior to the change.

ACKNOWLEDGMENTS

This study was financially supported by Universiti Malaysia Sabah through *Skim Bantuan Penyelidikkan Universiti Malaysia Sabah* and partially funded by SOS Rhino (Borneo) Bhd., presently known as Borneo Rhino Alliances (BORA). We are grateful to the people of Tidong community and staff of BORA for their wonderful hospitality during this study.

REFERENCES

Adams, W. M., & Hulme, D. (2001). If community conservation is the answer, what is the question? *Oryx*, *35*(3), 193–200.

Alfred, R., Abdul Hamid, A., Payne, J., Williams, C., & Ambu, L. (2010). Density and population estimation of the Bornean elephants (*Elephas maximus borneensis*) in Sabah. *Journal of Biological Sciences*, *10*(2), 92–102.

Ament, R., Clevenger, A. P., Yu, O., & Hardy, A. (2008). An assessment of road impacts on wildlife population in U.S. national parks. *Environmental Management*, *42*(3), 480–496.

Ancrenaz, M., Calaque, R., & Lackman-Ancrenaz, I. (2004). Orang-utan (*Pongo pygmaeus*) nesting behavior in disturbed forest (Sabah, Malaysia): Implications for nest census. *International Journal of Primatology*, *25*(5), 983–1000.

Aryal, R. S. (2002). Wildlife trade in Nepal. *Environment*, *7*(8), 1–5.

Auzel, P., & Wilkie, D. S. (2000). Wildlife use in northern Congo: Hunting in a commercial logging concession. In J. G. Robinson & E. L. Bennett (Eds.), *Hunting for sustainability in tropical forests* (pp. 413–426). New York, NY: Columbia University Press.

Bennett, E. L., Milner-Gulland, E. J., Bakarr, M., Eves, H. E., Robinson, J. G., & Wilkie, D. S. (2002). Hunting the world's wildlife to extinction. *Oryx*, *36*, 328–329.

Bennett, E. L., & Robinson, J. G. (2000). *Hunting of wildlife in tropical forests. Implications for biodiversity and forest peoples*. Washington, DC: The World Bank.

Bennett, E. L., Nyaoi, A. J., & Sompud, J. (1999). Saving Borneo's bacon: The sustainability of hunting in Sarawak and Sabah. In J. Robinson & E. L. Bennett (Eds.), *Hunting for sustainability in tropical forests* (pp. 305–324). New York, NY: Columbia University Press.

Bernard, M., Husson, S., Page, S. E., & Rieley, J. O. (2003). Population status of the Bornean orang-utan (Pongo pygmaeus) in the Sebangau peat swamp forest, Central Kalimantan, Indonesia. *Biological Conservation, 110*, 141–152.

Bosi, E. J. (2003). Report on the Sumatran rhino survey. In M. Maryati, M. Andau, & M. Schithuizen (Eds.), *Tabin limestone scientific expedition 2000* (pp. 145–148). Kota Kinabalu: Universiti Malaysia Sabah.

Broad, S., Mulliken, T., & Roe, D. (2003). The nature and extent of legal and illegal trade in wildlife. In S. Oldfield (Ed.), *The trade in wildlife. Regulation for conservation. Flora and fauna international* (pp. 3–22). London: Earthscan.

Buckland, H. (2005). *The oil for ape scandal.* London: Friends of the Earth.

Bulte, E., & Horan, R. (2003). Habitat conservation, wildlife extraction and agricultural expansion. *Journal of Environmental Economics and Management, 45*, 109–127.

Burns, P. M., & Barrie, S. (2009). Race, space and 'our own piece of Africa': Doing good in Luphisi village? *Journal of Sustainable Tourism, 13*(5), 468–485.

Butcher, J. (2007). *Ecotourism, NGOs and development.* London: Routledge.

Cottrell, S. P., Vaske, J. J., Shen, F., & Ritter, P. (2007). Resident perceptions of sustainable tourism in Chongdugou, China. *Society and Natural Resources, 20*(6), 511–525.

Davies, G., Heydon, M., Leader-Williams, N., MacKinnon, J., & Newing, H. (2001). The effects of logging on tropical forest ungulates. In R. A. Fimbel, A. Grajal, & J. G. Robinson (Eds.), *The cutting edge: Conserving wildlife in logged tropical forest.* New York, NY: Columbia University Press.

de Haas, H. (2002). Sustainability of small-scale ecotourism: The case of Niue, South Pacific. *Current Issues in Tourism, 5*(3&4), 319–337.

Dixon, J. A., & Sherman, P. B. (1990). *Economics of protected areas: A new look at benefits and costs.* London: Earthscan.

Eliason, S. L. (2003). Illegal hunting and angling: The neutralization of wildlife law violations. *Society and Animals, 11*, 3.

Ellis, R. (2005). *Tiger bone and rhino horn: The destruction of wildlife for traditional Chinese medicine.* Washington, DC: Island Press/Shearwater Books.

Erb, M. (2005). Limiting tourism and the limits of tourism: The production and consumption of tourist attractions in Western Flores. In C. Ryan & M. E. Aicken (Eds.), *Indigenous tourism: The commodification and management of culture* (pp. 155–180). Oxford: Elsevier.

Eyler, A. A., Mayer, J., Rafi, R., Housemann, R., Brownson, R. C., & King, A. C. (1999). Key informant surveys as a tool to implement and evaluate physical activity interventions in the community. *Health Education Research, 14*(2), 289.

Ferraro, P., & Kiss, A. (2002). Direct payments to conserve biodiversity. *Science, 298*, 1718–1719.

Fischer, C. (2010). Does trade help or hinder the conservation of natural resources? *Review of Environmental Economics and Policy, Winter 2010, 4*(1), 103–121.

Gibson, C. C., & Marks, S. A. (1995). Transforming rural hunters into conservationists: An assessment of community-based wildlife management programs in Africa. *World Development, 23*, 941–957.

Goodwin, H. (2002). Local Community involvement in tourism around national parks: opportunities and constraints. *Current Issues in Tourism, 5*(3&4), 338–360.

Harrison, D. (2010). Tourism and development: Looking back and looking ahead – More of the same? In D. G. Pearce & R. W. Butler (Eds.), *Tourism research: A 20–20 vision* (pp. 40–52). Oxford: Goodfellow Publishing.

Honey, M. (2008). *Ecotourism and sustainable development: Who owns paradise?* Washington, DC: Island Press.

Kaltenborn, B. P., Nyahongo, J. W., & Tingstad, K. M. (2005). The nature of hunting around the western corridor of Serengeti national park, Tanzania. *European Journal of Wildlife Research, 51*(4), 213–222.

Kinnaird, M. F., Sanderson, E. W., O'Brien, T. G., Wibisono, H. T., & Woolmer, G. (2003). Deforestation trends in a tropical landscape and implications for endangered large mammals. *Conservation Biology, 17*, 245–257.

Kiss, A. (2004). Is community-based ecotourism a good use of biodiversity conservation funds? *TREE, 19*, 232–237.

Kontogeorgopoulos, N. (2005). *Community-based ecotourism in Phuket and Ao phangnga.* Thailand: Partial Victories and Bittersweet Remedies. *Journal of Sustainable Tourism, 13*(1), 4–23.

Krupnich, G., & Kress, W. (2003). Hotspots and ecoregions: A test of conservation priorities using taxonomic data. *Biodiversity and Conservation, 12*, 2237–2253.

Leader-Williams, N., & Milner-Gulland, E. J. (1993). Policies and enforcement of wildlife laws: The balance between detection and penalties in Luangwa Valley, Zambia. *Conservation Biology, 7*, 611–617.

Lele, S., Wilshusen, P., Brockington, D., Seidler, R., & Bawa, K. (2010). Beyond exclusion: Alternative approaches to biodiversity conservation in the developing tropics. *Current Opinion in Environmental Sustainability, 2*, 94–100.

Linkie, M., Martyr, D. J., Holden, J., Yanuar, A., Hartana, A. T., Sugardjito, J., & Leader Williams, N. (2003). Habitat destruction and poaching threaten the Sumatran tiger in Kerinci Seblat national park, Sumatra. *Oryx, 37*, 41–48.

Magige, F. J., Holmern, T., Stokke, S., Mlingwa, C., & Røskaft, E. (2008). Does illegal hunting affect density and behavior of African grassland birds? A case study on ostrich (*Struthio camelus*). *Biodiversity and Conservation, 18*(5), 1361–1373.

Majail, J. (1996). *Cooperating with local communities on conservation, proposal & recommendations.* Unpublished. Sabah Biodiversity Conservation Project, Malaysia. Ministry of Tourism & Environmental Development, Sabah/DANCED.

Manyara, G., & Jones, E. (2007). Community-based tourism enterprises development in Kenya: An exploration of their potential as avenues of poverty reduction. *Journal of Sustainable Tourism, 15*(6), 628–664.

Maryati, M., Suleiman, M., & Hashimoto, T. (2006). Biodiversity and Conservation: Research for science and people: Proceeding of Research Seminar at the Institute for Tropical Biology and Conservation BBEC Publication No. 55. Universiti Malaysia Sabah. (p. 178).

Matarrita-Cascante, D., Brennan, M. A., & Luloff, A. E. (2010). Community agency and sustainable tourism development: The case of La Fortuna, Costa Rica. *Journal of Sustainable Tourism, 18*(6), 735–756.

Mehta, J. N., & Heinen, J. T. (2001). Does community-based conservation shape favorable attitudes among locals? An empirical study from Nepal. *Environmental Management, 28*(2), 165–177.

Meijaard, E., Sheil, D., Rosenbaum, B., Iskandar, D., Augeri, D., Setyawati, T., ... O'Brien, T. (2005). *Life after logging: Reconciling wildlife conservation and production forestry in Indonesian Borneo.* Bogor: CIFOR, WCS and UNESCO.

Mendoza-Ramos, A., & Prideaux, B. (2014). Indigenous ecotourism in the Mayan rainforest of Palenque: Empowerment issues in sustainable development. *Journal of Sustainable Tourism, 22*(3), 461–479.

Messer, K. (2000). The poacher's dilemma: The economics of poaching and enforcement. *Endangered Species Update*, 7(3), 50–56.

Mittermeier, R. (2010). Foreword. In T. Nadler, B. Rawson, & V. N. Thinh (Eds.), *Conservation of primates in Indochina, Frankfurt zoological society – Vietnam primate conservation program*. Hanoi: Frankfurt Zoological Society.

Moyle, B. (2003). Regulation, conservation, and incentives. In S. Oldfield (Ed.), *The trade in wildlife. Regulation for conservation. Flora and fauna international* (pp. 41–51). London: Earthscan.

Myers, N., Mittermeier, R., Mittermeier, G., Da Fonseca, G., & Kent, J. (2000). Biodiversity hotspots for conservation priorities. *Nature*, *403*, 853–858.

Nijman, V. (2005). *Hanging in the balance: An assessment of trade in Orang-utans and Gibbons in Kalimantan*. Indonesia: TRAFFIC Southeast Asia.

Noraini, N. (2005). *Tabin wildlife reserve: A potential nature tourism site. Institute for tropical biology and conservation*. M.Sc. Thesis. Universiti Malaysia Sabah.

Redford, K. H. (1992). The empty forest. *BioScience*, *42*, 412–422.

Robertson, J. M. Y., & van Schaik, C. P. (2001). Causal factors underlying the dramatic decline of the Sumatran orang-utan. *Oryx*, *35*, 26–38.

Rodrigues, C., & Prideaux, B. (2012). Backpacker tourism in the Brazilian amazon: Challenges and opportunities. In G. Lohmann & D. Dredge (Eds.), *Tourism in Brazil environment, management and segments* (pp. 123–140). Oxon: Routledge.

Saarinen, J. (2006). Traditions of sustainability in tourism studies. *Annals of Tourism Research*, *33*, 1121–1140.

Sabah Tourism Board. (2014). *Tourism statistics*. Retrieved from http://www.sabahtourism.com/business/statistic. Accessed on June 10, 2014.

Sakata, H., & Prideaux, B. (2012). An alternative approach to community-based ecotourism: A bottom-up locally initiated non-monetised project in Papua New Guinea. *Journal of Sustainable Tourism*, *21*(6), 880–899.

Salazar, N. (2012). Community-based cultural tourism: Issues, threats and opportunities. *Journal of Sustainable Tourism*, *20*(1), 9–22.

Sekhar, N. U. (2003). Local people's attitude towards conservation and wildlife tourism around Sariska tiger reserve, India. *Journal of Environmental Management*, *69*, 339–347.

Snyman, S. (2014). Partnership between a private sector ecotourism operator and a local community in the Okavango Delta, Botswana: The case of the Okavango community trust and wilderness safaris. *Journal of Ecotourism*, *13*(2–3), 110–127.

Stronza, A., & Gordillo, J. (2008). Community views of ecotourism: Redefining benefits. *Annals of Tourism Research*, *5*(2), 444–468.

Timothy, D., & White, K. (1999). Community-based ecotourism development on the periphery of Belize. *Current Issues in Tourism*, *2*(2), 226–242.

Tosun, C. (2006). Expected nature of community participation in tourism development. *Tourism Management*, *27*, 493–504.

Trombulack, S. C., & Frissell, C. A. (2000). Review of ecological effects of roads on terrestrial and aquatic communities. *Conservation Biology*, *14*, 18–30.

Vincent, V., & Thompson, W. (2002). Assessing community support and sustainability for ecotourism development. *Journal of Travel Research*, *41*(2), 153–160.

Von Kroff, M., Wickizer, T., Maeser, J., O'Leary, P., Pearson, D., & Beery, W. (1992). Community activation and health promotion: Identification of key organizations. *American Journal of Health Promotion*, *7*, 110–117.

Walker, S., Brower, A. L., Stephens, R. T. T., & Lee, W. G. (2009). Why bartering biodiversity fails. Conservation letters. *Journal of the Society for Conservation Biology, 2*, 149–157.

Wallace, G. N. (1993). Wildlands and ecotourism in Latin America. *Journal of Forestry, 91*(2), 37–40.

Walter, P., & Regmi, K. D. (2016). Conceptualising host learning in community-based ecotourism. *Journal of Ecotourism, 15*(1), 51–63.

Wang, Y. (2010). *Reducing the amount of poaching in Asia.* DIMUN Research Report. Dulwich College, Shunyi, Beijing.

Wearing, S., McDonald, M., & Ponting, J. (2005). Building a decommodified research paradigm in tourism: The contribution of NGOs. *Journal of Sustainable Tourism, 13*(5), 424–439.

West, P. (2006). *Conservation is our government now: The politics of ecology in Papua New Guinea.* London: Duke University Press.

Wyler, L. S., & Sheikh, P. A. (2008). *International illegal trade in wildlife.* Hauppauge: Nova Science Publishers.

Yasuma, S., & Andau, M. (2000). *Mammals of Sabah: Habitat and ecology.* Kota Kinabalu: Japan International Co-operation Agency (JICA) and Sabah Wildlife Department. Ministry of Tourism Development, Environment, Science and Technology, Malaysia.

INDUSTRIAL AGGLOMERATION MODEL IN CULTURE TOURISM SYSTEM: EMPIRICAL STUDY IN MAINLAND CHINA

Chunyu Yang and Jue Huang

ABSTRACT

Spatial integration and industrial clustering have become an important feature of the culture tourism business. When the core elements in both the culture industry and tourism industry are integrated, a model based on system science is constructed that combines the resources and capacity of the two entities to envisage the ways of creating integrated products and services from the two sectors. Guided by the system science, this study proposes a culture tourism system revealing the clustering and hierarchical structure of the industrial elements. The system contains two subsystems: internal system and external system. The agglomeration model of the system includes 26 indices and the PEF methods, which involved the Parallelogram Law, Entropy-weight Method, and Fuzzy Membership Function. Finally, this study deploys an empirical study involving all provincial territories (N = 31) in mainland China. It analyzes the variability and degree of balanced development of the system.

Advances in Hospitality and Leisure, Volume 12, 145–165
ISSN: 1745-3542/doi:10.1108/S1745-354220160000012007

In addition, through the resultant data this research adds a typology of culture tourism system along with policy recommendations.

Keywords: Culture tourism; industrial agglomeration model; system science

INTRODUCTION

In recent years, China has witnessed an increasing prominence of the culture and tourism industry, both of which have been regarded as the pillar business of national economy. Due to the inherent interconnection between the two industries, a hybrid between the two has given rise to the development of culture tourism industry across the country and the central and local governments have invested heavily in numerous culture parks. However, not all of the endeavors come to fruition and it is imperative to examine the dynamics that underlie the development of the culture tourism industry. This study presents a model for the culture tourism that is embedded in a systems approach as the identification of advancing and blocking mechanisms within the system could provide insights for specifying key policy issues.

The coupled development and spatial concentration of the culture and tourism industries have attracted broad attention from scholars. In the earlier days, researchers examined this topic mainly from an economic perspective, focusing on the production, consumption, and business opportunities of the culture tourism products (McKercher, Ho, & du Cros, 2005; Richards, 1996; Silberberg, 1995). Currently, the research focus has shifted toward the authenticity of tourist experience, tourist gaze, and the reproduction of culture tourism (Richards & Wilson, 2006; Theopisti, 2011; Tufts & Milne, 1999). However, researchers in China tend to pay more attention to other topics, such as the coupling relations between the culture and the tourism industries, quantitative modeling of industrial clustering (Bao & Wang, 2010; Liu & Yang, 2011; Wei, 2011; Yin & Lu, 2009; Zhang & Zhu, 2012), and construction of performance evaluation indices (Liu & Yang, 2013; Ma & Chen, 2012; Zhang & Wang, 2010; Zhang, Wang, & Tian, 2010). This stream of research has a strong interest in public policy intervention to promote the clustering of the culture and tourism industries. In general, in China research on culture tourism stays mainly at the exploratory stage of modeling industrial agglomeration and constructing evaluation indices. Investigation of the components of culture tourism industry from a system theory perspective, as well as the dynamic mechanism for industrial development, has so far received limited attention. In reality, the agglomeration and clustering of culture and tourism industries are not a simple addition of two sectors. Instead, a hierarchical and multifactor system should emerge through the integration of critical determinants of both industries, suggesting the paths of creating new products and services relevant to both sectors.

Gaines (1979) viewed constructing system as a way to delineating the possible casual phenomenon among interrelated factors of interest. The coupling relation among elements within a system provides the dynamic to the evolution of the system (Yang, 2010). Although the system approach is a useful tool in building agglomeration and clustering of the tourism business, only a handful of studies deal with system framework construction (Ding & Chen, 2002; Guo, 2008; Guo & Yang, 2012; Hjalager, 2009; Leiper, 1990; Mattsson, Sundbo, & Fussing-Jensen, 2005; Song, Ji, Lv, & Li, 2012; Sundbo & Gallouj, 2000; Zhang & Liu, 2007).

Aims of Study

From a review of tourism literature, as part of the present study found that till date there is no empirical study examining both tourism and culture systems collectively by using a system modeling. Supplying the above deficiency, this study intends to utilize a system model to build an analytical framework with respect to culture tourism in China. Subsequently, this study proposes a sectoral system based on the clustering of both culture and tourism industries. In sum, it presents a clustering model of the culture tourism industry and its measurement on a basis of the dynamic mechanism of system. Finally, this study tests the proposed model by using empirical data from all 31 provincial territories in China.

A Proposed Model of Culture Tourism System

Based on the system approach (Laszlo & Krippner, 1998), this study constructs a culture tourism system that entails the internal and external system. The internal system entails the basic endowment of the culture tourism industry (e.g., resources, capability, and actors) and plays a fundamental role in fostering the development of the industry. It contains four subsystems, including (1) magnitude of resources, (2) characteristic of actors, (3) financial strengths, and (4) level of innovativeness. The external

system consists of external conditions (e.g., policy and market environment) that would influence the development of the culture tourism system.
It includes factors that could either boost or impede the development of the
system, and contains the following four main external forces: (1) policy
environments, (2) knowledge sharing, (3) market environments, and
(4) openness to the outside world (see Fig. 1).

Interaction among the elements of the system originates from consumer
demand and the resulting exchange of resources, energy, and information
both within the system and with the outside world. During the process, the
coupling relationship among the components of the system exists generally
in the form of forces between elements as well as between subsystems.
Moreover, the coupling relationship is constantly changing and the outcomes of the initial adaptive process become the causes for the next round
of adaptive process. Thus, it forms a circular causality and dynamic

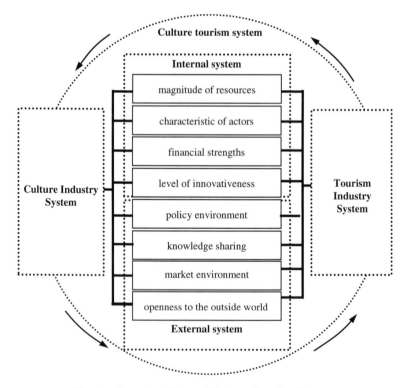

Fig. 1. Structure Chart of Culture Tourism System.

network and manifests itself as a steady structural pattern within certain temporal, spatial, and configuration scope. Namely, a new structural format — the culture tourism industry cluster — is constructed, which differentiates itself from other systems and the environment. As it should be, the confining and external forces contend with each other due to the coupling relationship among the elements of the system. However, their role is not to petrify the system, but rather to endow it with rules or order in its movement and evolution. Table 1 and Fig. 2 reveal the dynamic situations of the system.

INDEX AND METRIC CONSTRUCTION FOR A CULTURE TOURISM INDUSTRY CLUSTER

Index Construction

Drawing on the work of Wu, Fang, and Zhao (2011) concerning general industrial agglomeration model and previous studies on culture tourism industry evaluation index (Han, Tao, & Xiao, 2012; Song & Li Qiu, 2011; Wang & Huang, 2010; Wu, Fang, & Zhao, 2010; Wu & Song, 2011), a preliminary hierarchical index is proposed for the measurement of the agglomeration of the culture tourism system. It takes into account the content, structure, and function of the system. Then, two rounds of expert panel reviews were conducted to evaluate the content validity of the indices. Unimportant and inappropriate items were deleted accordingly. Finally, the index was amended based on the entropy-weight method and is discussed in the following section. The final index was composed of 1 overall system, 2 second-order systems, 8 third-order systems, and 26 indices (see Table 2).

Methodology for Model Construction

The current study developed a model deriving from the methods of parallelogram law, entropy-weight method, and fuzzy membership function (PEF) to provide a metric for the culture tourism industry clustering. The model measures the dynamic mechanism of culture and tourism industrial clusters. The following briefly introduces each of the methods, and then the

Table 1. The Dynamic Situation Analysis Table of Culture Tourism System.

	Stage of the Culture Tourism System	Resultant Force: F	Quadrant of the External Force, F_R	Status of the Component Forces	Situation Analysis	Notes
Model 1	Growth stage	$F = OR + OI$	Quadrant I	$F_k > 0$ $F_R > 0$ $F > 0$	The resultant force F is positive. When $F_k > F_R$, the internal force predominates. When $F_R > F_k$, the external force predominates.	$F > F_R$ and $F > F_k$
Model 2	Maturity stage	$F = OI + OR$	Quadrant II	$F_k > 0$ $F_R > 0$ $F > 0$	The resultant force F is positive. When $F_k > F_R$, the internal force predominates. When $F_R > F_k$, the external force predominates.	$F_k > F > F_R$ or $F_R > F > F_k$
Model 3	Decline stage	$F = OI - OR$	Quadrant III	$F_k > 0$ $F_R < 0$ $F > 0$	$F_k > F_R$, indicating that although the external force is negative, the internal force is still strong enough to maintain the development of the system, albeit in declining speed.	The situation for negative external force (i.e., $F_R < 0$) exists as a theoretical assumption. It is not within the research focus of the present study.
Model 4	Recession stage	$F = OI - OR$	Quadrant IV	$F_k > 0$ $F_R < 0$ $F < 0$	$F_R > F_k$, indicating that the negative external force restrains the development of the industry and leads to economic recession.	Same as above

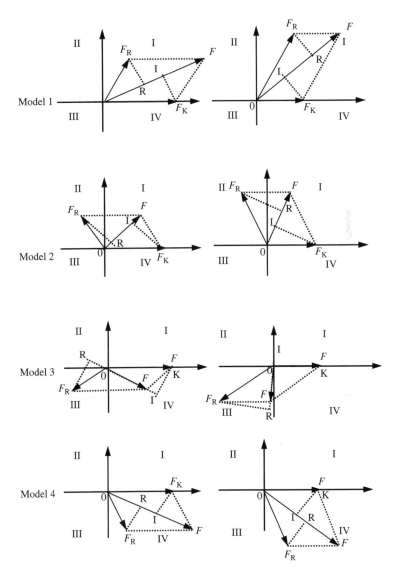

Fig. 2. The Dynamic Situation Analysis Figure of Culture Tourism System.

Table 2. Indices of the Culture Tourism Industry System Cluster.

Overall System	Second-Order System (K, R)	Third-Order System (K_m, R_n)	Indices (k_{mj}, R_{nk})
Culture tourism industry system	Internal System (k)	Magnitude of Resources (K_1)	Quantity of static culture tourism attractions (K_{11})
			Quantity of dynamic culture tourism attractions (K_{12})
		Characteristic of Actors (K_2)	Percentage of employees with professional titles of intermediate level and above (K_{21})
			Number of tourism institutions of higher learning (and research institutes) (K_{22})
			Number of top national companies for culture exports (K_{23})
			Number of companies in the culture tourism industry (K_{24})
		Financial Strengths (K_3)	Output of the culture tourism industry as a percentage of the overall GDP of the region (K_{31})
			Added value created by the culture tourism industry in the region (K_{32})
			Output of the culture tourism industry as a percentage of the overall output of the tertiary industry in the region (K_{33})
		Level of Innovativeness (K_4)	Number of innovation awards conferred by the Ministry of Culture (K_{41})
			Number of national exemplary sites for culture industry development (K_{42})
			Number of culture tourism research projects at the provincial level and above (K_{43})
	External System (R)	Policy Environment (R_1)	Public funding in culture undertakings as a percentage of the national financial expenditure (R_{11})
			Number of laws and regulations governing the culture tourism industry (R_{12})
			Amount of public fund allocated to the culture industry (R_{13})
		Knowledge Sharing (R_2)	Number of culture tourism related academic conferences and forums (R_{21})

	Number of registered trademarks in the culture tourism industry in the region (R_{22})
Market Environments (R_3)	Number of domestic tourist arrivals in the region (R_{31})
	The level of urbanization in the region (R_{32})
	Domestic tourism revenue in the region (R_{33})
	Percentage of population in the region with an educational level of diploma and above (R_{34})
	Per capita disposable income of urban residents in the region (R_{35})
Openness to the Outside World (R_4)	Number of inbound tourist arrivals in the region (R_{41})
	Foreign exchange earnings from the tourism industry (R_{42})
	Number of national key culture tourism projects (R_{43})
	Number of outbound visits by art performance groups in the region (R_{44})

Note: m, n, j, k = 1, 2, 3,....

computational methods used to construct a metric for the culture tourism system are explained.

(1) *Parallelogram Law*: As discussed above, the system for the culture tourism sector is composed of internal and external subsystems. The internal force (F_k) is a combination of the four internal forces (e.g., magnitude of resources), as described above, within the internal system, and its magnitude depends on the strength of the elements within the subsystem. It is the driving force that promotes development of the industry. The internal force presents a vector indicating a certain amount of magnitude and direction for system evolution. Similarly, the external force (F_R) is the resultant force from externalities (e.g., political situation). Its magnitude and direction are variable due to the dynamic and changeable characteristics of the external system. The net force of the system is the summation the internal force (F_k) and external force (F_R). Because these forces are all vectors with both magnitude and direction, the Parallelogram Law could be applied to obtain the sum of the vectors.

(2) *Entropy-Weight Method*: Information entropy is a measure for a system's degree of disorder/uncertainty. If an index has a lower information entropy, it contains information that is more reliable. Compared with other methods (e.g., expert scoring method), the entropy-weight method is a more objective method to establish the weights of evaluation indices by making full use of the inherent information.

(3) *Fuzzy Membership Function*: Because the indices contain different measurement units, non-dimensionalization was conducted to remove the units so that the sum of the indices could be calculated. In the current study, the indices were vectors with positive directions; therefore, semi-trapezoid fuzzy membership function was deployed in the computation. The non-dimensionalized equations were written as:

$$\phi(X_{ij}) = \frac{X_{ij} - X_{in}}{X_{im} - X_{in}} = \begin{cases} 1 & X_{ij} \geq X_{im} \\ \dfrac{X_{ij} - X_{in}}{X_{im} - X_{in}} & X_{in} < X_{ij} < X_{im} \\ 0 & X_{ij} \leq X_{in} \end{cases}$$

where X_{im} and X_{in} is the maximum and minimum values of the index i respectively. X_{ij} is the jth observed value for the index i. $\phi(X_{ij})$ denotes the membership grade (i.e., the non-dimensionalized value) and ranges from 0 to 1. The indices are normalized based on the above arithmetical function as a bigger value indicates that the observed value is closer to the maximum value. Conversely, the smaller the observed value is, the closer it is to the minimum value.

(4) *Computational methods for constructing the metric of the culture tourism system.* With the PEF operational methods for clustering model of culture tourism system, computation starts with the individual indices, and then moves up stepwise to the subsystem and system levels. For the internal system, the fuzzy membership function is applied first to determine the non-dimensionalized values based upon the position of the observed values in the membership range. Then, the entropy-weight method is used to establish the weights of indices and finally, weighted average of the non-dimensionalized values is computed as the dynamic of the internal system (F_k).

Similarly, non-dimensionalized values and weights are computed first for each of the indices in the external system. Then the resultant forces at the subsystem level are calculated with the Parallelogram Law. Next, the Parallelogram Law is applied again to obtain the dynamic of the external system (F_R). Finally, the integrated dynamic (F) of the overall system is computed as the resultant force of the dynamics of the internal system (F_k) and the external system (F_R) based on the Parallelogram Law.

AN EMPIRICAL STUDY OF 31 CHINESE PROVINCIAL TERRITORIES

After the above agglomeration model (including the indices and computational methods) of culture tourism cluster was established, an empirical study based on all Chinese provincial territories ($N = 31$) in mainland China was conducted.

Data Collection

Secondary data was collected from the 31 regions from the most recent 5–10 years (depending on the availability of the data), consisting of official statistics from the following three sources.

(1) Government statistical yearbooks, including the China statistical year-
    book, yearbook of China tourism statistics, yearbook of China culture
    and culture relics statistics, China basic units statistical yearbook,
    China statistical yearbook for regional economy, and statistical year-
    books at the provincial (autonomous region and municipality) level.
(2) Online databases, including SOSHOO, CNKI China economic and
    social development statistics database, National data, National social
    science foundation projects database, Datatang, and corresponding
    databases at the provincial (autonomous region and municipality)
    level.
(3) Official data from various government websites embodying the
    Ministry of culture, Website for the China culture Industries, the China
    national tourism administration, the China information system for
    laws and regulations, Project search database for the National natural
    science foundation of China, China trademark registration, as well as
    local tourism administration and statistics bureau.

Results of the Empirical Study

Based on the PEF method, dynamics of the overall system (F), the internal
system (F_k), and the external system (F_R) for each of the 31 provincial territories were computed and ranked in Table 3.

Variability of the Dynamic Scores among the 31 Regions

The variability of the dynamic scores among the 31 regions revealed the
difference in the level of development of culture tourism industry across the
country. Based on the integrated dynamic (F), it was apparent that culture
tourism industry was at relatively low level of development across all
regions in the country (see Table 3). Beijing took the leading position with
a mark of 68.47 and was the only territory that scored a mark over 60. The
distribution of the integrated dynamic scores for the 31 territories
resembled the shape of an olive, with the majority (61%) of the regions
obtaining marks between 20 and 40. Moreover, big gaps were obvious
between the highest and lowest scores for the overall system. Tibet ranked
last (16.35 marks) on the integrated dynamic, which was 52.15 below that
of Beijing. For the external system, again, Beijing ranked first (66.75
marks) and Tibet ranked last (14.10 marks). The two regions had a

Table 3. Ranking of the 31 Provincial Territories Dynamic Scores of the Culture Tourism System.

	Integrated Dynamic		Dynamic of the Internal System		Dynamic of the External System	
	Scores	Ranking	Scores	Ranking	Scores	Ranking
Beijing	68.47	1	70.45	1	66.75	1
Guangdong	59.99	2	57.67	3	61.99	2
Zhejiang	58.36	3	56.27	4	60.15	3
Jiangshu	55.83	4	59.10	2	54.15	4
Shanghai	47.03	5	44.84	8	48.91	5
Shandong	46.24	6	49.55	5	43.42	6
Sichuan	43.63	7	48.41	6	39.54	7
Yunnan	42.28	8	46.14	7	38.98	9
Liaoning	39.85	9	40.26	9	39.52	8
Henan	37.32	10	36.44	13	38.08	10
Hunan	35.21	11	38.82	10	32.12	12
Hubei	34.78	12	38.74	11	31.40	14
Fujian	34.31	13	32.83	17	35.58	11
Anhui	32.54	14	38.05	12	27.81	18
Guangxi	30.81	15	33.72	15	28.32	15
Shanxi	30.51	16	33.38	16	28.05	16
Tianjin	30.13	17	28.61	22	31.43	13
Guizhou	28.28	18	35.09	14	22.44	24
Shaanxi	28.03	19	30.01	20	26.34	20
Jilin	27.87	20	27.79	24	27.95	17
Heilongjiang	27.63	21	29.49	21	26.03	21
Hebei	27.55	22	30.81	19	24.76	22
Chongqing	27.31	23	30.90	18	24.24	23
Neimenggu	25.09	24	23.47	26	26.49	19
Jiangxi	23.82	25	27.92	23	20.30	26
Xinjiang	21.96	26	22.21	27	21.75	25
Gansu	20.61	27	24.39	25	17.37	29
Hainan	18.49	28	17.90	29	18.99	27
Qinghai	17.42	29	17.68	30	17.19	30
Ningxia	16.48	30	14.56	31	18.13	28
Tibet (Xizang)	16.35	31	18.98	28	14.10	31

difference of 52.65 marks. For the internal system, Beijing ranked first (70.45 marks) and Ningxia ranked last (14.56 marks), with a gap of 55.89 between the two.

Meanwhile, the results also revealed territorial differences in the eastern and western parts of China. The regions falling within the four bands of scores were shown in the map of China (Fig. 3) with different shades of color. For the overall system, the regions in the eastern part of China had an average score of 44.20, much higher than the average of 26.12 of the regions in the west. This suggested that, in general, the culture tourism industry in the eastern part of China was better developed than its counterpart in western China. Nevertheless, the top 10 regions based on the ranking of the integrated dynamic scores were not exclusively located in eastern China. Henan (in the middle part of China), Sichuan, and Yunan (in the western part of China) were also listed on the top 10. This could be attributed to their high quality culture tourism resources and relatively well-developed tourism markets. Spatial difference in the scores of the internal and external systems also revealed lower levels of development when moving from east to

Fig. 3. Distribution of All 31 Provincial Territories in China Integrated Dynamic Scores of the Culture Tourism System.

west. In addition, rankings based on the integrated dynamic scores were, in general, consistent with those based on the scores of the external system. The results suggested that the external dynamic appeared to dominate the overall development of the system.

Degree of Balanced Development of the System

The overall system was made up of different subsystems or components. Besides the aggregated dynamic scores for the overall system, it was also important to examine the dispersion of scores of the components therein. The degree of dispersion revealed the level of balanced development among subsystems for a particular region, and it could be measured with mean deviation, standard deviation, coefficient of variation, etc. The measure of variation applied in the current study was the range of ranking orders of scores of subsystems for a particular region, calculated as the difference between the maximum and minimum ranking orders. A large range indicated a big gap between the relative strength and weakness among the subsystems, and vice versa.

The range between the rankings of the internal and external systems was analyzed for each region. This aimed to uncover whether the two subsystems within the overall system were equal in strength for each of the regions under study. If the range between the rankings was small (i.e., the rank orders of scores of subsystems for a particular region were in close proximity to each other), it indicated that this region had balanced development in the two subsystems, and vice versa.

For 24 of the 31 regions, the range between the rankings of both subsystems was 5 or less. This indicated that most of the regions were able to keep balanced development for their internal and external subsystems. However, a few regions showed uneven rankings of the two subsystems. For example, Anhui, Guizhou, and Chongqing scored much higher for their internal systems than for their external systems respectively. It suggested that the three regions enjoyed relative advantage in their resource elements for culture tourism development, but the external environment that was conducive to industrial development was not in place currently. The lagging standings of these regions in the external system led to their low rankings in the overall system. On the other hand, Fujian, Tianjin, Jilin, and Neimenggu scored much higher for their external systems than for their internal systems respectively. The results implied that these regions needed to nurture and strengthen their basic resources and capacity to promote the development of culture tourism industry.

The four regions (Guizhou, Tianjin, Jilin, and Neimenggu) with the most conspicuous unbalanced development were, nevertheless, not the regions that ranked last on the integrated dynamic scores. They simply had wide difference in development between their internal and external subsystems. Meanwhile, among the 10 regions that ranked the last on the integrated dynamic scores, eight (Tibet, Ningxia, Qinghai, Hainan, Gansu, Xinjiang, Jiangxi, and Hebei) experienced moderately balanced development, with a range score from 2 to 4. The results suggested that the culture tourism industry was under-developed in these regions because they received low scores for both the internal and external subsystems.

Typology of the Culture Tourism System

A typology of culture tourism system was constructed to reveal the patterns in the development of the culture tourism sector across the regions. As discussed previously, the integrated dynamic (F) of the overall system was the resultant force of the dynamics of the internal system (F_k) and the external system (F_R). The dynamic scores of the internal and external systems represented the two dimensions used to classify the 31 regions. They were specified as the x- and y-axes respectively. The coordinate system was divided into four sections by mean scores of the dynamics of the two systems. Thus, the system of 31 regions could be classified into four segments, corresponding to the four sections in the coordinate plane. Fig. 4 shows the results of classification model.

(1) *Category I:* Regions falling within this section had above average dynamic scores for both the internal and external systems. They included Beijing, Guangdong, Zhejiang, Jiangsu, Shanghai, and Shandong. For example, the coordinates of Beijing were (70.45, 66.75), much higher than the other regions. This was in line with Beijing's position as the national political, economic, and culture center.

(2) *Category II:* This model represented a pattern of culture tourism development that scored low for the internal system but high for the external system. Currently, none of the 31 regions fell within this section. The internal system included the essential endowment and resources that were fundamental to the development of the culture tourism sector. Thus, if the basis upon which the culture tourism sector depended was

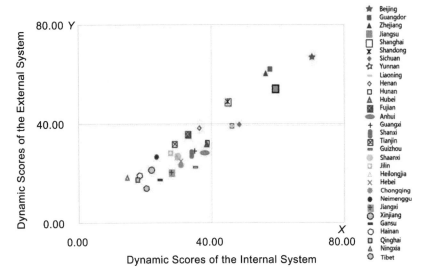

Fig. 4. Culture Tourism System Typology Based on Dynamic Mechanism.

unavailable, it was unlikely for a region to invest in external environment (e.g., government policy, market environment) that was conducive to the development of the sector.

(3) *Category III:* Regions falling within this section scored low for both systems. Among the 31 regions, 22 (71%) were classified into this typology. The results suggested that culture tourism industry was generally at a very low level of development nationwide. Taking Tibet as an example, it had coordinates of (18.98, 14.10), indicating its severe lack of essential resources and external environment for the development of culture tourism. This could be attributed to the status quo of Tibet's location in the inland plateau, its inaccessibility, low level of openness to the outside world, and backward economic development.

(4) *Category IV:* Regions falling within this section scored high for the internal system but low for the external system. Altogether, three regions were classified into this typology, including Yunnan, Liaoning, and Sichuan, for instance, Yunnan had coordinates of (46.14, 38.98), as shown in Fig. 4, it lacked behind those regions in Category I on both dimensions. However, compared with the majority of the regions in Category III, it contained substantial comparative advantages in essential resources for culture tourism development. Its great potential for

culture tourism development could come to fruition through further development of its culture tourism resources, brand building, and increased investment. Efforts to improve the efficacy of its external system could bring about a huge leap forward in its culture tourism industry, thus moving from Category IV to Category I.

CONCLUSION

Using the system science as guidance, this study constructs an agglomeration model for the culture tourism industry cluster. An empirical study is conducted using secondary data from all Chinese provincial territories. The results presented a general overview of the status of culture tourism development in the country. The typology of the culture tourism system is explored and policy recommendations were proposed.

Nevertheless, it is suggested that further studies relevant to policies and development could be proposed to address the issue rising from the resultant data. Furthermore, it is worthwhile to examine the relative role played by each subsystem (as listed in Table 2) in determining the actual output of culture tourism industry, so that significant driving forces in the system affecting culture tourism development could be pinpointed.

In summary, the empirical results suggest that culture tourism industry in China was under steady development. It is manifested by the integrated dynamic scores falling between the scores of the internal and external systems. The results are in line with the fact that in recent years the government has recognized the culture tourism industry as an important component for economic growth and policies were put in place to nurture its development. The justifiable results also lend support to the face validity of the proposed agglomeration model for the culture tourism cluster.

In addition, the agglomeration model may be used as a diagnostic tool to gauge the overall status of the culture tourism industry, and particularly to pinpoint the weakness in the culture tourism system that may have hindered the development of the industry. Results of such analysis could offer directions for public policy intervention to promote the development of the culture tourism industry.

Moreover, a city or region could formulate appropriate developmental strategy that is commensurate with its relative competitive advantages. For example, for the majority of regions falling within the Category III (as listed in Fig. 5), they had low dynamic scores for both the internal and

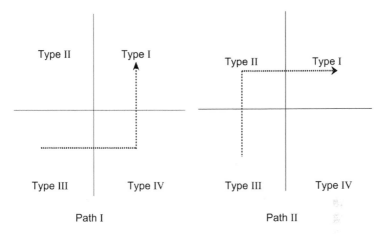

Fig. 5. Evolutionary Path of Culture Tourism Typology.

external systems. They could follow different evolutionary paths to develop their culture tourism industry, depending on their relative strength in the dynamics of the subsystems. For those that lack basic culture tourism resources, they could follow the path from Category III to Category IV first, and then to Category I. Namely, their priority is to build and nurture the basic culture tourism resources first, and then gradually implement policies to create constructive external environment to foster the development of the industry. In the end, their culture tourism industry could develop at a higher level, with coordination between elements in the internal and external systems. On the other hand, those who scored relatively high for the internal system in comparison with the external system, their priority is to lay down preferential policies so that their potentials in the culture tourism resources could be converted into realistic productive forces. In other words, these regions could adopt an evolutionary path from Category III to Category II first, and finally move to Category I to achieve harmony between the internal and external systems to a higher standard.

ACKNOWLEDGMENT

This study was funded by National Social Science Foundation of China (No. 12XJY025), Tourism Youth Expert Training Program of China National Tourism Administration (No. TYETP201342), Soft Science

Project funds of Science and Technology of Guizhou Province (No. [2014] 7277), and tourism planning project of tourism economy and management institute of Guizhou province.

REFERENCES

Bao, H., & Wang, S. (2010). Coupling analysis of culture industry and tourism industry. *Industrial Technology & Economy*, *29*(8), 74–78.

Ding, H., & Chen, L. (2002). The primary research of mountain tourism system on the fringe of metropolis—A study of Shenzhen city. *Journal of Mountain Science*, *20*(3), 307–312.

Gaines, B. R. (1979). General systems research: Quo Vadis. *General Systems Yearbook*, *24*, 1–9. Louisville, Kentucky, Society for General Systems Research.

Guo, L., & Yang, Z. (2012). The concept, characteristics and construction of meaning of tourism system. *Commercial Time*, *30*(36), 109–111.

Guo, S. (2008). Systematic operation in the regional culture tourism industry. *Areal Research and Development*, *27*(6), 57–60.

Han, S., Tao, Z., & Xiao, Z. (2012). The evaluation of regional culture-creative index in china and its influence on economic growth. *Economic Geography*, *31*(4), 96–102.

Hjalager, A. M. (2009). Culture tourism systems—The Roskilde festival. *Scandinavian Journal of Hospitality and Tourism*, *9*(2–3), 266–287.

Laszlo, A., & Krippner, S. (1998). In J. S. Jordan (Ed.), *Systems theories and a priori aspects of perception* (Ch. 3, pp. 47–74). Amsterdam: Elsevier Science.

Leiper, N. (1990). *Tourism systems—An interdisciplinary perspective.* Palmerston North: Occasional Papers: Business Studies Faculty.

Liu, D., & Yang, Y. (2011). Coupling coordinative degree of regional economy-tourism-ecological environment—A case study of Anhui province. *Resources and Environment in the Yangtze Basin*, *19*(7), 892–896.

Liu, G., & Yang, W. (2013). DEA-based investment efficiency model and a positive analysis of the culture tourism industry. *Tourism Tribune*, *28*(1), 77–84.

Ma, Y., & Chen, H. (2012). A research on the establishment of the appraisal index system of tourism culture industry. *Journal of Central South University of Forestry & Technology (Social Sciences)*, *10*(1), 4–7.

Mattsson, J., Sundbo, J., & Fussing-Jensen, C. (2005). Innovation systems in tourism: The roles of attractors and scene-takers. *Industry and Innovation*, *12*(3), 357–381.

McKercher, B., Ho, P. S. Y., & du Cros, H. (2005). Relationship between tourism and culture heritage management: Evidence from Hong Kong. *Tourism Management*, *26*(4), 539–548.

Richards, G. (1996). Production and consumption of European culture tourism. *Annals of Tourism Research*, *23*(2), 261–283.

Richards, G., & Wilson, J. (2006). Developing creativity in tourist experiences: A solution to the serial reproduction of culture? *Tourism Management*, *27*(6), 1209–1223.

Silberberg, T. (1995). Culture tourism and business opportunities for museums and heritage sites. *Tourism Management*, *16*(5), 361–365.

Song, Z., Ji, X., Lv, L., & Li, Y. (2012). A study on the structure and properties of culture tourism system. *Tourism Tribune*, *27*(2), 80–87.

Song, Z., & Li Qiu, Q. (2011). A research on urban culture capital and culture tourism development. *Tourism Science, 24*(4), 1–9.

Sundbo, J., & Gallouj, F. (2000). Innovation as a loosely coupled system in services. *International Journal of Services Technology and Management, 1*(1), 15–36.

Theopisti, S. (2011). Gazing from home: Culture tourism and art museums. *Annals of Tourism Research, 38*(2), 403–421.

Tufts, S., & Milne, S. (1999). Museums: A supply side perspective. *Annals of Tourism Research, 26*(3), 613–631.

Wang, Z., & Huang, X. (2010). The dynamical mechanism and countermeasures research of the development of culture tourism creative industry. *Shandong Social Sciences, 23*(9), 118–122.

Wei, F. (2011). Coupling and innovation: The originality of national culture and the development of regional tourism—The new perspective of the readjustment of economic structure and development in western ethnic regions. *Study of Ethnics in Guangxi, 26*(1), 174–179.

Wu, F., Fang, C., & Zhao, Y. (2010). The progresses of urban industrial agglomeration dynamic mechanism and patterns. *Progress in Geography, 28*(10), 1201–1208.

Wu, F., Fang, C., & Zhao, Y. (2011). PAF model of study on urban industrial agglomeration dynamic mechanism and patterns. *Geographical Research, 29*(1), 71–82.

Wu, J., & Song, Z. (2011). Study on the development of movie-induced tourism from the perspective of industrial merging. *Tourism Tribune, 26*(6), 29–35.

Yang, C. (2010). *Research of tourism area complex system evolution theory, method and practice* (pp. 23–31). Beijing: Science Publishing House.

Yin, Y., & Lu, M. (2009). On the coupled development of tourism industry and creative industry in ethnic areas. *Tourism Tribune, 24*(3), 42–48.

Zhang, C., & Liu, Z. (2007). Analysis of culture tourism industry in Henan Province—Based on dynamics system. *Management World, 22*(5), 152–154.

Zhang, H., Wang, L., & Tian, X. (2010). Study on the agglomerative performance of regional tourism industry cluster and the comparison of its competitive situation—Based on the empirical analysis of 21 cities in Guangdong Province. *Economic Geography, 30*(12), 2116–2121.

Zhang, H., & Wang, Z. (2010). Evaluation research on competitiveness of culture and tourism industry—Based on perspective of industry convergence. *Resource Development & Market, 16*(8), 743–746.

Zhang, Y., & Zhu, H. (2012). Regional differences research on coupling development of the culture industries and tourism industry—Based on empirical research though provincial panel data. *East China Economic Management, 26*(10), 54–59.

RESEARCH NOTES

TOURIST'S EXPERIENCE VALUES AND PEOPLE INTERACTION

Joseph S. Chen, Nina K. Prebensen and Uysal Muzaffer

ABSTRACT

This research examines the effect of people interaction on value creation of tourist experiences by reconstructing a scale of value perception. It gathers a set of on-site survey data collected from tourists visiting Norwegian Arctic destinations that contain 579 useful questionnaires. A 19-item value measurement is first validated by confirmatory factor analyses (CFA) that results in a 13-item, five-factor parsimonious model. The CFA results also suggest a high-order factor solution; it finds two convergent factors explicated by five value domains. The derived high-order factors are labeled as tangible value and intangible value. Further analyses show significant relationships between experience values and people interaction. That is the intangible domain of value could create significant mediating effect on people interaction. Specifically, novelty and social values tend to moderate tourist experience. The conclusion furnishes implications in theory advancement and service innovation along with suggestions for research study.

Keywords: Value perception; people interaction; second-order factor analysis; Arctic destinations

Advances in Hospitality and Leisure, Volume 12, 169–179
Copyright © 2017 by Emerald Group Publishing Limited
All rights of reproduction in any form reserved
ISSN: 1745-3542/doi:10.1108/S1745-354220160000012008

INTRODUCTION

The emergence of informatics era supplies abundant opportunities to consumers who are able to make optimal acquisition decisions so as to enhance their service experiences via information technologies. As the trend persists, consumers in the current market place are more informed on the quality of the services of interest. In the words, it is likely that proactive consumers are able to quickly access the literature concerning the quality of service they intend to experience. Furthermore, their reviews on the consumption experience of services may also be freely and rapidly disseminated to mass audience via various e-channels. Retrospectively, such a technological advantage propelled by informational networks may have engendered new business ventures to service providers. This tenet may be epitomized by a study (Bakhat & Sajjad-ul-Aziz, 2012) of customer's valuation of restaurant services that information technology services like webpage and online delivery are an important apparatus to moderate customer's valuation perception of service.

Perceived Personal Values

For decades, market researchers and practitioners have expressed great interest in exploring the meanings of value in the minds of the consumers in general and the consequences of consumer's evaluation of value on satisfaction and loyalty. There are two sets of discussions on consumer values. One looks at consumer values from a macroperspective that is to use nationality or Hofstede's culture taxonomy as a unit of analysis whereas the other explores consumer value at personal level which is influenced by lifestyle and culture context in which the consumer lives (Ladhari, Pons, Bressollers, & Zins, 2011).

Concerning personal values, in the early stage of its concept development several embryonic frameworks have emerged in academia. Rokeach (1968), for instance, envisaged the value as an intrinsic stimulus affecting attitudes and behavioral intention. Individual's valuation of products and services builds on a hierarchical thought process (Rokeach, 1979) that one value (e.g., money) may have a greater consideration than the other (e.g., time). Consumer researchers (Schwartz & Bilsky, 1987) have advocated a best way of utilizing the notion of value to foresee behavioral variations. That is to consider value as a domain consisting of few with an akin value characteristic instead of as a single descriptor. In the other words, personal value may be explicated by various mutually exclusive value domains that embody multivariate traits of value. This tenet may be best illustrated by the proposition of Ledden, Kalafatis, and Samouel (2007) that defines value from the perception of consumers instead of sellers and regards value as a multifaced and complex construct.

As tourism and hospitality emerged as an academic discipline, scholars have been teeming to exploit the value domain in marketing research and then apply it to tourism issues. The effort could be represented by three streams of investigative tasks, differentiated by the nature of research and the first stream deals with market segmentation. Indeed, the early application of value concept appears in market segmentation studies (Luk, de Leon, Leong, & Li, 1994; Madrigal & Kahle, 1994; Muller, 1991; Pitts & Woodside, 1986) that posit to strategy development in product and service. Those studies using value as descriptor for partitioning the study sample into various mutually exclusive groups either centers on overall value (Madrigal & Kahle, 1994) or a specific value such as price value (Bojanic, 1996; Murphy & Pritchard, 1997) and social value (Blamey & Braithwaite, 1997). The other type of segmentation study could be found in marketing studies (Petrick, 2002) which use value as one of the comparison attributes between/among resultants.

The second stream rests on scale development. In a bid for valid assessments on the value domains, tourism researchers have started constructing scales of value perception for different sectors of tourism. Petrick (2002), through an empirical investigation of a value scale concerning scale reliability and validity, unveiled a 25-item measurement of customer's perceived value of services in tourism and recreation that is explained by five value domains. From a different study setting that relates to hotel services, Al-Sabbahy, Ekinci, and Riley (2004) conceptualized the personal value as a two-dimensional domain including acquisition value and transactional value. Later, Gallarza and Gil (2008), expanding the early value framework of Holbrook (1999), underlined five value domains (e.g., efficiency, quality, play, aesthetical, and social) using college students as samples. The third stream relates to causal modeling. As a recent example, in revelation of adventure tourist's future intention, Williams and Soutar (2009) probed the significant predictors of satisfaction based on a value scale. Further, Chen and Chen (2010) initiated a similar approach to study tourist's behavioral intention, however, in a different setting — heritage site. Above all, value domains have been regarded as a viable measurement in assessing moderating and mediating effects on tourist behavioral consequences.

In addition, empirical works concerning the evolution of value concept in tourism have in large emerged from the field of marketing. Rokeach's work (1973) may have long influenced the contemporary tourism research in value perception, exhibited by Madrigal and Kahle's study (1994). The Rokeach's Value Survey nesting on 18 instrumental values and 18 terminal values (RVS) illuminates a primitive version of value measurement in marketing. Recently a more parsimony version emerged that is the List of Values (LOV) scale which has been widely tested on different types of samples. Further, a tourism study by Madrigal and Kahle (1994) modified the LOV, by deriving four value dimensions: external, enjoyment/excitement, achievement, and egocentrism. From a different perspective, Williams and Soutar (2009), slightly revising Sweeney and Soutar's (2001) four-dimensional value scale on product and service in general, proposed a value scale with five dimensions (e.g., functional, monetary, emotional, social, and novel) fitting into tourism phenomenon. Both scales of Madrigal and Kahle (1994) and Sweeney and Soutar (2001) are able to demonstrate a predictive property in a hierarchical order comparing to the LOV scale. However, Williams and Soutar's (2009) scale is considered more updated and complying with tourism setting for model testing. Seemingly, it is plausible to incorporate the scale by Williams and Soutar (2009) into tourism research.

People Interaction

In the field of tourism and hospitality, literature on people interaction has been chiefly reflected on the social aspect of interaction. In reference to the parties involved in social interaction, the literature (Armenski, Dragičević, Pejović, Lukić, & Djurdjev, 2011) has examined the relationship between tourists and local residents. Such interaction is likely to modify the local residents' attitudes toward tourism development. Retrospectively, Armenski et al. (2011) reckoned that tourist's interaction with locals shapes the tourist's perceptions of the destination. Nevertheless, it is noted that the resident's attitude toward tourist–host interaction may be moderated by personality and ethnicity (Zhang, Inbakaran, & Jackson, 2006). For example, Reisinger and Turner (1998) articulated the cultural differences between Chinese tourists and Australian hosts and their impacts on tourist–guest interaction.

It is evidenced that encountering has been considered as a channel for exchanging relationships between buyers and sellers (Czepiel, 1990) that manifests a defining setting for establishing relationship marketing. Like interactions between customers and service personnel, customer-to-customer (C-to-C) interactions often occurring in tourism settings has recently been the center stage in service encounter study in tourism. In a survey of outbound travelers, Wu (2007) noted through current marketing literature that in a C-to-C interaction customer homogeneity contributes to customer satisfaction. Huang and Hsu (2010) further delineated that a quality C-to-C interaction alters vacation satisfaction in cruise settings.

Moreover, the barriers of social interaction deriving from the C-to-C channel have been discussed. A recent study by Papathanassis (2012) underlined that cultural compatibility between/among customers involved in social interaction is a factor impacting the continuity of social interaction. This study also depicted the intentionality of tourists in participating in a social interaction and that cruise tourists tend to perform a social screening to identify a compatible cohort consisting of people with shared routines and experiences before partaking in more intense social interaction. Furthermore, tourism literature has also documented that in a different travel setting individuals may pose a different level of desire to interact with others, given that people interaction may constitute an important part of a particular type of itinerary. Murphy, Pritchard, and Smith (2000) found that packagers are motivated to interact with follow packagers for social as well as destination information inquiry. Individuals visiting alternative destinations, such as a farm, are inclined to interact with people surrounding the destination to enhance their trip experience and therefore give rise to a satisfactory state of being as long as the outcome of social interaction is deemed to be positive (Choo & Petrick, 2014).

The forgoing literature view on perceived value and personal interaction suggests a new investigative theme to extend the current theory that links experience value creation with people interaction. In this spirit, his research aims to further cross-validate the scale of value perception and use it as a rhetorical underpinning to understand how personal interaction affects tourist's perceived value of a trip taken. Specifically, to accomplish the aim of study, this research furnishes two study questions as follows: (1) What is a robust scale of value perception? (2) Is there a positive relationship between perceived values and personal interaction? The first question strives to reexamine the value scale by Williams and Soutar (2009) while the second question aims to test the monological validity of scale and extend the current theory of value perception by including people interaction into the examination something which has not been evaluated previously.

METHOD

The present research deployed a questionnaire survey in three counties in Northern Norway encompassing Nordland, Troms, and Finnmark. Two nature-based attractions (a lift to the mountain and an aquarium) and three cultural and natural hybrid attractions (a zoo with historical stories, a visitor center, and a Viking museum) were selected as study sites where a structured questionnaire was given to the tourists. This study transpired between June and September 2011. The study instrument contained questions regarding tourists' perceived value of the destination under study as well as respondents' demographic variables and trip information. As presented in the literature section, several scales have been deployed to measure perceived value in consumer products and this study adopted the value framework proposed by Williams and Soutar (2009). The value scale covers five dimensions: (1) functional, (2) monetary, (3) emotional, (4) social, and (5) novel that are explained by 19 indicators assessed by a five-point Likert-type, disagreement-agreement scale from one (strongly disagree) to five (strongly agree).

Survey questions were first developed in Norwegian language and transformed to both English and German versions of questionnaires. To secure the content validity, 20 academic professionals were invited to provide comments to screen the clarity and readability of the study questionnaire. Literature shows that a large number of tourists visiting Norway are from United Kingdom and Germany (VisitNorway.com, 2013) and therefore, the Norwegian survey questionnaire was translated into English and German to obtain opinions from foreign visitors.

RESULTS

Reliability tests were conducted on the value scale to assess the subscales as well as the overall scale internal consistency. Since a commonly accepted Cronbach's alpha coefficient is 0.70 (Nunnally & Bernstein, 1994), Cronbach's alpha scores for five dimensions was found to be .849, .861. .834, .921, and .710, which indicated an acceptable consistency of the dimension and the total scale reliability was .89.

A confirmatory factor analysis (CFA) was performed to determine if the 19 indicators could accurately measure perceived values. The model fit was determined by a chi-square ratio and the fit indexes of Comparative Fit

Index (CFI), Goodness of Fit (GFI), and Root Mean Square Error of Approximation (RMSEA). From the CFA results, the fit indexes were not satisfactory. Thus, it went through the procedure of model modification by deleting five indicators that improved the model fit. After this model trimming process, a tenable model emerged, coming with good fit indices ($\chi^2 = 164$, df = 55, $\chi^2/df = 3$, CFI = .97, GFI = .96, NFI = .96, RMSEA = .05). In sum, the final model included 14 indicators explaining five first-order perceived values (see Table 1). The five resultant dimensions were illustrated by two to three indicators respectively.

In the above CFA procedure, the correlation matrix of independent factors suggested the dimensions of functional and money could be further merged. Thus, this study conducted a second-order factor analysis. The resultant model showed good fix indices (CFI = .96, GFI = .95,

Table 1. Reliability of the Resultant CFA Model on Perceived Value on Destinations.

Dimensions and Indicators	Path Coefficient	CR[a]
1. Functional value		.63
Consistent service quality	.48	
Well-organized services	.60	
2. Money value		.86
Reasonable service fees	.68	
Great value for money	.89	
Spending money meaningfully	.80	
3. Emotion value		
Well-being	.53	.68
Happiness	.59	
4. Social value		.94
Transforming viewpoint	.93	
Making one think about others	.98	
Giving social approval	.96	
5. Novel value		.69
Satisfying curiosity	.58	
Authentic experiences	.64	
Ample opportunity for activity pursuit	.57	

[a]CR, composite reliability.

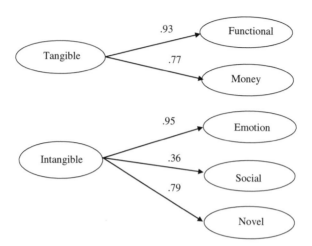

Fig. 1.   Second-Order Factors of Value Domain.

NFI = .95, RMSEA = .06), indicating that functional and money dimensions contribute to a second-order factor labeled as tangible value, while emotional, social, and novel values are the other second-order factor intangible values (see Fig. 1). Function value had a stronger relationship with tangible dimension (.93) while emotional value showed a strongest impact (.95) on intangible dimension.

Further analyses revealed the relation between perceived value and people interaction. This study found that two intangible value dimensions, including social and novel values, tended to influence the respondent's attitude toward people interaction (e.g., tourist−resident, tourist−service staff, and tourist−tourist). In terms of type of interaction involved, tourist−resident, tourist−service staff, and tourist−tourist interactions were significantly affected by tourist's judgment of social value.

CONCLUSION

This research has revalidated a five-dimension scale developed by Williams and Soutar (2009) and consequently streamlined the scale. It renders two major discoveries. Firstly, the total number of the value indicator is reduced to 13 that collectively explain the five value dimensions in a parsimonious way. Second, the five value domains are able to be consolidated into two high-order factors labeled as tangible and intangible values. Nevertheless, to build a robust scale in experience value the following three issues may be examined in future studies. Firstly, since two value domains only contain two measurement items, these two dimensions should respectively add one or more indicators to increase the explained variance of the dimensions. Secondly, it is important to evaluate the three value domains showing a composite reliability score lower than .70. Thirdly, the value scale may be revalidated by using a set of survey data drawn from individuals visiting Arctic destinations.

It is enlightening to know that the social value represents the key drive for partaking in people interaction followed by the novelty value. In other words, the respondents are not inclined to look for other types of values like functional, monetary, and emotional values when interacting with people at destinations. As for functional value, due to the prevalence of informational technology, travel public is capable of retrieving needy information timely via different communicative devices such as smart phones and tablets. It seems that nowadays consumers have lesser reliance on service staffs or other people at destinations in comparison to innovative technologies. It is reasonable to assume that Arctic tourists have a stronger interest in enjoying wildness and scenery in the Arctic than interacting with people. So the monetary value of the trip may be largely reflected by what the tourists have seen, instead of having met. For the emotion value, the nature wonder has nourished and occupied the tourist's mind that makes people interaction a less critical agenda in enhancing emotion values.

Lastly, it is important to recognize the limitation of study that the study population is individuals visiting Norwegian Arctic destinations. Readers may be cautious in interpreting the results as the experience value of Arctic tourists may differ from that of mass tourists. It is suggested that further studies be deployed on non-Arctic tourists to cross-validate the results from the current study.

REFERENCES

Al-Sabbahy, H. Z., Ekinci, Y., & Riley, M. (2004). An investigation of perceived value dimensions: Implications for hospitality research. *Journal of Travel Research, 42*(3), 226–234.
Armenski, T., Dragičević, V., Pejović, L., Lukić, T., & Djurdjev, B. (2011). Interaction between tourists and residents: Influence on tourism development. *Polish Sociological Review, 173*, 107–118.

Bakhat, M. S., & Sajjad-ul-Aziz. (2012). The impact of information technology on hospitality services on consumer satisfactions-A case study of fast food industry in Pakistan. *Interdisciplinary Journal of Contemporary Research in Business, 4*(6), 360–390.

Blamey, R. K., & Braithwaite, V. A. (1997). A social value segmentation of the potential eco-tourism market. *Journal of Sustainable Tourism, 5*(1), 29–45.

Bojanic, D. C. (1996). Consumer perceptions of price, value and satisfaction in the hotel industry: an exploratory study. *Journal of Leisure and Hospitality Marketing, 4*(1), 5–22.

Chen, C.-F., & Chen, F.-S. (2010). Experience quality, perceived value, satisfaction and behavioral intentions for heritage tourists. *Tourism Management, 31*(1), 29–35.

Choo, H., & Petrick, J. F. (2014). Social interactions and intentions to revisit for agritourism service encounters. *Tourism Management, 40*, 372–381.

Czepiel, J. A. (1990). Service encounters and service relationships: Implications for research. *Journal of Business Research, 20*(1), 13–21.

Gallarza, M. G., & Gil, I. (2008). The concept of value and its dimensions: A tool for analysing tourism experiences. *Tourism Review, 63*(3), 4–20.

Holbrook, M. B. (1999). *Consumer value: A framework for analysis and research.* London: Psychology Press.

Huang, J., & Hsu, C. H. (2010). The impact of customer-to-customer interaction on cruise experience and vacation satisfaction. *Journal of Travel Research, 49*(1), 79–92.

Ladhari, R., Pons, F., Bressollers, G., & Zins, M. (2011). Culture and personal values: How they influence perceived service quality. *Journal of Business Research, 64*, 951–957.

Ledden, L., Kalafatis, S. P., & Samouel, P. (2007). The relationship between personal values and perceived value of education. *Journal of Business Research, 60*, 965–974.

Luk, S. T., de Leon, D. C. T., Leong, F.-W., & Li, E. L. (1994). Value segmentation of tourists' expectations of service quality. *Journal of Travel & Tourism Marketing, 2*(4), 23–38.

Madrigal, R., & Kahle, L. R. (1994). Predicting vacation activity preferences on the basis of value-system segmentation. *Journal of Travel Research, 32*(3), 22–28.

Muller, T. E. (1991). Using personal values to define segments in an international tourism market. *International Marketing Review, 8*(1), 57–70.

Murphy, P. E., & Pritchard, M. P. (1997). Destination price-value perceptions: An examination of origin and seasonal influences. *Journal of Travel Research, 35*(3), 16–22.

Murphy, P. E., Pritchard, M. P., & Smith, B. (2000). Destination product and its impact on traveler perceptions. *Tourism Management, 21*, 43–52.

Nunnally, J. C., & Bernstein, I. H. (1994). *Psychometric theory* (3rd ed.). New York, NY: McGraw-Hill Education.

Papathanassis, A. (2012). Guest-to-guest interaction on board cruise ships: Exploring social dynamics and the role of situational factors. *Tourism Management, 33*(5), 1148–1158.

Petrick, J. F. (2002). Development of a multi-dimensional scale for measuring the perceived value of a service. *Journal of Leisure Research, 34*(2), 119–134.

Pitts, R. E., & Woodside, A. G. (1986). Personal values and travel decisions. *Journal of Travel Research, 25*(1), 20–25.

Reisinger, Y., & Turner, L. (1998). Cultural differences between Mandarin-speaking tourists and Australian hosts and their impact on cross-cultural tourist-host interaction. *Journal of Business Research, 42*(2), 175–187.

Rokeach, M. (1968). *Beliefs, attitudes and values: A theory of organization and change.* San Francisco, CA: Jossey-Bass.

Rokeach, M. (1973). *The nature of human values* (Vol. 438). New York, NY: Free Press.

Rokeach, M. (1979). From individual to institutional values: With special reference to the values of science. *Understanding human values, 47,* 70.

Schwartz, S. H., & Bilsky, W. (1987). Toward a universal psychological structure of human values. *Journal of Personality and Social Psychology, 53,* 550–562.

Sweeney, J. C., & Soutar, G. N. (2001). Consumer perceived value: The development of a multiple item scale. *Journal of Retailing, 77*(2), 203–220.

VisitNorway.com. (2013). *Tourism in Norway: Statistics.* Retrieved from http://www.visitnorway.com/us/Media–press/Facts-about-Norway/Tourism-in-Norway/. Accessed on October 6, 2013.

Williams, P., & Soutar, G. N. (2009). Value, satisfaction and behavioral intentions in an adventure tourism context. *Annals of Tourism Research, 36*(3), 413–438.

Wu, C. H. J. (2007). The impact of customer-to-customer interaction and customer homogeneity on customer satisfaction in tourism service—The service encounter prospective. *Tourism Management, 28*(6), 1518–1528.

Zhang, J., Inbakaran, R. J., & Jackson, M. S. (2006). Understanding community attitudes towards tourism and host—Guest interaction in the urban–rural border region. *Tourism Geographies, 8*(2), 182–204.

THE RESTORATIVE POWER OF FORESTS: THE TREE HOUSE HOTEL PHENOMENA IN GERMANY

Philip Sloan, Willy Legrand and Sonja Kinski

ABSTRACT

Tourism and hospitality have experienced strong diversification during the past few years. One of the latest trends in the field of nature-based tourism is the phenomenon of tree house hotels. The unique character of these hotels appeals not only to childhood memories but fulfills desires of adventure and novelty, romanticism, and uniqueness. The restorative power of nature is examined in this setting and the evidence suggests there are physiological and psychological benefits from forest recreation and sleeping in treetops. Surveys of potential clients, actual guests, and tree house hoteliers gave new insights into the perception of tree house accommodation and an understanding in the choice and provision of tree house hotels. The findings suggest that tree house hotels respond to a human need in urbanized societies to reconnect with nature and gain relaxation, restored health, and well-being. Environmentally friendly and noninvasive, this new form of hospitality may well stimulate sustainable

Advances in Hospitality and Leisure, Volume 12, 181−189
ISSN: 1745-3542/doi:10.1108/S1745-354220160000012009

tourism policymaking based on increasing human interaction with the forest ecosystem services that nature provides.

Keywords: Tree house hotels; human−nature relation; well-being; environmental psychology

INTRODUCTION

The tourism and hospitality industries are amongst the fastest growing industries worldwide, especially nature-based tourism is showing steady growth (UNWTO, 2014) Booking a trip to stay in an eco-lodge in Chile or doing volunteer work in Africa has never been easier to organize thanks to the existence of many web sites offering what was considered not long ago to be marginal tourism activities (Kirig, Huber, Kelber, & Rützler, 2011). With ever-expanding air routes to the most previously inaccessible destinations along with falling prices even the farthest place on earth is within reach of today's affluent travelers (Gössling, 2002).

People and society are experiencing a shift towards changing values, such as well-being and self-fulfillment (Schulze, 2005). Holidays are essentially seen as a means to balance body and soul, to enhance health and well-being (Kirig et al., 2011). City dwellers are yearning for nature as natural surroundings vanish under concrete and according to Kirig et al. (2011) many are turning to the wilderness experience instead of a beach holiday. Many references can be found in the literature from recent decades that demonstrate the positive effect of nature on urbanized societies (Herzog & Strevey, 2008; Louv, 2011; Ulrich et al., 1991). According to the Millennium Ecosystem Assessment, nature, forests, and trees are known as an ecosystem service (2005). They provide, regulate, and perform cultural services that directly benefit people. Forests regulate climate, biodiversity, and produce revenue not only in terms of timber and other products but also in terms of recreation and well-being, thus, forests represent a potential revenue source to the tourism and hospitality industries (Millennium Ecosystem Assessment, 2005). Tree house hotels designed to create minimum environmental impact while producing a healthy, pleasurable experience for guests and revenue for the hotelier meet the criteria for a sustainable hotel (Sloan, Legrand, & Chen, 2013).

Health and Well-Being Benefits

In a time that is defined by urbanization and consumerism the tourism industry is in need of innovative products more than ever before. Informed customers want to be awed and experience something new every time they embark on a holiday. At the same time, there is a longing for relaxation, health, and nature as a break from the busy, humdrum of city life. Holidays are increasingly seen as a means to balance body and soul, to enhance health and well-being (Kirig et al., 2011). People's innate desire to be in and engage with nature is a topic that has brought forward many questions among researchers of various fields. Different theories and opinions from anthropology, biology, evolutionary theory, psychology, medicine, geography, and architecture have been compiled together in the new multidisciplinary field of environmental psychology established in the 1960s (Craik, 1973). This scientific area closely examines the effects of humans on the environment and vice versa. In the late 1970s and early 1980s, Wilson developed his *biophilia theory* defined as "the innate tendency [of humans] to focus on life and lifelike processes" (Wilson, 1984, p. 1). In a similar way, Orian drew on previously developed theories from the field of anthropology to develop the *savannah theory* where he argued that people long for nature as they are genetically and evolutionarily connected to all living things and thus not able to leave their attraction for nature, and especially landscapes like that of the African savannah, behind (Wilson, 1984, p. 110).

Over the last two decades, research has shifted more towards the social and health benefits of nature and towards the examination of how to improve urban landscaping and green design through use of trees (Kopec, 2012; Maller, Townsend, Pryor, Brown, & Leger, 2005). The most recent studies consider the effect that nature deprivation has on humans and how to offset these negative repercussions (Maller et al., 2005). Louv (2011) has coined this disengagement from nature and people's inability "to find meaning in the life that surrounds [them]" as nature-deficit disorder (p. 11). Louv further outlined the possibilities of improving personal well-being and health through contact with nature in the discipline he has named as eco-therapy (2011).

In his 18th century treatise *Scienza Nuova* (New Science), Giambattista Vico claimed "this is the order of human institutions: first, the forests, after that the huts, then the villages, next the cities, and finally the academies" (Vico, 1725, p. 239). Human engagement with forests clearly goes back to the earliest days of humankind. However, in the context of urbanized societies there is generally less concern with the contribution that forests may make to basic requirements of survival and more with what Maslow and others have termed "higher level" needs (Maslow, 1954) associated with well-being, fulfillment, and pleasure. A comparatively recent field of research focuses on the "restorative" effects of nature (Hartig, 2007). Similar to the eco-therapy concept of Louv, the so-called *restoration theory* of Kaplan (Kaplan, 1995) is another approach to explaining why certain types of environments, particularly natural ones, appear to be effective in stress reduction and restoration from fatigue. The theory suggests that directed attention used in coping with complex patterns of daily life, including work, is a highly limited resource, easily exhausted if there are no opportunities for recovery. People recover best in environments where this system can rest and where their minds are drawn to involuntary attention or "soft fascination" – which the natural environment is particularly well-suited to supplying. There is evidence to show that people suffering from mental fatigue, looking out of a window at a scene that includes natural elements such as trees, plants, or flowers, the mental restoration time is considerably speeded up when compared with a break where only built elements are visible.

Being in or viewing wooded or natural environments has been shown to reduce physiological measures of stress including blood pressure, heart rate, skin conductance, and muscle tension (Ulrich et al., 1991). In Japan, a study exploring the effect of a walk in the forest ("Shinrin-yoku" – taking in the forest atmosphere) has shown that such environments can promote lower concentrations of cortisol, lower pulse rate, lower blood pressure, greater parasympathetic nerve activity, and lower sympathetic nerve activity when compared to city environments (Lee et al., 2011). Recent, innovative work in the United Kingdom has shown how increased contact with nature by people from deprived urban communities lowers stress, especially amongst children suffering from "mental disorder" (Roe & Aspinall, 2011a).

Stevens (2010) argued that losing touch with nature can lead to a number of "psychological symptoms such as anxiety, frustration and depression" (p. 267). Stevens claimed that an important aspect of eco-therapy is the way in which it reconnects patients with natural environments by not solely considering the illness as a human defect, but also acknowledging that every human being is connected with its surroundings. Hence, changing these environments is integral to eco-therapeutic practices. The restorative properties of natural settings are used and patients are given the chance to benefit from nature's positive influences. For the future, the suggestion is made to also use nature as a preventive means in individual and public health care (Louv, 2011; Maller et al., 2005; Stevens, 2010).

The History of Tree Houses

Typically, in western societies of the 21st century, the idea of tree houses can be said to commonly refer to children's playgrounds set up in a tree in the backyard. Stories such as The Adventures of Huckleberry Finn or Winnie the Pooh — dating back to the late 19th and early 20th centuries — draw pictures of little houses set up in old, rugged trees that do not only give shelter, but also tell of adventure and secrecy (Milnes, 2005; Twain, 2009). Closer to reality is the usage of tree houses as actual accommodation. It used to be common for many tribes in South East Asia and the Pacific to build their houses in the trees for safety reasons. Due to the height at which the huts were built, protection from predatory animals and also from mosquitos was guaranteed. From high up in the trees one could also see the approaches of other tribes, while simultaneously avoiding being seen. Today, the Korowai tribe of Papua New Guinea still lives in houses built high up in the trees. Their wooden huts are constructed at a height of 10–35 meters in the sturdy banyan trees and can only be accessed via ladder constructions that also function as a warning sign of anything attempting to climb up the tree (Todays Whisper, 2012). The commercialization of tree houses as an accommodation has in fact developed into a recent trend. Globally, tree house hotels exist in Australia, Africa, the Americas and Asia, as well as in Europe (Tiny Houses, 2013). In Turkey for instance, Kadir's Tree Houses have existed since the 1980s (Kadirs Tree Houses, 2014). Similar properties are now located in France, England, Germany, Switzerland, Austria, Italy, and Sweden (Tiny Houses, 2013).

In the modern era of chain hotels bearing strong resemblance to each other, hotel entrepreneurs are in a quest to capture the interest of potential guests with an innovative concept just as much as they need to meet expected service standards. Those businesses that offer an extraordinary location and design automatically offer a unique selling point (Kopec, 2012). Generally, the German hospitality sector can be described as highly individualized. In 2012, it is still characterized by almost 47% of all accommodation being small privately-owned hotels which have less than 20 rooms and are typically family-operated (IHA, 2013). The tendency of this traditional accommodation format is, however, steadily decreasing, leading to a shift towards larger properties and chains (IHA, 2013, p. 40).

One special characteristic of tree house hotels is that, they are all unique in design. Tree house hotels can feasibly be described as design or lifestyle hotels since their unique architecture could be argued to make them fit both definitions. However, when looking through the web site of Design Hotels, no tree house hotel appears in their collection of hotels (designhotels.com, 2013). In total, there are currently 15 tree house hotels established in Germany of which one was opened in July 2013. Two additional establishments were opened in 2014.

Overall Research Aim

The main aim of this research was to determine the image of tree house hotels held by customers prior to their visit and to determine which criteria are salient in choosing this form of lodging in the consumer decision making process. The following questions are answered:

- How important is the aspect of nature and the notion of sustainability in the decision making process?
- How can the marketing potential be enhanced?
- What makes the idea of a tree house hotel so appealing to potential guests?
- Do the opinions of tree house hoteliers converge with those of their guests?

METHOD AND FINDINGS

This paper is an exploratory research, applying an inductive research approach using a combination of quantitative and qualitative data in three different data sets. Non-probability sampling methods were used to collect the data in an online survey using the queSTat survey tool. All respondents were of German nationality, as the focus of the study was on the German market. The evaluation of the online survey was facilitated by using the statistics tool PASW Statistics 18. The survey was sent to a sample of 180 people and a total of 96 responses were collected, resulting in a response rate of 53.33%. For assessing the results, the authors worked with an N of 89, leading to a final response rate of 49.44% for the online survey.

The second data set was an offline survey using the guests of Hofgut Hafnerleiten in Bavaria as a convenience sample where the survey took place over a period of two weeks. A short questionnaire was employed consisting of 10 closed-ending questions. The last data set was from one of tree house hoteliers who answered nine closed-ending questions.

A summary of the findings is provided due to the limitations in scale of this present paper. All three data sets highlighted the unique experience value of tree house hotels as extraordinary alternatives to every day hotel overnight stays. The image people hold is one of an adventurous way to spend a night away from home in a destination with novel character. Sustainability (ecosystem services) and closeness to nature represented important factors for choosing and providing tree house accommodation in all data sets obtained. Interestingly, the sustainability of the concept was in most cases not valued as important as being in and experiencing nature. In turn, the motivation to enhance personal well-being through nature was not, nevertheless, the chief perceived unique selling proposition for the tree house hotelier. The respondents did highly value closeness to nature and sustainability, but primarily their aim was to enjoy an extraordinary over-night stay.

CONCLUSIONS AND IMPLICATIONS

This study showed that the general image of tree house hotels held by the people surveyed largely matches the intentions that the tree house hoteliers wish to convey. Thus, it can be assumed that their communication strategy is working since the findings show that customers choose this type of accommodation for its unique character. Secondly, the repeat and future visit potential seems to be proven. The only reasons found for not wanting to stay were those of insecurity about safety and accessibility, as well as an assumed lack of comfort prior to the visit. With a little imagination and entrepreneurship, tree house hoteliers could make some small changes to their product while enhancing positive images of their accommodation. With improved marketing the general awareness and demand for this type of hospitality experience is set to increase. Given the huge interest in wild-erness and eco-tourism coupled with the proven demand for sustainability in hospitality, the future of this sector appears rosy especially when overall awareness of tree house hotels in general and particularly in Germany is low.

The subject area of human engagement with forest environments for physical and mental health and well-being is well-developed and the upsurge in research and application witnessed in the new millennium seems set to continue. As populations become more and more urbanized, the well-documented evidence pointing to the hugely beneficial effects of nature and specifically forests on health and well-being is rising up in European Union policy agendas (EU Biodiversity Strategy to 2020, 2014). Likewise, proof that forests are a true ecosystem service under the terms of the 2005 Millennium Ecosystem Assessment is undeniable. The repercussions of the Millennium Ecosystem Assessment are that forests as recreational sites will receive priority funding from the Millennium Ecosystem Assessment (2005) under tourism policy development. Of course, increased use of forests by walkers, cyclists, and other hobbyists will require more accommodation, thus, the future development of more tree house hotels looks bright.

REFERENCES

Craik, K. H. (1973). Environmental psychology. *Annual Review of Psychology, 24,* 403–422.

Gössling, S. (2002). Human-environmental relations with tourism. *Annals of Tourism Research, 29*(2), 539–556.

Hartig, T. (2007). Three steps to understanding restorative environments as health resources. In C. Ward Thompson & P. Travlou (Eds.), *Open space: People space* (pp. 163–179). Abingdon: Taylor and Francis.

Herzog, T. R., & Strevey, S. J. (2008). Contact with nature, sense of humor, and psychological well-being. *Environment and Behavior, 40*(6), 747–776.

IHA. (2013). *Hotelmarkt Deutschland (The German Hotel Market).* Industry Report 2013, German International Hotel Association (IHA)/Deloitte.

Kadirs Tree Houses. (2014). Retrieved from http://www.kadirstreehouses.com/en/index

Kaplan, S. (1995). The restorative benefits of nature: Toward an integrative framework. *Journal of Environmental Psychology, 15,* 169–182.

Kirig, A., Huber, T., Kelber, C., & Rützler, H. (Eds.). (2011). *BuSINNess: Der Wandel der Genusskultur* [Business: The change of the culture of consumption]. Kelkheim: Zukunftsinstitut.

Kopec, D. (2012). *Environmental psychology for design* (2nd ed.). New York, NY: Fairchild Books.

Lee, J., Park, B. J., Tsunetsugu, Y., Ohira, T., Kagawa, T., & Miyazaki, Y. (2011). Effect of forest bathing on physiological and psychological responses in young Japanese male subjects. *Public Health, 125*(2), 93–100.

Louv, R. (2011). *The nature principle – Reconnecting with life in a virtual age.* Chapel Hill, NC: Algonquin Books.

Maller, C., Townsend, M., Pryor, A., Brown, P., & Leger, L., St. (2005). Healthy nature healthy people: "Contact with nature" as an upstream health promotion intervention for populations. *Health Promotion International, 21*(1), 45–54.

Maslow, A. (1954). *Motivation and personality.* New York, NY: Harper and Row.

Millennium Ecosystem Assessment. (2005). Retrieved from http://www.millenniumassessment. org/en/index.html

Milne, A. A. (2005). *Winnie-the-Pooh*. New York, NY: Puffin Books.

Roe, J., & Aspinall, P. (2011a). The restorative outcomes of forest versus indoor settings in young people with varying behaviour states. *Urban For Urban Green, 10*, 205–212.

Schulze, G. (2005). *Die Erlebnisgesellschaft – Kultursoziologie der Gegenwart [The experiential society: Cultural sociology of the present]* (2nd ed.). Frankfurt am Main: Campus Bibliothek.

Sloan, P., Legrand, W., & Chen, J. S. (2013). *Sustainability in the hospitality industry – Principles of sustainable operations* (2nd ed.). London: Routledge.

Stevens, P. (2010). Embedment in the environment: A new paradigm for well-being? *Perspectives in Public Health, 130*(6), 265–269.

Tiny Houses. (2013). *Tree house hotels all over the world*. Retrieved from http://tiny-houses.de/baumhaus/baumhaushotel/

Todays Whisper. (2012). *Tree houses of the Korowai tribe of New Guinea*. Retrieved from http://todayswhisper.com/tree-houses-of-the-korowai-tribe-of-new-guinea

Twain, M. (2009). *Adventures of Huckleberry Finn*. Cranford, NJ: Dover Publications.

Ulrich, R. S., Simons, R. F., Losito, B. D., Fiorito, E., Miles, M. A., & Zelson, M. (1991). Stress recovery during exposure to natural and urban environments. *Journal of Environmental Psychology, 11*(3), 201–230.

UNWTO. (2014). *UNWTO annual report 2014*. Retrieved from http://www2.unwto.org/annualreport2014

Vico, G. (1725). *Scienza Nuova [The new science]*. Naples: Stamperia Museana.

Wilson, E. O. (1984). *Biophilia*. Cambridge, MA: Harvard University Press.

INDEX